SECOND ACT

SECOND ACT

WHAT LATE BLOOMERS CAN TELL YOU ABOUT REINVENTING YOUR LIFE

Henry Oliver

First published in Great Britain by John Murray One in 2024
An imprint of John Murray Press

1

A CIP catalogue record for this title is available from the British Library

Hardback ISBN 978 1 399 81331 0
ebook ISBN 978 1 399 81330 3

Typeset in Adobe Garamond Pro by 11/15 by Integra Software Services Pvt. Ltd.,
Pondicherry, India

Printed and bound in Great Britain by Clays Ltd, Elcograf S.p.A.

John Murray Press policy is to use papers that are natural, renewable and recyclable products
and made from wood grown in sustainable forests. The logging and manufacturing processes
are expected to conform to the environmental regulations of the country of origin.

John Murray Press   Nicholas Brealey Publishing
Carmelite House   Hachette Book Group
50 Victoria Embankment   Market Place, Center 53, State Street
London EC4Y 0DZ   Boston, MA 02109, USA

www.johnmurraypress.co.uk

John Murray Press, part of Hodder & Stoughton Limited
An Hachette UK company

To all the potential late bloomers out there…

'People are always speculating – why am I as I am? To understand that of any person, his whole life, from birth, must be reviewed. All of our experiences fuse into our personality. Everything that ever happened to us is an ingredient.'

Malcolm X, *The Autobiography of Malcolm X: As Told to Alex Haley*

'Men who have multiple careers are to be envied.'

David Ogilvy, *Blood, Brains and Beer*

CONTENTS

INTRODUCTION: THE SWITCH

Katharine Graham became the CEO of the Washington Post Company – a major publishing business that owned radio and television stations, as well as *Newsweek* and the *Washington Post* – one summer afternoon in 1962, at the age of forty-five, when her husband shot himself. She had no idea what was going to happen. For most of her life, she had been so denigrated and mocked by her mother and husband that she lacked the confidence to dress herself for a party, let alone believe herself capable of running a major corporation. Despite the fact that her father had owned the *Post*, and nurtured her talent, she believed that running a business was never in her blood. She said that when she bought a house in her late twenties, she did not know the difference between income and capital. She was obsessed by news and politics but bored by advertising and balance sheets. And so, when she woke up from a nap that August afternoon to find her husband – alcoholic, manic depressive, adulterous, verbally abusive – shot dead, Katharine Graham faced a transformative moment. For the six months before Phil Graham died, Katharine had worried that he would take the *Post* away from her, after he started a bitter-minded legal attempt to take control of the company. In her grief, she faced a challenge. She could either run the business herself or let it go out of the family. She was advised to sell. She declined.

Katharine Graham went on to become one of the most successful CEOs of the twentieth century, and one of the few women of her time to hold so much commercial and political power.

To the people around her – and perhaps to herself – Katharine Graham's success as a CEO came out of the blue. She had no training in business. She lacked confidence. But she had everything a late bloomer needs to succeed. She didn't come out of the blue at all. She had just been overlooked. Her talents were always there, but they were unappreciated.

Katharine Graham never lacked the qualities she needed for success. What was missing was opportunity. In among the long years of self-doubt, there were many flashes of the steel, signals of the character that would later see her acclaimed as one of the most powerful people in Washington and one of the most successful CEOs in the United States, in whose company Warren Buffett confidently invested and whose salons became essential attendance for new presidents. From her abusers, she drew resilience. From her elite background she had acquired the skills for success. Circumstances that might have crushed other people didn't quite crush Katharine Graham.

Graham's story exemplifies many of the ways in which late bloomers flourish. Because she was a woman, she wasn't going to be just given the opportunity to run the company. In a perverse, tragic way, she got a lucky break. But she was prepared to take that break. She was well educated, knew the newspaper business in detail, had been acquainted with the *Post* from her childhood. She was networked with the right people and learned from the good influences of her upbringing and education. Above all, she was resilient. Persistence is a perpetual theme of late blooming, and Katharine Graham persisted and persisted and persisted, no matter what. She shows us that simply deciding to act when faced with a challenge can reveal new depths of capability. The more she did, the more capable she became. 'Do your work,' said Ralph Waldo Emerson, 'and you shall reinforce yourself.'[1]

This book is going to examine the factors that made Katharine Graham – and others like her, in fields ranging from painting to entrepreneurship – a late bloomer, so that we can better understand what a late bloomer is and how we might find more of them.

•••

Graham's life pivoted on a single tragic moment. But she chose to make the switch, from one life to another. By deciding to own the Washington Post Company, rather than sell it, she chose to move from the drawing room to the boardroom. This wasn't so much a transition as a translocation. It was as if Fate snapped its fingers and she found herself in strange new surroundings.

How then did she become one of the most successful CEOs of the twentieth century?

The answer can be found in a recent study of the careers of scientists, film directors and artists. This study, which was conducted by academics at Northwestern University, looked at hot streaks in people's careers – intense periods of high achievement, lasting a decade or more. What conditions have to be present for a hot streak to occur? The study found that before the hot streak begins there is an exploration phase, when new ideas are gathered, which is followed by a period of exploitation, when those new ideas are turned into original and impactful work.

This is similar to the explore/exploit dynamic, an idea from computer science, which says that to make the best decisions we should find the correct balance between gathering information (exploring our options) and making the most of what we know (exploiting that information). To make the best decisions, we need to balance exploration and exploitation.

What the research on artists, filmmakers, and scientists found was not that either exploration or exploitation alone was critical to a hot streak: it was the transition from explore to exploit that mattered. Exploring before exploiting means you can discover the most productive ideas and expand your creative possibilities. What matters is the *switch*.[2]

Too much exploration can be risky: you end up as a dabbler, a dilettante. Too much exploitation can be boring: you don't discover enough new information to do interesting, original work. To have a hot streak, a burst of your best work, you need to switch from explore to exploit. Importantly, these findings were robust whether the hot streak came early in a career or late.[3] You can make the switch later in your career and still see the same effect.

This broad pattern, of shifting from exploring to exploiting, can be observed in the lives of late bloomers.

•••

Like Katharine Graham, most late bloomers go through these two stages. First, they take a long and winding road, an essentially unplanned career path. Then, they get the opportunity for success through some combination of the right people, the right place and the right time. Their network, the culture they move to, a personal transformation – or some combination of these – take the disparate experiences of the first stage and turn them into the focused output of the second stage. They make the switch from explore to exploit and enter a hot streak. They just happen to do it later than their peers.

Late bloomers rarely take conventional career paths to success; if they did, perhaps they would not be late. Their progress is punctuated and disrupted, not smooth and steady. In this stage, their careers are often either dormant or patchwork, made of seemingly disparate parts. This might look listless, directionless or inefficient: rather than working towards a specific goal, late bloomers prepare for the unknown, the unexpected, the unstated. As with the explore mode, this stage has many influences, and what eventually triggers their transition to success might not be the most obvious or most expected thing. The idea that gets exploited is rarely the most popular, mostly highly cited or most recently discovered idea. It's the most interesting.

Second, late bloomers find their niche or opportunity – some turn in their luck, some discovery, some change in their circumstances comes along and makes them a channel for their talents. They get direction, focus, challenge, resources, support, opportunity. This is when they exploit the capabilities and preparation from the first stage. We shall see, again and again, the importance of preparing for your luck – chance really does favour the prepared mind.

This second stage has three conditions, which are not all present in all cases, but which are reasonably consistent: right people, right place, right time. To understand how late bloomers leave the long and winding road and arrive at the place where they achieve so much, how they switch from explore to exploit, we need to look at their networks, the culture they live and work in, and the transformational moments in their lives, or their crisis points.

What we will see is that weak ties – the phrase sociologists use to describe people we are only slightly acquainted with – are the people who can change our prospects, but *only* if they are influential. Good networking is not about knowing all the best people, but the few who can be credible and persuasive to the people we need to reach.

Personal transformation happens through cultural immersion, sampling the world and changing our surroundings. In new circumstances, gradually sampling our way into a new mode of thinking, living or working, we can change our opportunities, perhaps even change ourselves.

Moments of crisis have to be taken advantage of, not ignored or suffered through, whether that's a personal tragedy, a moment of inspiration, or a gradual attrition of your will, caused dissatisfaction that culminates in desperation to change. Sometimes there are good reasons to have a midlife crisis, not to accept a slump but to use it as a pivot point.

•••

As we see examples of late bloomers making these transitions across various fields of endeavour, three characteristics will recur:

PERSISTENT. Though they often don't work towards a specific goal, neither do late bloomers lavish their life away on useless trifles, in Samuel Johnson's phrase. They persist in following their interests and ambitions; they are unable to let it go, but, sometimes by necessity, sometimes by choice, they have to be flexible about how and when this persistence accrues into a tangible achievement or accomplishment.

EARNEST. Late bloomers are serious, perhaps intense, obsessive, occasionally eccentric, volatile, or weird. Not infrequently, the people around them don't quite understand who they are capable of being. Their earnestness can make them seem strange, off-putting, and makes it difficult to see how and where their talent could flourish: their capability often hides in plain sight.

QUIET. Their ambitions are usually secret, or unknown to themselves for a long time. They pursue their interests quietly. Their ability and confidence grow with experience. It might be quite late in the day when they realize that their capabilities actually make them fit for some exceptional enterprise.

So, despite the fact that late bloomers are often overlooked, they are often quietly, persistently developing the qualities, on the long and winding road that will eventually lead them to success, when the right opportunity comes along. Importantly, the more active they are in this process, the more likely they are to find that opportunity and turn it to their advantage.

•••

To understand how late bloomers flourish, and because late bloomers are individuals, this book relies on biographical stories as well as social science research. Their stories teach us lessons about how people can be helped to flourish earlier. But more often they also demonstrate the many different ways talents come to fruition.

Knowing an idea in theory is not enough to change our lives. We need to see how it works in the mess of real life. We want to know what it is like to become a late bloomer so that we can live differently. We need to see the story before the success.

It's one thing to know about the way our brains develop as we age, the importance of deliberate practice to achieving mastery, or the way that changing who we associate with can change what we achieve. It's quite another thing to see those ideas in the complications of real life. If we want to change ourselves, or spot the potential for change in other people, we need examples alongside scientific theory. To the aspiring late bloomer, to the manager looking to make a new sort of hire, or to someone who believes in a friend, partner or spouse, scientific research is of limited help. We need to know *how* late bloomers do it. In addition to asking questions like 'How much does our brain really decline as we age?' or 'What sort of networks do we need to be part of to succeed?' we will explore examples of people changing their lives, from all disciplines and time periods: businesspeople, innovators, writers, salespeople, scientists, academics, politicians.

These stories of real people's lives will show what it takes to change yourself, in ways big and small, profound and mundane. Some of the people in this book battled failure for decades, quietly preparing for whatever opportunity came their way. Some great leaders spent years in obscurity, as no one's prediction to take the top job. Some will reveal that following the rules is often the wrong approach.

The book compares late bloomers' stories, revealing patterns and showing the many different scenarios in which they thrive. All of the people featured here are highly accomplished people who changed the world in some way or made a serious contribution to their field. This is because, as Warren Bennis and Patricia Ward Biederman say in *Organizing Genius* – their study of collaborations that produced amazing success – 'Excellence is a better teacher than mediocrity.'[4] We should be inspired by the best. We're interested in these people because of what their example might breathe into us.

•••

In 1932, aged forty-five (the same age Katharine Graham was when she took control of the Washington Post Company), American author Walter Pitkin published *Life Begins at Forty*, which exhorted people to realize that ever improving life expectancy meant their lives were more full of possibility than ever before. 'The annals of the great,' said Pitkin, 'are filled with tales of dull youth blossoming late.'[5] Ninety years later, his message is truer than ever. When Pitkin published his book, life expectancy in the United States was 62.0 for men and 63.5 for women. In 2019, the United Nations estimated that global average life expectancy was 72.6 years.[6] We are living longer, healthier and more productive lives. Many more of us can become late bloomers, if we want to.

Life Begins at Forty was a big hit. Pitkin had caught the spirit of the times. The title became a catchphrase. Songs and films were named after Pitkin's book, and he became a regular radio pundit. It is now a common idiom. The idea has kept pace with changing times, too. Today, you are more likely to hear that fifty is the new forty. Or even sixty.

Pitkin's core idea is that slow development is normal, and age should not necessarily mean decline. We should not despair if we are not yet everything we want to be or if we are behind our peers. 'The slow growing human,' he says, 'is one regular and normal variety.'[7] This is a message we need to hear again. Since Pitkin's time, re-education and career changes have become normal. Retirements are long affairs during which people learn new skills and take up hobbies. The proportion of women over the age of fifty in employment in the UK has risen from 42 per cent in 1992 to 66 per cent today.[8] In both the UK and the United States, rates of employment among the over-sixty-fives have increased significantly since the 1990s. After the 2008 financial crash, large numbers of workers over the age of fifty re-entered the workforce. That might have been driven by financial necessity, but it is a reminder of our ongoing ability to change our lives and keep working. As journalist Connie Goldman wrote, 'Ageing does not have to be the end: It can be another beginning.'[9]

Some will see this book as a denial of the reality of ageing. We do become less capable as we grow older, and we should accept that rather than contribute to a stigma against the reality of ageing. It is precisely because we all lose our faculties at some point – if not to age or dementia, then to death – that I am writing this book. Our time is not guaranteed to be well spent. How many people every year are lost to weariness, laziness, mental decline, exhaustion, redundancy? As Jimmy Carter wrote in his memoir of post-presidential life, *The Virtues of Aging*, 'Each of us is old when we *think* we are – when we accept an attitude of dormancy… a substantial limitation on our physical and mental activity… As I know from experience, this is not tied very closely to the number of years we have lived.'10

It is important to acknowledge the realities of ageing and not make older people feel marginal or unacceptable. It is equally important to encourage people to make the most of whatever life they have left and not to succumb to an 'attitude of dormancy' before they need to. I have seen too many colleagues dropped by the office because they were no longer seen as being fresh enough, and too many lives not lived as they could have been. One of my grandmothers was a widow for forty years. The other outlived two of her children. 'Sometimes it is the body which is the first to surrender to old age,' says Montaigne, 'sometimes the soul.'11 The best way not to get caught out by your death, or old age, is to act like it's closer than you think. We all know people who died young, or grew old before their time: they are the warning that motivates this book. As it says in the Gospel of John, 'the night cometh when no man can work.'12

Despite the popularity of Pitkin's claim, we do not expect as much of ourselves and others as we age. We don't expect as much of older people as we do of those in life's earlier stages. Inevitably, surely, there has to be a period of decline. Age is the enemy of success. The 'thirty under thirty' list remains prevalent. The 'fifty over fifty' list, less so.

But Emma Rowena Gatewood became the first woman to solo hike the Appalachian Trail aged sixty-seven. Freeman Dyson published a new solution to the prisoner's dilemma aged eighty-eight. Mary Delany invented a form of paper-cutting in her seventies and created nearly a thousand detailed illustrations of botanical specimens. Ray Charles won a Grammy aged seventy-four. Laura Ingalls Wilder started writing *Little House on the Prairie* at sixty-five. Gertrude Jekyll, the famous garden designer, started her career in her forties. John Goodenough developed the lithium-ion battery the year before he was forced to retire from Oxford. He is still an active professor in Texas aged ninety-nine and is the oldest Nobel laureate in history. Knut Wicksell spent fourteen years in graduate school. He later made significant contributions in economics. Marjorie Rice was in her fifties when she discovered new forms of pentagonal tessellation in geometry. She was an amateur with only a high school diploma. Ynés Mexía started studying botany aged fifty-one and went on to discover fifty new species of plants. Michael Ramsay founded TiVo aged forty-seven.

It is difficult to spot late bloomers before they emerge. Often, this is because we're too focused on external markers of success, rather than a person's character. For example, psychologist Shane Snow has said: 'Neither age nor speed of political climb was correlated with... success as a president. Instead, the best presidents were the most *adaptable* and *open-minded*... age, it turns out, had nothing to do with it.'[13] This is not just true of presidents. In a review of a hundred years of psychological research, age was found to have zero predictive power in recruitment. Just knowing how old someone is tells you almost nothing about how well suited they are to do a job.

Rather than looking for a particular measure of potential late bloomers, we need to start from Pitkin's premise that they are 'one regular and normal variety'.[14] Late bloomers are not always people who might otherwise have flourished but who were held back, the way Katharine

Graham was. We will see many examples of late bloomers who were never going to succeed early. Late bloomers are not merely delayed prodigies: they are a complicated, diverse group of people we need to pay more attention to.

•••

There are many other ways to define a late bloomer. For children, a late bloomer is someone whose academic development is slower than that of their peers, such as the inventor Thomas Edison or the scientist Pierre Curie, who were unimpressive pupils at elementary school. Some people are late bloomers in terms of public recognition. Economist Scott Sumner was a successful academic in his thirties; it was not until twenty years later, when he became a blogger, that his ideas influenced monetary policy after the 2008 financial crisis. And there are people like Helen Downie who started painting aged fifty. By posting her work on Instagram, Downie ended up collaborating with Gucci. Now she has 250,000 followers. Nor does late blooming have to be about creative or intellectual accomplishment. People in their thirties are being diagnosed with autism; people in their forties are discovering their sexuality; and people in their fifties are achieving educational and business successes unavailable to them earlier in life. The nurse Bronnie Ware's book *The Top Five Regrets of the Dying* records her terminally ill patients' regrets about their lives.[15] They often regretted having worked too much on something they didn't especially care about, when they didn't need the money, to the neglect of other areas of their lives. Addiction to success, habit, and love of status had prevented them from travelling or seeing their children. One important type of late bloomer is someone who successfully changes the balance of their life.

Beyond accomplishment in a professional or creative field, many people have the potential to live more spiritually, emotionally or mentally fulfilling lives. Ruth Wilson, a former elocution teacher in Australia, emerged from a depression in her sixties by rereading Jane Austen. Wilson went on to achieve a PhD in Jane Austen aged eighty-eight and has recently published a book about her experiences.[16] How many more people are out there who might confound expectations, whether other people's or their own?

•••

This is a book about late-blooming talent. Talent that flourishes after it is expected to, that confounds or surprises expectations. Late bloomers are found in all kinds of activities – politics, sports, business, writing, finance, art, exploration, even revolutions. Gladys Burrill completed the Honolulu Marathon aged ninety-two. Robin Chase was a stay-at-home mother with an MBA before she founded Zipcar, aged forty-two. (She doesn't think of herself as a late bloomer.) Siphiwe Baleka nearly became an Olympic swimmer aged fifty. (He was denied the chance to represent Guinea-Bissau because of a technicality.) Barry Diller is a late-blooming self-made man. He was a company executive who did no independent work at all for the first thirty years of his career. Then he took over US teleshopping network QVC and became a phenomenal success. Independent financial success – what he called 'running his own shop' – came late to Diller relative to his other corporate achievements. Not every company executive can make it big on their own after thirty years, perhaps not most of them. Gerald Stratford became famous online for growing big vegetables in his retirement; he is now the 'Twitter King of Big Veg' and has published a book.[17] Before this, he was a butcher and a barge controller on the Thames. Carl Allamby was an auto mechanic for twenty-five years before he went to medical school aged forty. 'Sometimes,' says Carl, 'you're just going to have to take a chance and believe in yourself.'[18] Cervantes wrote *Don Quixote* from prison late in life. The mathematician Eugène Ehrhart graduated high school aged twenty-two and finished his PhD aged sixty. Charles Spearman, the psychologist who developed the theory of general intelligence, started his PhD aged thirty-four, paused it to fight in the Second Boer War, and completed it aged forty-one. Toussaint Louverture began leading the Haitian Revolution aged forty-eight; he had been a slave himself until the age of thirty-three, and a property owner after that.

There is no single cut-off age and no simple formula for identifying late bloomers. They blossom late relative to expectations or to their life trajectory. Obviously, someone like Grandma Moses, who took up painting in retirement, was a late bloomer. But you can be a late bloomer at twenty, if you are a basketball player like Stephen Curry or a tennis player like Martina Navratilova. Similarly, a mathematician who gets serious in their twenties would be a late bloomer, relative to the usual pattern in their field. Alan Kay was one of the oldest PhDs to join the Californian research and development company PARC. He studied mathematics and molecular biology, computer science not being a degree at that time; he learned to code aged twenty-two in the US Air Force; he got his undergraduate degree aged twenty-six and his PhD aged twenty-nine. Kay is not a late bloomer compared to most people, but he came to his niche somewhat later than his peers. At twenty, Malcolm Little was in jail, showing no signs of his later brilliance as a preacher, political communicator, orator, and civil rights leader. No one was expecting great things of him. But prison acted as a period of withdrawal for reflection, and he had a spiritual and intellectual conversion that changed the course of his life. By twenty-five, he was Malcolm X, a late bloomer. Similarly, Jay-Z is often named as a late bloomer in hip hop because he didn't release his first album until he was twenty-six. Rani Hamid only started playing chess aged thirty-four and went on to become Bangladesh's first International Woman Master.

Here then is the definition I will work from: a late bloomer is someone who succeeds when no one expects them to.

The phrase I heard that got me started researching this book was – *people who haven't done something yet but maybe they will.* This book is about those people whose careers change trajectory later than expected, and surprise everyone around them.

•••

Finding this talent really matters. Late bloomers built some of the great cathedrals of the Renaissance. They were essential to the campaign to abolish slavery. Has any poem or song changed the world more than 'Amazing Grace'? It was written by the late bloomer John Newton. Late bloomers have written some of the most important books of philosophy and made scientific and mathematical discoveries that changed the world. They've composed great poems and produced great art – think of Francisco Goya's dark paintings, created in his seventies. Famous novels like *The Big Sleep*, *The Wind in the Willows*, and *Beloved* were written by late starters. It was the late bloomer Anne Clough who pioneered women's education in the UK. Late bloomers have founded some of the most successful businesses in the world. They are fundamental to the story of Silicon Valley. Many of the world's most notable politicians got a late start. Winston Churchill's career was thought to be finished before the Second World War. There has been a recent vogue for Stoicism among young people – we should remember that Seneca wrote his famous letters in his final years.

But this book is not a manifesto for easy optimism. People do not wake up one day and discover that they are in fact a fully formed Paul Cézanne or Toni Morrison. Some people *do* just wake up one day and blossom. Reddit has forums dedicated to sexual and emotional late bloomers, who realize their sexuality or discover happiness in midlife, for example.

Because late bloomers are 'one regular and normal variety', there is great range in the ways people flourish. This is not a case of looking for a single answer. There's no one piece of the puzzle missing – late bloomers are an entirely new sort of puzzle. Late bloomers often face substantial obstacles, especially when they are women or members of marginalized groups. They tend to be smart (which doesn't have to mean successful at school), self-educating and self-directing. They follow their own interests and take lifelong education seriously. They never stop teaching themselves; often, they set their own agenda. One early sign of a late bloomer is often earnestness, which can be off-putting to many people. Another thing that characterizes many late bloomers is a period of withdrawal for reflection. What might look like an unexplained career break for most people will often be a sign of development in late bloomers. Harry Truman wrote: 'In 1924 I was ingloriously defeated… I spent two years thinking.'[19] It was that sort of reflection that took him, however unexpectedly, from small-town farmer to Cold War president.

Many people do not fully realize themselves until later in life. They might be highly accomplished, like eminent English philosopher Mary Midgley, who wrote her first book at fifty-nine. Or they might be like Annunziata Murgia, who went back to school in Italy aged ninety, after her original studies were interrupted by the Second World War. What these two people have in common is that they carried within them early seeds that took an unusually long time to germinate. Midgley was a member of the Elizabeth Anscombe circle in Oxford, then moved to Newcastle and worked as a lecturer, fiction reviewer and a stay-at-home mother before writing books in her fifties, a much later start than many of her colleagues. All her experiences contributed to her writing. Viola Davis spent decades playing mainly supporting roles before becoming a television, and now film, star later in her career: 'I was trying to fit in, stifling my voice, stifling who I was, in order to be seen as pretty, in order for people to like me. And then going home, not being able to sleep and having anxiety. I have found that the labelling of me, and having to fit into that box, has cost me a great deal. I've had a lot of lost years.'[20]

Truly remarkable people, no matter how accomplished they are, often seem to come out of the blue. Their talents flourish in seemingly unpredictable and astonishing ways. We will meet many people like this: a novelist who started writing aged sixty; an out-of-fashion architect who did his most radical work in his seventies and eighties; a cloistered nun who became a global television star. In reality, these people live through long periods of inefficient or indirect preparation – when they switch from the explore to the exploit phase. They only *seem* to come out of the blue – the signs of their ability were there all along.

Talent hides in the open all around us. We simply don't know how many people *could* be late bloomers, given the opportunity.

•••

The pervasive spirit of this book is the word 'perhaps'. I am not arguing that I can prove something definitive. There is no law of late blooming. I don't know for certain how many more people could be late bloomers or whether *you* could be a late bloomer. I am not presenting these biographical examples as incontrovertible, pure or morally exceptional. What I do argue is that in all fields – including fields like maths, where late blooming seems unfeasible – we underrate the potential of hidden talent.

All the studies I quote and the findings I rely on are part of an argument that begins with 'perhaps'. This is not a grand unifying theory. No great secrets are revealed, no hacks or tricks to leapfrog you to a new life. Instead, all this is meant as inspiration, one that might start you living differently or that might help you find other people who could change. There are dozens of examples in this book, in a huge range of activities, of people who show that many more of us can make achievements later in life than we think. Their stories are remarkably contingent: the power of 'perhaps' is strong in their lives.

This is why there is a combination of biography and social science. The biographical stories also show that, instead of looking at someone's record and deciding that they have nothing else to give, we ought more often to be saying, perhaps they could do something else, given the right circumstances. What happens in your second act is determined, to a greater or lesser extent, by what happens in your first act. But the past is a prologue, not a prediction.

To understand late bloomers, we need to be open to the range of ways an individual life can flourish. By combining scientific studies and biographical stories, this book aims to give a new taxonomy of late blooming. Instead of providing information and insights which you can agree or disagree with, or giving you a checklist to change your life, this book aims to make you think that, whether or not the idea that talent can flourish late in life is true, there is truth in that idea; that you might be or know a late bloomer; that you can learn something about how to live from the people profiled here.

Perhaps…

Part One
Meandering Career Paths

'All rising to great place is by a winding stair.'

Francis Bacon, 'Of Great Place'

1

Katharine Graham's transformation to Mrs Graham, CEO

To begin with, Katharine Graham was privileged. Although raised for success, she was treated with coldness and belittled. This created competing impulses of ambition and achievement but also self-doubt and despair. One of her sisters said of their family: 'We have all felt a compulsion to be terrific! And that is a dangerous thing.'[1]

Katharine Graham (1917–2001) was the daughter of Eugene Meyer, a financier who used part of his great wealth to cover the losses made by the newspaper he bought at auction, the *Washington Post*, and Agnes Meyer, a writer. It was a volatile and somewhat unhappy home. Agnes rarely showed her any love. Eugene was hot tempered and autocratic. 'I had more or less to bring myself up emotionally,' said Graham.[2] Her mother and nanny took a strict view of illness – that it was to be ignored. Young Katharine was routinely sent to school with dreadful coughs and was later told she had scarred lungs from tuberculosis. In 1989, Graham recalled:

> We five children were brought up very strictly and rather spartanly, which was odd because we lived in very large houses that were run rather grandly, even for those days. We had small allowances, walked to school rain or shine, worked hard, and believed that you had to work – that no one could sit back and do nothing.[3]

It was also a competitive and illustrious environment, and Katharine was surrounded by eminent people. Guests included H. G. Wells, the French ambassador and members of the Cabinet.[4] During the First

World War, Eugene gave up investment banking for public service. Agnes was a successful journalist and expert on Chinese art. Although Agnes belittled and bullied the children, Eugene made space for them to debate current events. He expected the children to excel at everything, including conversation. He once put out a sign on the breakfast table which read, 'Every father can sometimes be right.'[5] In 1931, some years after she had left home, the eldest daughter wrote to Eugene, 'I wish we'd had time to talk more before we both went in opposite directions.'[6] It was a businesslike family, not a close-knit one.

Graham did learn one valuable lesson from her mother. This extract from her mother's diary represents the philosophy 'imposed' on Graham and her siblings:

> It is interesting to learn once more how much further one can go on one's second wind. I think that it is an important lesson for everyone to learn for it should also be applied to one's mental efforts. Most people go through life without ever discovering the existence of that whole field of endeavour which we describe as a second wind. Whether mentally or physically most people give up at the first appearance of exhaustion. Thus they never learn the glory and the exhilaration of genuine effort...[7]

As well as the extensive informal education she received from her parents, travelling to Europe, mountaineering and visiting Einstein, as a small child Graham had a Montessori education where she was 'encouraged to pursue our own interests'. She would later compare her experience of taking over the *Post* – 'learning by doing' – to the Montessori method.[8] Aged eight, she moved to a more traditional school and learned to 'get along in whatever world one is deposited'.[9] Both of these would prove to be vital lessons when Graham's second wind was forced on her by her husband's suicide.

Graham had a sense when young that she wanted people to know who she was. This came true after Watergate. Fame didn't corrupt her, though. 'The shadow of my mother's enormous ego lent the whole thing an enormous reality check.'[10] So far did this reality check go that Graham was determined not to repeat her parents' egoism – even as the famous proprietor of the *Washington Post*, she never complained when given a bad table at a restaurant. 'I just go meekly,' she said.[11]

Perhaps the earliest sign of Graham's later talents was her consistent ability to withstand difficult situations. From a young age, she was forged of steel, even though her self-image was self-deprecating: 'I knew I wasn't any of the things that were held out as desirable.' Her family was rich but she owned far fewer clothes than other children. Nothing personal was discussed. Neither sex nor menstruation was explained to Katharine. What she did take from her childhood was a remote but certain sense that her father believed in her: 'That was what saved me.'[12]

That and the fact that when she was sixteen, her father, recently retired as governor of the Federal Reserve, bought the *Washington Post*. It was something he had long talked of. He came downstairs one day, a few weeks into his retirement, and said to Agnes, 'This house is not properly run.' She retaliated, 'You'd better go buy the *Washington Post*.'[13] And he did. He was fifty-seven and his biographer called this purchase 'the greatest adventure of his lifetime'.[14]

No one even told Katharine about the purchase. She overheard the news in her parents' conversation.[15] An attentive reader, she sent her father corrective advice about layouts and content. Graham was interested in journalism early, working on the school paper and then the college one. She took vacation jobs on local papers.

When Graham arrived at college she lacked practicality, the result of growing up in a house with a dozen servants. She had to be prompted by other students to launder her cardigan. She showed the ability to hold her own counsel, though. She switched from Vassar to the University of Chicago, realizing she had gone to Vassar because 'it simply was the place to be'. This prescient self-awareness was matched with self-direction. She got a D on a history paper, having failed to follow her tutor's advice: 'She has taught history ten years too long… I do history my own way and enjoy it.'[16] In those words we can hear the future proprietor who would make the hard choices – against the advice of many – that allowed the publication of the Pentagon Papers and reports of the Watergate scandal.

During college she became closer to her father. Attending the founding of the American Student Union as a reporter, she arrived to find herself nominated to the National Executive Committee, a ploy by left wingers to bring credibility to their scheme. Her father advised her against the position. She took his advice on board but joined the committee anyway, interested in new experiences. He then sent her the second piece of wisdom she absorbed from her peculiar parents: 'I do not think I would be helpful in advising you too strongly. I do not even feel the need of doing that because I have so much confidence in your having really good judgement.' He wrote to her as well suggesting she would soon be a journalist at the *Post*. 'What I didn't grasp at the time,' Graham reflected, 'was my father's real bias in my favour.'[17] His belief in her would be invaluable in the years to come.

At the University of Chicago she took a great books course taught by Richard Hutchins and Mortimer Adler, renowned and intimidating pioneers of that sort of course, who barked questions at their students. 'The methods they used often taught you most about bullying *back*.'[18] She learned to thrive in these classes, and it is hard not to see the later Katharine Graham, the first woman CEO of a major corporation, developing at that seminar table. Despite her professed lack of self-confidence, which wasn't helped by the fact that her mother had already read everything she encountered in college, we can see flashes of steel beneath Graham's shy exterior. The woman who would one day face down Richard Nixon was being formed.

As a graduate she took a job at the *San Francisco News*. She wanted to quit after a week, but Eugene persuaded her to stay. She then moved to the *Washington Post*, where she was given rotations, including editorial. As the only Meyer child to show any interest in journalism, Eugene gave her favourable opportunities.[19] She was treated differently in other ways. Her sisters were both persuaded by their parents not to marry their first choice of husband, but it never occurred to Katharine that she would need her parents' permission about who to marry.[20] Their indifference – her mother had been 'too busy' to attend her daughter's graduation, which reduced Katharine to tears[21] – held some advantage.

While working for the *Post*, Katharine met Philip Graham, a vibrant, brilliant, aspirational young man who came into her life like a rainbow and left it like a storm. David Halberstam, the journalist and author, who conducted dozens of interviews for his history of American journalism *The Powers That Be*, described Phil Graham as 'incandescent' and said 'no one in Washington could match him'.[22] Katharine and Philip got married somewhat to his parents' discomfort and settled down in Washington where he clerked for a Supreme Court justice. At this point, it was horrifying to Philip that Katharine could be a mere housewife, waiting for him while he worked.[23] She continued to write for the *Post*; at one point, he found her working at 2 A.M.[24] They married in 1940. Katharine was pregnant the next year and stopped working. 'I resigned myself quite contentedly to the quiet life of a vegetable,' she wrote to a friend. She was, at that time, very happy.[25] (Carol Felsenthal, one of Katharine's biographers, believes Katharine's strong desire to be a mother and homemaker was a way of being the opposite of her own mother.) Then, in quick succession, she had a miscarriage and Philip went to war. Loneliness and depression became part of their lives. Kay blamed herself for their first child being stillborn and her family's suffocating wealth for Phil's intense moods.[26]

Katharine makes no mention of his despair this early in their marriage, but Halberstam records that Philip 'on occasion in the privacy of his own home came completely apart, scenes of tears and deep depression, telling his young wife he was not worthy of what others expected of him'.[27] In the early days, Philip brought Katharine 'laughter, gaiety, irreverence for rules, and originality'. He also freed her from her family.[28] Halberstam writes that Philip 'did what no-one else had done for Katharine Meyer before. He made her laugh and he made her feel young and pretty and he got her outside herself.'[29] Only later would she realize that he completely dominated her: 'Always, it was he who decided and I who responded.' She was, she said, a 'doormat wife'.[30]

During the Second World War, Katharine spent more time with her father. Philip was away and her mother was in England. They shared no intimate conversation but became quietly 'very close and very dependent on each other'. They talked extensively, of course, about newspapers. He gave her a part-time job reading other papers to get ideas for stories.[31] At this time, the *Post* was one of several newspapers in Washington, and it struggled to survive. Everyone in town assumed it would go broke.[32]

In 1942, Eugene started thinking about who would take over the *Post*. He chose Phil and was reported to have said that no man should have to work for his wife.[33] But there was more to it than that. Katharine had written to her sister years earlier that she did not want to work for her father (which surprised her when she researched her autobiography) and that she was interested in reporting, not in the business side of things. 'I detest beyond description advertising and circulation.' Even when she did take over, twenty years later, she confessed, 'The mere mention of terms like "liquidity" made my eyes glaze over.'[34] By then, though, her motivation was very different.

So Katharine endorsed her husband going to work at the *Post* as a journalist while she went off 'to lead the life of wife, mother, and good works'.[35] And although women had done a lot of newspaper work during the war, the old ways were slow to die. 'The only possible heir,' she wrote, 'would have been a male.' At the time, she thought nothing of this. 'It never crossed my mind that he [Eugene] might have viewed me as someone to take on an important job at the paper.'[36] Halberstam notes that Eugene was more admiring of Katharine than his other daughters: 'Kay, he liked to boast, was most like him.' Still, he was a 'German-Jewish patrician of the old generation', and girls didn't inherit newspapers.

Katharine was 'more sure of her politics than she was of herself'.[37] She was prepared to stand up for Roosevelt against her Republican parents, but not to stand up for herself. Eugene's biographer says:

> While he had been grooming Katharine for a larger role at the *Post*, she was still too young and inexperienced for a managerial assignment, and in any event it would be difficult to give a daughter responsibilities at the paper that he had denied to his wife. But if Graham would interest himself in the paper, with Kay at his side, that might be the ideal solution.[38]

This suggests that Eugene always intended for Katharine to be involved. Phil was a 'solution' to the problem that Agnes was indiscreet and handing over to Katharine would inflame family tensions. Eugene's son was the first to decline the offer. Phil also hesitated. 'For a long time he mulled over his problem, in consultation with Kay, but without any urging from her.'[39] Felix Morley, a *Post* editor, thought Kay was being groomed to take over.[40]

It is worth considering just how much Phil diverted Katharine's ambition: 'I became the drudge and, what's more, accepted my role as a second class citizen... increasingly unsure of myself.'[41] Interestingly, as late as 1945, when she bought a house in Washington, Graham didn't know the distinction between income and capital.[42] Her parents never talked money. She believed herself incapacitated by privilege.

Something similar happened when she had her first baby, who she only saw twice a day because she was looked after by a nurse. Being sheltered like this 'impeded my learning'.[43]

She never felt capable as a young mother, but she was constantly having to learn how to run a home, how to raise children. This intense learning process, often going against the grain of her natural abilities – she says, for example, that she lacked the patience young children require – was exhausting.[44] But it clearly prepared her for the second burst of learning she would go through. Consider what her life would have been like if she and Phil had gone to Florida and he had run for office, as he had wanted to. Being a candidate's wife was a much less attractive proposition than staying in Washington, and that may have been part of Eugene's thinking.[45] She was trapped between her mother and her husband.

By 1946, Phil was Eugene's assistant, and was running the *Post* aged thirty-one. Deborah Davis sees Katharine's self-appointed role at this time as being to 'ease' Philip into 'the style of the rich', perhaps feeling obliged because she was keeping him in Washington.[46] She made his breakfast, looked after the children, and drove him to work. She also got money from her father to buy an impressive house, which Phil disliked.[47]

Phil persuaded Eugene to go into the broadcasting business, a decision that bore fruit for many decades.[48] Katharine said of Phil's abilities: 'His early memoranda to his executives are stunning in their detailed outline of problems, potential, and objectives in business and editorial areas.' He was concerned with everything: use of editorial space, research quality, maintaining street-sales in summer, payroll costs, expenses, typos, misprints, mechanical problems, promotion, suburban coverage. He was involved in everything: recruitment, labour negotiations, redecorating the office, promoting the paper to schools, writing sales letters, changing the size of the comics. He knew all the staff on personal terms.[49] Eugene's biographer says

Phil minimized tensions with his 'genius for getting along with people'.[50] He succeeded through tireless exertion. Katharine says he knew nothing about newspapers but his 'brains and ability served him well'.[51] Isiah Berlin said of Phil, 'If he believed in something, no effort was spared. Phil was really a man of action and, above all, not a loser.'[52] Katharine saw all this, and learned from it.

Within a year, Phil was on top of his brief. She was the same, years later. They were both highly capable learners. So intense was Phil's work that when Katharine started having contractions for the birth of their third child, he had no idea what was going on. Between the war and the *Post* he had missed the births of his first two children.[53]

Philip was never going back to Florida: he was a Meyer now. But he didn't want to be a kept son-in-law. He was the only one who could resolve the hot disputes among the Meyer family – too close to them, perhaps, to be able to think of himself as an independent person. Years later, in 1957, when Eugene was old and ill, Agnes wrote to Kay about Eugene's vicious behaviour:

> When he was strong, I could fight back. That is out of the question now. He conquers through weakness and I am helpless. The only people who can help me, therefore, are you and let's admit it, especially Phil who can say anything because he is the one person who can do no wrong.[54]

Katharine kept the details of Phil's problems secret. But Eugene wasn't blind. 'Phil is too skinny and too high-powered,' he commented, worried that Phil lacked the toughness to withstand the pressure of his position.[55] People had worried about Phil before. As editor of the *Harvard Law Review* he had been emaciated, sleep-deprived, smoked too much, and would 'browbeat people if he had to and he wanted to'.[56] Phil was brilliant but, unlike Katharine, lacked resilience. Everyone had talented-spotted him rather than her because they were looking at the wrong indicators. His brilliance was obvious; his limitations became visible later. She was the other way around. As one journalist described her, Katharine was 'an unusual mixture of outward diffidence and inner self-confidence, an observer rather than a joiner, a very private person'.[57]

In 1947, Katharine didn't want to go back to work. She felt it would be too confusing for both her and Phil to be on the *Post* together. He disagreed. 'His concern for what my life was becoming led him to suggest that I start writing a weekly column.' He told his sister it would make Kay 'a little less stupid and domestic'. Kay came to feel he had done it to keep her close to the *Post* but away from the business side.[58]

In 1948, Phil made a serious bid for the *Post* to buy out their main competitor, the *Times-Herald*, which Eugene had first tried to buy in 1935.[59] It played strongly on his nerves and he was crushed when the sale fell through. 'I'm going to die for six weeks,' he told Katharine. For weeks he hardly slept, obsessively reading biographies of newspaper titans. When he realized they had 'all pulled it together' in their late twenties and early thirties he told Kay, 'I'm still in my early thirties. We're going to make it.'[60] It wasn't just Phil. Katharine wept at breakfast when she heard the purchase had fallen through.[61]

In 1948, Eugene retired. Philip bought 70 per cent of his stock, Katharine the other 30 per cent. Agnes gave Phil the money.[62] A trust was established that had veto power over the paper's future ownership.[63] It would not be possible to undercut the paper's 'principles of independence and public service' through any future sale.[64] In recompense for Phil's debts to her mother, Katharine now covered *all* their expenses other than Phil's personal expenses, something she later came to regret.[65] In 1952, Phil had another depressive episode, taking three months off.[66] His confidence never quite recovered. As Halberstam said, Phil was in his mid-thirties, no longer the boy wonder, and the *Post* was changing more slowly than he wanted.[67]

Phil eventually did buy the *Times-Herald*, and worked exhaustively to maintain circulation and quality.[68] This was the start of the *Post*'s rise. It was now in a position to challenge the *Star*, Washington, DC's leading paper. As more young, liberal people came to work in the expanding federal government, the *Post* became their paper.[69] Phil bought the *Times-Herald* in 1954; by 1955, the *Post* was profitable for the first time. By 1959, it was bigger than the *Star*.[70] Phil Graham was building his empire.

Katharine's interest in political affairs was still evident. At upper-class parties, men and women still went into separate rooms after dinner. Katharine used to go into the room where the men were talking politics, which the other wives did not. She was submissive but curious. She recalled in 1989, 'The only preparation I had was the same passionate attachment to newspapers, magazines, and television stations, and what they are about, that I had gained from indirect participation with my father and husband.'[71] Whatever else was going on in her life, she was absorbing important lessons from the culture she had spent her life in.

Under pressure and with shrinking confidence, Philip started treating Katharine badly in public, making derogatory comments about her in front of *Post* staff. These comments continued to circulate in the office after Phil was dead.[72] Katharine watched Phil with what Halberstam calls 'admiration, fear, and, on occasion, resentment'.[73] His success put more pressure on her as a hostess, which further dented her confidence. He continued what her mother had started – sour, imperious moods that made Katharine feel inadequate to even dress herself for a party. The old dynamic in her personality – deep insecurity punctuated with flashes of steel – resurfaced.

Old friends began to notice that there were, in fact, two Kay Grahams. One was the woman who accompanied Phil to parties, and who seemed awkward and unsure of herself, determined never to say anything when he was talking, or to cost him even a tiny share of the spotlight. The other was the Kay who, when Phil was busy or out of town, came alone, and though shy and reserved seemed to be a woman of considerable intelligence, depth and curiosity. Once, when they had just been married, the Grahams had been having a dinner party and Phil had said, 'Do you know the first thing Kay does every morning?' There was a pause and then he said, 'She looks in the mirror and says how lucky she is to be married to me.' Everyone laughed at the time. It seemed to be said with kindness and with so little malice it was fun, and besides everything Phil said made people laugh. But he would not have been able to say something like that now. It had become a little too true. He had grown more dashing and she had grown dowdier, and there would have been nothing to laugh about.[74]

Phil's divergent personality – vibrant in public, depressed in private – was a secret Kay had to manage on her own. Success frayed his nerves as he pushed for more than he could cope with. Katharine had Galatea syndrome: 'I felt as though he had created me.'[75]

But she was more than a Galatea. Phil was more interested in power than printing the news and became close to Lyndon Johnson, then a senator. One night, Johnson blurted out that all newspaper men could be bought for a bottle of whiskey. Phil let the comment pass; Katharine did not. When they went upstairs, Katharine 'denounced Lyndon for saying what he had said, and Phil for letting it go 'unchallenged'.[76] Her newspaper instincts were just as good, perhaps better than his. In 1957, Phil pushed himself too far helping Lyndon Johnson pass a civil rights bill; it was a monumental effort. Frenzy gave way to a breakdown. It was now obvious that he had a serious mental condition, albeit one not well understood. Katharine's warnings about his work load were ignored.[77] During a desegregation crisis shortly afterwards, he worked with hysterical energy, calling people at 3 A.M. Then it happened. 'In the middle of the night, he broke... He was racked with pain and in despair.'[78]

When the crash came, Kay took him to Virginia to rest and all he could do was ridicule her.[79] From then on, he was a seesaw of manic moods. He was also an alcoholic. She found him a psychiatrist, but had no one to talk to herself. 'If I had any strength later, it came from surviving these exhausting months.'[80] Phil's psychiatrist, Dr Farber, caused more problems. He got Phil to read Dostoyevsky, prescribed no drugs, and refused to 'label' his condition. Katharine never heard the term 'manic depression' until years later. Most bizarrely, Farber started seeing Katharine as a patient. There were periods when she was seeing Farber regularly but Phil was not. As she said, Farber was weak and Phil was in control.[81] Tellingly, it was Phil's idea for Katharine to see Farber. Seeing his friend John Kennedy get elected to the Senate set off Phil's neurotic regrets. If he had gone to Florida and started a political career instead of joining the *Post*, he too could be in the Senate. He began to feel bitter.[82]

In 1959, Philip started an affair. Katharine was tearful a lot of the time, told by friends to divorce the absent and erratic Phil. His drinking shattered her confidence. 'When I saw the drinking begin, I started to freeze; dreading the inevitable fight.'[83] They never fully realized his volatile behaviour had been a presage to manic depression. And he retained his brilliance: the way he recounted parties was so vivid, his memory so photographic, that 'it was almost better than being there, since he had a great sense of what was interesting and funny'.[84] As well as being vile and volcanic in private, 'Phil was the fizz in our lives... He had the ideas, the jokes, the games... His ideas dominated our lives. Everything rotated around him, and I willingly participated.' She would need the energy, optimism, focus, and determination she learned from him when she took over the *Post*, qualities she had not been much exposed to in childhood. 'His energy was infectious.'[85]

In 1961, Phil bought *Newsweek*. So intense were the negotiations that when Katharine's doctor told her she had tuberculosis and ought to go in for tests, she delayed her treatment and ignored her doctor's advice, going to see Phil and staying up late in smoky rooms. 'Not telling Phil,' she recalled, 'was the only thing to do.'[86] Shortly after the purchase, Katharine was put on bedrest and medication. During her confinement, she read Proust.[87]

In 1962, things reached a head. Phil's bad behaviour was more public. Often, 'he just wanted to be abusive'. Senior people at the *Post* were covering for him.[88] During an outburst at a business dinner, he was escorted from a restaurant.[89] Katharine found out about the affair when she and Phil picked up separate phones on the same line and she overheard him talking to the woman he was seeing – on Christmas Eve. Shortly afterwards, Katharine's mother gave her some earrings of hers, an unusual and touching gesture; Phil told Katharine to give them to their daughter. She did so and then went to the pantry where she burst into tears.[90]

Phil was drinking to excess, being verbally abusive, and Katharine was keeping it secret from their teenage children, one of whom found out during a particularly bad night of his drinking. Katharine was gracious and understanding about the woman Phil had been sleeping with, a journalist called Robin Webb, describing her as 'charmed out of her mind' by Phil and knowing none of the context.[91] Even now, Katharine told Phil she was there to support him, even after he walked out one day and went to New York to see Robin. Weeks later, he asked for a divorce. There were months of separation when he lived with Robin. Throughout 1962 and 1963, his mental health worsened and he was in and out of hospital. At this time Phil said to President Kennedy, 'Do you know who you're talking to?' and Kennedy replied, 'I know I'm not talking to the Phil Graham I have so much admiration for.'[92]

Phil left Katharine and was using lawyers to try to get her shares in the *Post*. This, finally, was a step too far. Remembering the years of losses her father had covered to keep the *Post* alive and the fact that she had enabled Phil to buy his share by paying their living expenses, Katharine knew she must stand firm. 'My bitterness about his plans was extreme, and my intention to dig in was total.'[93] Her steel was back. As Phil seemed to prosper during their separation, she became depressed: 'I felt that no-one cared, that I didn't count anymore, and that life was passing me by; all good things were going to Phil.'[94] What she knew, though, was that she wouldn't let him divorce her *and* keep a controlling interest in the paper.

Katharine then had the 'complicated relief' of having Phil come back to her. In a depression so bad one friend said he was almost 'paralysed', Phil broke off with Robin and was readmitted to a psychiatric hospital. It was only at this point that the diagnosis of manic depression was made. Katharine hadn't yet learned that untreated manic depression could be fatal.[95] In August 1963, having talked his way out of the hospital for the weekend – he organized a vote among the other patients as part of his manipulation; he was described as magnetic, dancing the devil's dance, by members of the hospital – Philip shot himself while Katharine was taking a nap.[96] She was forty-five and suddenly in control of the *Washington Post*. Her circumstances had changed, and now, so did she. 'Left alone, no matter at what age or under what circumstance, you have to remake your life.'[97] And she did. As is often the case with life-changing decisions, Katharine 'had no conception of the role I was eventually to fill'.[98]

Graham now undertook what the *New York Times* later called a 'mythic act of self-transformation'.[99] She refused advice to sell the *Post*, appointed a new editor after realizing the paper had been stagnating (she picked Ben Bradlee, supposedly because 'he seemed a man who could get things done'),[100] and oversaw one of the most important periods of newspaper reporting in the twentieth century. The fact that she never let herself get entirely detached from the *Post*, and the continuing resonance of her father's example, were important.

> Some of my friends suggested that I hire someone to run it; others, that I sell it; others, that I marry again. But I had been so closely associated with the struggle that had gone into getting where we were that it never occurred to me to do anything but go to work.[101]

She told a friend the *Post* was a family business and there was a 'new generation' to think about.[102] It took time to get her new colleagues' respect. Howard Simons, the managing editor, said she was like 'a shaky little doe, coming in on wobbly legs out of the forest'.[103] But Graham 'evolved into a regal, sometimes intimidating and always principled force'. She picked mentors for herself, changing when she needed to. Ruthless perhaps, she knew she lacked time. She loved news and had an instinct for the speed at which political business had to be conducted. 'Her view was that she could not dither; her mistakes had to be corrected quickly.'[104] The *Post* became more profitable, bought new titles and television stations, and went public under her leadership. Such was her enthusiasm, she loitered at reporters' desks during breaking stories. She had become quite a different person.

Graham's personality was a combination of strong ego and low self-esteem. This meant people saw her as a binary whereas she was a paradox. Warren Buffett, one of the few people who actually got to know Katharine, described her as 'Fearful but willful. Patrician but democratic. Wounded by the people she cared most about.'[105] As she was at the University of Chicago, so she was at the *Post*: a woman who was clever and self-directing, but who also often lacked the confidence to trust her own judgement. In an interview with Buffett's biographer, one of the *Washington Post*'s board members gave an account of Graham's character that shows the paradox at work.

> She would second-guess herself. She would fall in and out of love with people. She could be bullied. She could get overwhelmed by certain people in the business. She would meet somebody and be sort of dazzled with them for a little while and think they knew all the answers. She thought men knew all about business and women didn't know anything. At bottom, that was the real problem. Her mother told her that and her husband told her that, over and over and over and over again.[106]

Describing Richard Hutchins and Mortimer Adler's course at the University of Chicago, Graham said, 'When I didn't do well the most awful depression set in, because so much depended on that performance. When I did do well, my elation carried over to everything else I was doing at the university.'[107] This volatility remained with her for the rest of her life. She never liked public speaking, getting into near-panics beforehand. Before one speech Buffett went to help her prepare. He could see what others could not and was able to give the simple, direct advice she needed: 'I just tried to convince her that she was a hell of a lot smarter than all of those dumb males.'[108] Once she realized how much her colleagues simply didn't respect her – Buffett reports that people would 'push her buttons just to watch her fall apart' – Buffett became almost her sole source of support for a period. What she needed wasn't advice, but encouragement. 'I would just make her make the damn decision.'[109]

In 1971, Graham and her editors decided to publish the Pentagon Papers, leaked documents about the American government's conduct of the Vietnam War. The *New York Times* had published a series of stories based on the documents and were prevented from publishing any more by federal courts. The papers were sent to the *Post*, creating a dilemma.

> All the writers and editors implored me to go ahead. The lawyers said 'Don't,' and the businesspeople said 'Take your time.' I was shocked when Fritz Beebe, who was chairman of the company… said that he would not go ahead. But somehow he very subtly left the door open for me to say 'Let's publish' if I thought it was the right thing to do. I realized that if I did, it would be the first time he and I had ever disagreed. My decision really had to be instinctive, and my instincts said 'Let's go.' We did.[110]

This was not just dramatic because the *Post* was confronting the courts and the White House. The *Post* had floated on the stock exchange two days before. There was a risk that this could be ruinous. Graham herself had a lot at stake. The editor Harry Rosenfeld happened to be in the courthouse one day during the hearing when the *Post* was being sued to prevent further publication. He asked her why she had made such a bold decision. It was celebrated by the journalists, but they had no money at risk. What made her do it? She told him that in the eight years since she'd taken over, the *Post* had become an 'enterprising paper' and was full of 'quality staff' – choosing not to publish would have put all that at risk.[111]

The following year, under threat of financial ruin from the White House and of prosecution from the Attorney General, the *Post* broke the Watergate scandal, the story that began the downfall of Richard Nixon. As with the Pentagon Papers, it was Graham's leadership that enabled the *Post* to follow the story. She was now the most significant decision-maker in American news.[112] That status relied most on her ability to withstand pressure, something she was all too familiar with. The White House tried to squash the newspaper's reporting by financially threatening the other parts of the company's interests.

> The first blood-chilling message I got came from the Nixon administration, even before Watergate, at the time of the Pentagon Papers. It was delivered at a social occasion attended by a *Post* reporter and his wife. They were told by Richard Kleindienst that the Justice Department might go forward with criminal prosecution. He thought someone should remind me that no one under criminal indictment could own television stations.[113]

We should not be surprised at Kay's resilience. Her father would not have been. Despite his worries about Phil's ability to withstand the pressure, Eugene wasn't worried about the future of the *Post*. He died before Phil shot himself, and didn't know that Kay would be called on to take over, but he knew she was there, in the background, as he had arranged when he appointed Phil. He once compared Kay to a doll that 'no matter how many times she might be knocked down, she always came up straight'.[114] He worried about Phil; he was reassured by Kay.

Katharine is sometimes talked of as being inferior to Phil, as if he had made the *Post* great and she had then managed it. This is not true. The most important decision in the history of the *Post* was the publication of the Pentagon Papers. It was a decision that had to be made at short notice and under intense pressure. The *New York Times* had been prevented by the courts from publishing a specific story ahead of time – a unique occurrence and a threat to the free press. If the *Post* had not published, it would have been the end of their aspiration to rival the *New York Times*. What would Phil have done? Perhaps he would have taken the risk. But he was concerned with power. He hobnobbed with politicians and acquired businesses. He wrote Lyndon Johnson's acceptance speech for the Vice Presidency slot of the JFK ticket. He was too involved. And too intense. James Reston, a senior figure at the *New York Times*, refused several offers to go to the *Post*. Phil was 'too hot for me, too involved in politics, felt too deeply about people, even his own people on the paper'.[115] Herb Klein, the journalist and politician, said when she died, 'Katharine Graham stayed above anything petty, and that's one of the qualities that even in a crisis you remember and admire her for.'[116] The same could never have been said of Phil. As her daughter said in a letter just before she started at the *Post*, Katharine Graham had 'good judgement, great ability to get along with people, earn their respect and discern their strengths and weaknesses and desire to follow things up which Pa was quite unwilling to do'.[117] She also made sound investments, just as Phil had done, purchasing a 45 per cent stake in the Paris edition of the *Herald Tribune*, which returned multiples of her investment.[118]

Katharine inherited a tired paper from Phil: the Managing Director was past his best, the editorial quality was declining, and the reporting lacked energy. She invested in talent, doubled the editorial budget and increased newsroom staff by a fifth after Bradlee arrived.[119] By the end of the 1960s, Graham and Bradlee made the *Post* a better paper than it had ever been. They made it fit to report stories like the Pentagon Papers and Watergate, not just to be a crux of power. Phil aspired to *The Times* of London, the 'thundering voice of the ruling class';[120] Kay achieved something much bigger and more vital – a paper that held the ruling class to account.

The Pentagon Papers decision came at the same time that the *Post* was being floated on the stock exchange. The decision required resilience. Phil's volatile, erratic, egoistical leadership would have been a risk. Would he have made a deal with the White House, like he had done with other stories? Who knows. Would he have been influenced by his political friendships? We can't say. We do know that Kay, with her ability, as her father said, to always come up straight when she got knocked down, made the right decision and transformed the business. David Remnick summed up the differences in their leadership:

> Under Phil Graham, the *Post* had a well-respected editorial page and mediocrity nearly everywhere else; it was not even the best paper in the city. Phil's greatest successes were in business: buying and absorbing the *Times-Herald* in 1954, purchasing *Newsweek* (for a song) in 1961, and making inroads against the dominant paper in town, the *Evening Star* (which folded in 1981).[121]

Phil made the *Post* the leading paper in Washington and made it into a political force among the elite. Katharine made it into an international mass media company, and a defender of free speech. She made it into a dominant newspaper.

They were different leaders with different skills – her achievement is bigger and longer lasting. She knew what Phil did not: she didn't have to hide her worries; she had to deal with them. There is a quotation, perhaps apocryphal, that shows Katharine's deep understanding of how to lead: 'I think that there are moments when looking helpless seems to help.'[122] She knew how to change her manner to suit the situation; and she knew that she had to stand firm and make the decision about the Pentagon Papers, a decision that reverberated throughout America and emboldened the entire *Post* staff. Phil had charm; Katharine had guts.

She was a strong-minded businessperson, too. In 1975, the *Post* saw down a union strike that could have broken the *Post* financially, as it employed over seven hundred unnecessary printing staff.[123] In one strike, machines were damaged and the pressroom foreman was beaten. The union couldn't be allowed to win. In the face of this behaviour, Katharine was resolved: she offered a wage increase, and said no one involved in the destruction could come back. The *Post* would reduce its workforce by attrition and control schedules. She also offered a lump sum. The response was bitter. Katharine was burned in effigy, and Charles Davis, a key lieutenant of the pressmen's leader, John Dugan, carried a placard that read 'Phil Shot the Wrong Graham'. The argument was fundamentally about the introduction of computers into the *Post*'s operations, and Katharine wasn't going to back down. The fight was the end of the union's power at the *Post* and profits recovered from their early 1970s' dip.[124] Katharine's inherent insecurity wasn't a problem anymore.

She was later criticized for this decision by people who thought she was in hock to Warren Buffett. She replied forcefully: 'I particularly detested the sexist implications of stories like these – always being depicted as the difficult woman, while whoever left the company was the victim of my female whims.'[125] She had got used to dealing with condescension early on. 'When you inherit editors who have known you... they condescend without knowing they're condescending.' To counteract this, she was firm about the way she would be addressed. One editor recalled, 'It was always Mrs., not Ms., and she insisted on her title of Chairman and not Chairwoman.'[126]

Kay Graham exemplifies all of the principles discussed in this book. She was prepared for her luck. She was networked. She was resilient. She was persistent. She was energetic. She had the advantages of natural intelligence, a patrician upbringing, inherent motivation, a resilient personality and a strong belief in the *Post*. All of that helped make her successful. But no one was expecting her to be able to take on the role, let alone succeed. It required something different. Mrs Graham the Chairman had come a long way from being Kay, whose husband teased her for being fat. When her son Donald took over in 1979, he said, 'The uniqueness of my mother's story is that she had something dropped in her lap. She had to fill in without warning and she performed brilliantly.'[127] Katharine Graham is an example of how putting people in new contexts often has surprising results. All of these ideas will be explored in more detail.

What ties it all together is that Katharine Graham did not take a direct path to her destination. It took a variety of seemingly unconnected experiences to make her into Mrs Graham, the Chairman. She had no MBA. Her experiences were sometimes beneficial, sometimes miserable. She was often a domestic person, out of the workforce. Her experience of managing people was gained in her family and her marriage more than in an office. The resilience she used to manage strikes and high-stakes business decisions was learned from her relationship with her mother. She had never been in a directly comparable business position before she became CEO, but her whole life had been preparation for the role.

She had a very inefficient preparation for being Mrs Graham, and that might have worked better than taking a more direct route to the top.

2
The benefits of inefficient preparation

Many late bloomers do not plan their success. Many do not know what they are aiming for much of the time. They have to rework their early attempts, re-experiment with their ideas, and persist until they find out what works. This isn't efficient. Discovering what you want to do with your life in your mid-thirties, starting your first successful business aged forty-five, switching careers in your fifties, or finally getting the time, resources, or courage to do what you want in retirement might suggest time wasted and opportunities lost. But the uncertain and inefficient path often gives late bloomers experiences and understanding they couldn't have got any other way.

This is well illustrated by the famous spaghetti and marshmallow experiment, which psychologist and design thinker Tom Wujec has run hundreds of times. The goal is to build a tower of spaghetti that will support the weight of a marshmallow. Business school graduates and corporate executives often do badly on this exercise. Kindergarten students routinely outperform them. The reason is simple: business graduates and executives spend too much time planning. They make team structures, appoint group leaders, debate different ideas, and look for the 'right' solution. They take an efficient approach. The children do none of this. They just build. Unlike the businesspeople, the children build many prototypes and learn from each iteration until they reach a successful tower. As you might expect, one of the most successful groups of all is engineers and architects. (Another successful group is CEOs, but only when they have an executive assistant with them. As we will see in the influence chapter, having the right people to manage the work process makes all the difference.)[1]

Late bloomers often think and work more like kindergarteners and engineers than business executives: they iterate until they succeed. The rest of this chapter will focus on the way meandering can create an effective career path through iteration or inefficient preparation. Inefficient preparation has two components: slow development and finding a calling. The examples in this chapter, from politics, business, and music, show that late bloomers are not always delayed, distracted or held back. Many people take the inefficient route for practical reasons, because of their luck, or because it fits with their personality. Not getting a head start doesn't stop them from flourishing later.

•••

In an interview with the *Harvard Business Review*, the comedian Jerry Seinfeld, who wrote and starred in the most successful sitcom of all time, praised inefficiency:

> **You and Larry David wrote Seinfeld together, without a traditional writers' room, and burnout was one reason you stopped. Was there a more sustainable way to do it? Could McKinsey or someone have helped you find a better model?**
>
> Who's McKinsey?
>
> **It's a consulting firm.**
>
> Are they funny?
>
> **No.**
>
> Then I don't need them. If you're efficient, you're doing it the wrong way. The right way is the hard way. The show was successful because I micromanaged it – every word, every line, every take, every edit, every casting. That's my way of life.[2]

If you're efficient, you're doing it the wrong way. That could be a motto for late bloomers. There are observed benefits to developing slowly. The legendary jazz guitarist Django Reinhardt was self-taught. He couldn't read music. He learned everything the hard way. That lack of formal training left him with huge inventiveness. This is a method of many creative and innovative musicians. Jack Cecchini, one of the few people who has mastered both jazz and classical guitar, told the journalist David Epstein that the slow and painful method of self-teaching was better than being taught.[3]

What Jerry Seinfeld and Jack Cecchini both realized is that easy learning doesn't stick. Manfred von Richthofen, the First World War fighter pilot known as the Red Baron, was a cavalry officer before joining the air force. He was a poor flying student. He crashed the first time he took the controls. Although he was never a natural showman, he was an impressive tactician and an excellent shot. He took down eighty enemy aircraft during the war. What might feel laborious to a late bloomer – or look inefficient to an outside observer – is often the best method for development.

The economist David Galenson has identified this inefficient development in late-blooming artists and writers. Galenson contrasts 'experimental artists', who peak in the second half of their careers, with 'conceptual artists', who tend to peak before they are thirty. Conceptual artists are systematic, have a clear vision early on, and make detailed plans of their work. They proceed from first principles.

Experimental artists learn by doing: their work is research. Each piece of work is a test, a discovery. Rather than seeing each painting as a finished execution or an instalment in a series of complete works, each is an experiment that gives results. These results accumulate and are constantly tested and taken into account in future works. In this way, experimental artists gradually accrue their vision and the techniques to achieve it. Chapter 3 shows how these ideas are relevant beyond art and literature and how they can be applied to the life of the late-blooming businessman Ray Kroc.

Inefficient preparation relies on stamina. You have to be able to keep going. Later on, we will consider Margaret Thatcher, who was a mother, housewife, and barrister, as well as prospective parliamentary candidate: she sometimes felt like she went around the house on roller skates and said that it is easier for a woman to give up power than a man because 'I can fill the time spring cleaning the house'.[4] Michelangelo, a late-blooming architect, had so much energy in his final decade that he made himself a hat that held candles, so he could sit up sculpting late into the night.

In their recent book about finding great talent, the economist Tyler Cowen and the venture capitalist Daniel Gross highlight the importance of stamina. Rather than endorse the psychological concepts of grit and conscientiousness, they point out that successful people have energy. This is a trait venture capitalists and other investors look for when deciding whether to support a start-up. Grit, popularized by the psychologist Angela Dworkin, emphasizes passion and perseverance. But it is the perseverance that matters.[5]

In *Range*, David Epstein shows how this affects schooling and education. Psychology has shown that intense, short-term pattern learning, the sort of thing we do for tests, has a high wear-off rate, whereas the long struggle to really understand concepts and systems creates lasting learning. We all know the difference between learning how to do something to pass a test and persisting until it all clicks into place. That second sort of learning enables more creative, individual thinking.

The financier John Paulson was described by the *New York Times* as 'a relatively unknown hedge fund manager' in 2007 with 'a reputation for running a solid if boring hedge fund that made bets on the outcomes of various mergers and acquisitions'.[6] He later became one of the most successful traders of all time by meandering and learning through persistence.

Paulson took a long and winding road to his success. He lacked direction in college, went to South America where he began selling shirts to Bloomingdale's, went back to Harvard Business School and joined Boston Consulting Group. By the time he was twenty-eight, he was frustrated with consulting and switched to finance. At Bear Stearns he rose to Managing Director within a few years but disliked the politics and wanted to make his own investments, so he left and joined a smaller firm. That didn't last long, and he took a career break to enjoy himself. Then he started his own hedge fund. He was moody, had a limited track record, and sometimes struggled to recruit people. All the way through his career, he had got top grades and rapid promotion, but he was running a tiny firm making no strides towards the great success he wanted. In 1996, aged forty-one, his firm managed $16 million of assets, 'small-fry in the hedge fund world'.[7] He settled down: stopped partying, got married, ate healthily. He was frustrated about missing the real estate boom, feeling 'under-utilized' in his merger and acquisition work, watching his classmates become far more successful than him.[8] But as he became more serious, the firm grew to $3 billion, still small but getting noticed.

Then Paulson hired another late bloomer, Paolo Pellegrini, who had been fired twice, was divorced, and had no net worth. In the world of finance, he was incredibly unsuccessful. Working with Paulson, Pellegrini became interested in the mortgage market. He immersed himself in the data to an absurdly obsessive degree, painstakingly investigating every angle from scratch. People joked that he would never take a shortcut, even to get to a nearby street. As we have seen, sometimes it's better to be inefficient and Pellegrini once said, 'It's more fascinating for me to do everything on my own and reinvent the wheel.'[9] Just like Jerry Seinfeld and Larry David writing *Seinfeld*, the only way Pellegrini could do his research well enough to get the answer was to do it exhaustingly. To others it looked crazy – but it worked. Pellegrini spotted that the complex array of loans and credit swaps in the mortgage market would implode when house prices went down – his immersion into historical interest rate data revealed that house prices were bound to go down. So he and Paulson bet against the market. Paulson's firm made $15 billion from that trade, perhaps the most successful investing position of all time.

•••

Late bloomers don't always have a specific goal, but they do have a vocation or sense of calling. The inefficient development of Jerry Seinfeld and Django Reinhardt was driven by creative compulsion. Katharine Graham had a passion for news, no matter what was happening. A calling or vocation can be more motivating than a specific goal. And wanting to do something just for the sake of doing it – because you love comedy or music, because you find political news compelling, because you just want to understand something – is often essential to discovering your goal.

According to the psychologists Jane Sturges and Catherine Bailey, there are several different ways people come to their callings. Sturges and Bailey distinguish between latent callings and lost callings. Latent callings are only discovered late in life, when your circumstances change. Lost callings are vocations we discover when we are young and then lose sight of in middle age as life takes over.

Latent callings are discovered when the context of someone's life changes to make their calling seem more valid. The late-blooming artists Grandma Moses and Bill Traylor are examples of people with latent callings. Moses started painting in her late seventies; Traylor began drawing aged eighty-five. Both had lived demanding, difficult lives. Moses worked from the age of twelve, had many children (several of whom died), and was required to work on her farm for most of her life. Traylor was born into slavery and became a sharecropper. Retirement in Moses' case and old-age homelessness in Traylor's were the contexts in which they could legitimately pursue their gifts; before that, it simply wasn't possible or sensible for them to do so. (Moses' story is examined in more detail in Chapter 6.)

While many people regret not being able to pursue their vocation early in life, people like Moses and Traylor do not; their callings are simply discovered later on. This can happen at any age. Mother Teresa felt her calling to leave the nunnery and work with the poor after twenty years as a nun. Madonna Buder is a nun who started athletic training aged forty-eight and began competing in Ironman competitions in her eighties. Ray Moon had polio as a child and was a heavy smoker and drinker as an adult. It was in his seventies that he was persuaded by a friend to take up bodybuilding. He then won several competitions in Australia. Mae Laborde became a television actress in her nineties. She had been a bank teller and department store worker, and had worked for the television star Lawrence Welk. It was only in late retirement that she found her calling.[10] There's a great benefit to having a latent calling. Sturges and Bailey show that people who immerse themselves in their interests in retirement, when they have the time and money to do so, get a surge of positive feelings.

Many people, though, abandon or lose their calling early on. Trying to enter a profession, especially a creative or artistic one, requires resources of time and money that people are unable or unwilling to make. Repeated failures use up the time you might be using to start earning money and developing a career. Often, it makes more practical sense to stop pursuing your vocation and get a job. Many people will also lack the network, peers or mentors that are often so important for success (as we will see in the chapter on influence, Chapter 6).

Sturges and Bailey interviewed thirty-two musicians who had set their calling aside earlier in life and pursued less vocational careers. All of them reported a very early response to music, from the age of two or three, and a moment of realizing music was essential to their life in some way. At some point in their teens or twenties, they abandoned the idea of a musical career. There were three reasons: working conditions, such as poor pay and job insecurity; a belief that they didn't have the required level of talent or personality; and finally, a sense of discouragement, either from relatives or through lack of opportunities.

Sturges and Bailey describe that there are three routes back to a lost calling: accommodation, emergent and deferred. Accommodation of a calling means keeping it as a hobby alongside your work. Emergent callings start off weak and become stronger as you age. Deferred callings are lost in middle life and have to be completely rediscovered. People who give up their callings – or who perhaps never felt them that strongly – often return to them with renewed vigour. And the ones who were least interested at the start might be the most dedicated learners and practitioners later on.

The musicians who accommodated their calling – keeping music as a hobby – maintained their musical practice, but with less commitment than a professional would have. They refused to let their interest die.[11] They changed where they worked or the hours they worked to make sure they had time to practise. It was unthinkable for them to live without music. This made it easier to transition into a musical retirement, by increasing their time commitment as work trailed off.

The musicians who deferred their calling – spending many years, sometimes decades, without music – simply could not fit music into their lives. One of them said: 'I was very interested in my work and you can't do everything.'[12] Some of them found this frustrating to the point of misery. One compared it to having a limb removed. Despite this, they mostly didn't regret the choices they had made. But once they reached retirement, some moment of inspiration reached them – hearing a choir as they passed a church, for example – and they started again with music, in some cases even learning a new instrument.

Those with an emergent calling – whose initial vocation was weaker but became stronger throughout their lives – found it easier to put music aside when they were young. These people reached a high level of accomplishment and reverting to amateur status was less appealing to them. They came back to music in two ways, either through a crisis or transformation moment, such as attending a funeral and realizing they were running out of time in their life, or because they needed to fill up the time they had available once they retired. Surprisingly, this group was the most likely to learn extensively: they studied for postgraduate degrees and set up orchestras. This emergent rediscovery of a vocation had a remarkably strong effect. As one of them said, 'It's reached the inner musician in me which nothing ever did when I was younger.'[13] Out of former accomplishment, a vocation emerged.

For many people in Sturges and Bailey's study, irrespective of how they came back to music, having kept it as a hobby rather than a profession increased their interest. Rather than experience the drudgery of a steady music job, or the fear of being asked to play something unfamiliar, their interest was kept lively by its marginal role in their lives. 'People say keep your passion as your hobby but not your career, because it will be more satisfying … I think in retrospect looking back that was probably sound advice.'[14] Amateurs have more agency, more room to develop slowly. They meander.

It is worth pausing here to note that a meta-study of the literature on 'callings' found that while having the intrinsic motivation of a calling can increase your wellbeing, people with a very strong calling also often experience the sort of stress we associate with overwork. People with a calling who aren't able to work at it, of course, will sometimes experience the unhappy effects of that dissonance, too. People who believe in the moral aspect of their calling so strongly that it cannot be achieved are also liable to be disappointed. The meta-study found little evidence to support this, instead finding that having a calling increases your wellbeing, often significantly. However, the studies the authors reviewed were largely quantitative and the qualitative studies they did not review were often based in more extreme contexts, like zookeepers and animal shelter workers. Those people are more likely to have an unattainable moral calling and thus to be disappointed in some way.[15]

Although late bloomers often exhibit early signs of their talents, the idea of a discovered vocation is important. We do not know everything we want to do with our lives when we are young. The psychologists Bryan J. Dik and Ryan D. Duffy have said that a calling is not always an undeniable or transcendent feeling early in life but can be 'an ongoing process of evaluating the purpose and meaningfulness of activities within a job and their contribution to the common good'.[16] In Dik and Duffy's view, a vocation is the result of the way a person views their work, not the work itself. You do not have to be a charity worker or teacher to have a sense of vocation; all jobs can produce a sense of vocation through approaching your work as a calling and seeing the social value of what you do.

Chris Gardner became a stockbroker despite having no experience, no college education, and an atypical background for a finance career at that time. It was a long journey of inefficient preparation, not just an inspirational moment, that made him successful. He only found his calling after several other jobs.

Gardner's childhood had been turbulent, his young adulthood uncertain. His stepfather was violent and abusive. As a child, Gardner spent time in foster homes. Although he was often isolated, withdrawn and struggling, he was also dedicated, focused, and strong. From his mother he learned self-reliance. She told him the cavalry was never going to arrive: it was up to him. From his uncle he took inspiration to join the navy, which he did as soon as he was old enough. In the navy, Gardner began working as a medical specialist, which connected him to a surgeon who later hired Gardner into his research lab. He intended to train as a doctor.

However, changes to the medical profession meant it was a difficult and less lucrative option. It would have taken Gardner a decade of training to become a surgeon and surgeons' earnings were going to decline. He was also bored by the fact that his practical ability far outstripped his qualifications: 'It was going to be ten more years of qualifications before I could officially do what I already was doing.'[17] Aged twenty-six, he decided to stop his medical training. At that time, his marriage was coming to an end, and he started an intense relationship with another person that involved skipping work due to his 'feverishly aroused state' and taking cocaine. Chris Gardner wasn't yet on the path to success. He did, however, become a father. Having a son inspired Gardner to find his biological father, whom he had never known. And a row with his new partner prompted him to find a new job that could support the family better than his modestly paid lab work did. He doubled his salary selling medical equipment.

Something about meeting his father helped settle what Gardner called his 'no daddy blues' and he became ambitious about business, trying to learn how to earn the $80,000 salary of the top man at his new firm. He learned a hard lesson: 'The best salespeople are born that way.'[18] Gardner was determined to do well but struggled to see how he could make it to the top. Leaving a sales call one day, calculating how far he was from the prized $80,000 salary, he saw a Ferrari circling the parking lot. Gardner asked the driver some questions and discovered that, as a stockbroker, the man earned $80,000 *a month*. He had found his calling. So intense was this realization, Gardner compared it to the first time he heard the music of Miles Davis.[19]

Gardner was twenty-seven. His circumstances were nothing like those of most people in stockbroking at that time: no degree, no connections, no experience. And he was Black. But he was so dedicated to this new calling that he was eventually jailed for non-payment of the parking tickets he amassed while he took meetings with stockbrokers to try to get a job. When he finally found someone to take a chance on him, Gardner quit his job in sales only to turn up to the brokerage and find out that the man who had hired him had been fired. He didn't have a new job after all. Now he was odd-jobbing with a child to support. After an altercation, his partner left with their son while he was in jail for the unpaid parking tickets, and he had to turn up to an interview in jeans and trainers. Rather than ruining his chances, this prompted the man interviewing him to relate stories of his three divorces. Gardner got the job.[20] The small stipend on this training programme meant Gardner had to stay with friends and acquaintances in rotation, and eventually get a room in a flophouse. He later came to see this as preparation for his biggest challenge – navigating homelessness with his son after he was returned to him by his partner.

Gardner's circumstances were a huge obstacle to his success, but they provided him with the preparation he needed once he had found his calling. Not only did he become a successful stockbroker, but he also founded his own multimillion-dollar firm.

His mother's lesson about self-reliance gave him the determination he needed to train as a stockbroker: even while homeless and a single parent, Gardner made two hundred calls a day and was routinely the best broker at the firm. When he worked in the laboratory, with plenty of medical experience from the navy but no degree, he was subject to the bigotry of white male medical students from elite universities. But the doctor running the institution made it clear: Gardner was in charge. It was up to him to run his lab, and he learned 'not to take some of their superior attitudes personally, in the same way I couldn't take it personally when my mentors put me in that position of control'. This reinforced what his mother had taught him: 'No one can take away your legitimacy or give you your legitimacy if you don't claim it for yourself.'[21] This taught Gardner about management and talent spotting, a crucial element of running a business. It might seem unconnected to his later career but it was an apprenticeship in how to be a leader. The way he learned to deal with the racism of injured sailors when he worked in the medical centre later paid off when he was able to withstand the abusive jokes of his highest paying client.

Gardner displays many other core qualities of a late bloomer that we will encounter in later chapters. Chance played a huge role in his life, for better and for worse, but he was able to turn those opportunities to his advantage, and it was partly his personality that created his good luck. This is discussed in Chapter 4. When he joined the navy, worked in the lab, quit medical training, and joined the stockbroker firm, Gardner changed his surroundings. He put himself under new, beneficial influences. In Chapter 8, we will see how changing your circumstances can change your life. And in Chapter 9, we will see this sort of persistent transformation again in the story of Audrey Sutherland. (Like Gardner, Sutherland believed in the importance of doing *something* now in service of your bigger goal.) Most of all, he had learned from working in a care home, a navy medical centre, a research lab, a sales job, that he could walk 'into jobs with no knowledge' and still succeed. As we will see in Chapter 8, once we become experts in one field it can be difficult to go back and start as a beginner again. By changing track several times, Chris Gardner had learned the value of being a learner quite early in life. He came late to his calling but a long period of inefficient preparation meant he was perfectly positioned to become a late-blooming stockbroker.

•••

Inefficient preparation involves finding a calling and achieving success through slow development. It might involve learning through a series of failures, rediscovering or re-engaging a lost vocation, or blending various interests into a new opportunity. The life of the novelist Penelope Fitzgerald (1916–2000) demonstrates all of these elements of inefficient preparation in the pursuit of a vocation.

Penelope Fitzgerald wrote some of the great fiction of the twentieth century. Her final novel, written in her seventies, won the National Book Critics Circle Award in the United States. Somewhat neglected in her lifetime, her reputation has grown since she died in 2000, and she is being recognized as one of the great writers of the twentieth century.[22] Philip Hensher said in 2001, 'Of all the novelists of the last quarter-century, she has the most unarguable claim on greatness.'[23] Fitzgerald had been expected to be a prodigy. She was from a demanding and intellectual family of writers. She went to the same Oxford college as her mother. When she left, she said that she was ready to start writing. The fact that she was fifty-eight, rather than twenty-one, when her first book came out is the big mystery of her life. Why did she start so late?

The standard answer is her husband, Desmond, whose drinking, failed career and erratic life pursued by creditors left Fitzgerald with no time or energy to write. The expectations of childhood might have been a burden, too. She began her first book just after her father died and her second as her husband lay dying. Critics point to her childhood stories, anonymous reviews for the *Times Literary Supplement*, her probable contributions to Desmond's history of the Irish Guards, and the literary magazine they ran together as examples of an early start. She wrote two short stories as a young child and two in the 1950s when she was a mother. It seems likely that she published a short story under her husband's name in 1951.[24] The most recent critical study says that Desmond held her back, and this early work shows her promise.[25]

But this overlooks many important facts about her life. Fitzgerald wasn't a frustrated prodigy. She was a late bloomer.

Fitzgerald herself said: 'I think you can write at any time of your life.'[26] Critics see such statements as a pose, false modesty. It is difficult to take her at face value because of her turbulent life. She's a prime example of a woman born during the First World War, held back because of her gender. But most people who write anonymous reviews for the *TLS* don't become genius novelists. This looks at her life backwards. As well as the vicissitudes of her life, there must be something about Fitzgerald herself that explains her lateness. We risk not taking her seriously if we think that a difficult marriage and a teaching job are enough to turn a potential genius into a mute inglorious Milton. Of course, there were times when it seemed as if life might have got her down for good. That is why Fitzgerald's story is so important. There is a long unwritten history of talent failing to prosper.

After Oxford, Fitzgerald worked for the BBC during the Second World War. She didn't lack material to write about: this was the basis of her fourth book, *Human Voices*, written when she was aged sixty-three. After the war, Desmond came home with trauma, screaming in the night. Penelope had a miscarriage and a baby who died shortly after birth. Her biographer, Hermione Lee, says 'there were signs of strain'[27] in Fitzgerald's work.

The question hanging over this period is whether she would have started writing fiction if it weren't for these difficulties. She *was* writing: scripts, film reviews, science and children's programmes, and a special for *Woman's Hour*. The Fitzgeralds took on the editorship of a literary magazine. She also decorated their house fashionably, with black walls and ceramics, some of them her own. She was taking pottery lessons in Hampstead and practising her drawing. She was regarded by acquaintances as knowledgeable, artistic and literary.[28] It is a mistake to think that there was no creative time available at this period. Desmond should not be blamed entirely. Fitzgerald once said 'nothing is ever all anybody's fault'.[29] After he died, she wrote to a friend, 'The truth is I was spoilt, as with all our ups and downs Desmond always thought everything I did was right.' She told the *Guardian* in 1998, 'The sort of men I like are life's losers. They struggle gallantly, but they really ought to be left in peace.'[30] These were partly years of impediment, partly, as her son-in-law says, 'The years when, as Cervantes said to explain his own long silence, she was living her life.'[31]

Her life, though, was exhausting. Her letters are full of her tiredness. The year Desmond died, she wrote to a friend:

> I think we middle-class ladies are really driving ourselves mad by doing all the things that were formerly done by a 'staff' and keeping up our cultural interests as well – tho' there you are, we can't help it. But when I lived in the council flat I noticed the other ladies seemed to have time to stand on their doorsteps and talk to each other all day, and I thought they managed better than I did.[32]

There is a clear image of a woman struggling under the many demands of her life here, but also of a woman with time, space and energy for cultural interests.

Importantly, she didn't only want to be a literary writer. Her son-in-law wrote, 'She is on record as saying in an ideal life she wouldn't have gone to Oxford to read English, but would have become an artist. Much of her writing in *World Review* (and her first book, *Burne-Jones*) was on art.'[33] There were discussions with a publisher as late as the 1970s about Penelope writing a book on flower symbolism in Renaissance art.[34] She arrived at literature; she wasn't entirely diverted from it. As late as 1981, when she had written four novels, she wrote to her editor, Richard Ollard, that she had been asked to look at William Morris's novel and 'a mysterious chestful of Pre-Raphaelite papers' as well as having her (ultimately never published) work on the Poetry Bookshop to keep her busy. 'Perhaps I'm better employed doing this... than in writing novels,' she mused. A response, no doubt, to the slow sales of *Human Voices* that year, but telling nonetheless.[35] She had won the Booker Prize at this point.

Her interest in the Arts and Crafts movement recurs in *The Beginning of Spring*. That novel was also informed by a package holiday she took to Moscow in 1975 and years of studying Russian, involving many 'lectures, films, theatres, exhibitions' with the Great Britain–USSR Association.[36] In 1979, she went to Florence, a visit that would re-emerge nearly a decade later in her novel *Innocence*.[37] She studied Spanish, German and Chinese; visited Venice, Germany, Elba, Turkey, Madrid, Greece, and other countries. Her letters mention studying Spanish grammar at night.[38] So esoteric was the influence of this cultural immersion that when she based *Human Voices* on a poem by Heinrich Heine no critic noticed.[39]

She helped her daughter study *Scènes de le vie de provence* for her A level. As her son-in-law says, that book influenced 'the moral atmosphere' of *The Bookshop*, and 'perhaps also some of the form (each chapter a scene)'.[40] For *The Blue Flower* she read the 'records of the salt mines from cover to cover in German'.[41] She had Novalis's letters and private documents out of the London Library for two years.[42] Wendy Lesser has shown that details of language, like the use of the definite article before a name in Germany, have a specific usage at the time period Fitzgerald was writing about, highlighting the immense subtlety of Fitzgerald's writing.[43] She simply could not have written like that when she was young. She was a novelist of great learning, in all senses, from books, classes, travel, culture, and living.

Her teaching experience was another part of her development. One of her pupils recalled, 'She taught literature like a novelist, always… getting us to look at *how it was being done*.'[44] There is tentative evidence that she was not undertaking her intensive self-education out of sheer curiosity. One of her notes on an exam paper with the question 'Should there be limits to curiosity?' reads, 'Scarcely an adult quality in itself – what is it an element of? Ambitious search for truth etc in biography.'[45] In her restless pursuit of the truth about literature and history, she was laying the foundations for her fiction.

Nor was being hassled for time an impediment when she was a novelist. She wrote in the staff room between lessons, scribbling on the back of envelopes.[46] She wrote that most women will always be 'kitchen-table writers'. Unable to write any other way, 'a woman, in my experience, can pick up her draft novel and go on with it, precisely until the telephone, the doorbell, the egg timer, or the alarm rings'. She was not romanticizing women's lives. But she said that once she left teaching, she missed the staff room 'full of undercurrents of exhaustion, worry, and reproach'. Those are the undercurrents of her fiction, too.

Fitzgerald's novels are also evocations of the Edwardian culture of her childhood. Writing to a friend in her eighties, she said, 'I suppose it's ridiculous to regret the Liberal Party, the Church of England, Lyons tea shops, Carter Paterson, telegrams and so on, but so many of them seemed to disappear at once.'[47] *The Knox Brothers*, a group biography of her uncles, is a study of that lost world. Years later, she said to her editor, when the book was being reissued, 'It seems to belong more and more to a vanished era.'[48] As a young woman, 'I tried to get away from them and do my own thing. I didn't realise until much later, indeed until after my father's death, how much there was to find out about them, and by that time it was almost too late.'[49] She had to go away and come back to contemplate this world properly – and then evoke it. Lyons and the Liberal Party recur in *Human Voices* and *The Bookshop*. As she said, 'All my books are before the 1960s as this was the last time anyone was stopped from doing anything for moral considerations.'[50]

The whole philosophy of Fitzgerald's writing, of having to ignore the reality of life if you are to get through it, comes out of her experiences. In *Human Voices*, Mrs Simmonds is 'generous enough to learn nothing from experience'. Sam says of Annie, 'She isn't carried out of herself... by the sheer injustice of life's coincidence.'[51]

She blinded herself, in short, by pretending for a while that human beings are not divided into exterminators and exterminatees, with the former, at any given moment, predominating. Will-power is useless without a sense of direction. Hers was at such a low ebb that it no longer gave her the instructions for survival.[52]

'Will-power is useless without a sense of direction' might easily describe Fitzgerald's earlier life. She said to a friend:

I'm not quite sure why I have taken to writing either, but it's better than weaving, hand-printing &c in that it represents a slight profit rather than a large loss for the amateur; also it struck me that I was getting to the end of my life and would like to write one or 2 biographies of people I loved and novels about people I didn't like.[53]

Maybe she wanted to finally live up to her family's expectations; maybe she needed to be free of them; maybe she had demons to exorcise; maybe she finally had the emotional space; maybe, maybe, maybe. Sometimes, the simple fact of change inspires further change. The most likely effect of her father's death was that she realized just how much of the old world that she had come to admire was slipping away. She wrote about her father on his deathbed:

He complained gently as people do when they're dying that the room was getting dark. We said that the lights were on. My father said 'of course they are. How absurd one is. [Very Edwardian. We've lost the secret.] But there's an awkward thing about dying — one gets so little practice.' I treasure that 'how absurd one is' and hope I won't forget it when the time comes.[54]

She also felt that studying literature was a slow, lifelong process. 'The truth is, though I would never <u>dare</u> say it in public, that the value of studying literature only really appears as you go on living.'[55] Literature is well suited to a late bloomer like Fitzgerald. She was a historical novelist, working from her carefully cultivated knowledge of European history and culture, and she was repeatedly rewriting her and her family's lives. She had to live the life she lived before she could become the writer she became.

There are other writers like this, unpredictable talents who schooled themselves with a long, perhaps unwitting, preparation for their work. For many years, Giuseppe di Lampedusa and his wife read out loud to each other from their favourite authors, including Proust, Tolstoy, and Joyce. Lampedusa had thought of writing a novel for many years, and did so at his wife's suggestion as a way to manage his nostalgia. Lampedusa had a bookseller friend who encouraged him to publish. As Penelope Fitzgerald did, Lampedusa travelled Europe.[56] *The Leopard*, Lampedusa's only novel, was published the year after he died aged sixty. Similarly, Norman Maclean was a literature professor for his whole career who became a writer on retirement, producing one book, *A River Runs Through It and Other Stories*, whose eponymous novella was, like *The Leopard*, an instant classic, based on the experiences of his earlier life. Laura Ingalls Wilder started writing the *Little House on the Prairie* series in her sixties, recasting her childhood experiences into fiction. Writing during the Depression, Wilder was re-invoking a lost time in America. Mary Wesley started writing novels in her seventies and looked back to a lost Britain of the Second World War and earlier.

For every writer like Jane Austen, who wrote the first drafts of *Pride and Prejudice* either as a teenager or in her early twenties, or F. Scott Fitzgerald, who, like Austen, produced his significant work before he was forty, there are writers like Cervantes, Dickens and George Eliot, who either started late or produced their greatest work in the second half of their career. Novels like *The Wide Sargasso Sea*, *The Brothers Karamazov*, *Dracula* and *The Big Sleep* are the products of maturity. Even poets, often mischaracterized in the youthful stereotype of Keats and Shelley, are often older. Robert Frost and Wallace Stevens wrote some of their most canonical work after they turned fifty. Amy Clampitt published her first book aged fifty-eight. Chaucer wrote *The Canterbury Tales* in his fifties. As we have seen and will see with other subjects, averages obscure the great variety of ways that people do their work. There is more than one route to success.

As well as the benefit of inefficient preparation, Penelope Fitzgerald's life demonstrates several lessons we will see in later chapters. She wrote her best novel in her eighties, when some might suppose her mental faculties would be in decline. She practised all her life – not deliberate practice, the way a pianist practises scales, but constantly reading, learning, studying languages and literature, travelling. She immersed herself in the European cultures she would later write about. Her circumstances changed and so did she: her traditional, stable, bourgeois, Christian, English upper-class background gave way to poverty and desperation via a period of London bohemia and the anxiety of a traumatized husband. This provided her novels with their unique perspective, which Frank Kermode called 'calm eccentric boldness' written from the perspective of 'oddly-angled observation'.[57] And she demonstrates the equal probability of success theory, winning prizes for her third and her final novels: her later work is her best. She was published without an agent, using a connection to get in touch with publishers, showing the importance of influence in a network.

•••

Inefficient preparation through a meandering career path can lead to a discovered vocation just as strong as one that you realize when you are young. Finding a vocation often involves learning from failure. This is not just something that happens to musicians and writers. In the next chapter, we will see how Ray Kroc, the man who made McDonald's into a multibillion-dollar global corporation, fits the same pattern of late blooming.

3
Ray Kroc's long apprenticeship

In 1954, a milkshake mixer salesman called Ray Kroc (1902–1984) pulled up to the parking lot of a small hamburger restaurant called McDonald's, run by two brothers, Richard and Maurice McDonald. Kroc had worked as a musician, a real-estate speculator and a paper cup salesman, before selling milkshake mixers. Had he not been dissatisfied with the low-ambition world of paper cups, he might have stayed in middle management. But sitting in that car park was a transformative moment. Kroc was stunned by what he saw. Unknown to him, or the McDonald brothers who ran the restaurant, Kroc would take this idea and turn it into one of the world's most successful businesses. This was the start of the most productive, intense and successful period of Kroc's life.

Kroc was captivated by the McDonald brothers' operation. Nothing else quite like it existed. This was the most efficient fast-food restaurant in America. No one else came close to producing such delicious food so quickly. The French fries were crisp on the outside, fluffy inside. The burgers had the perfect fat-to-meat ratio. People were queuing for the food and the queue moved quickly. Other burger joints were so slow that the food was cold by the time you ate it. At McDonald's, they served their food hot. A burger, fries and shake came out every fifty seconds.

This was a moment of inspiration for Kroc. 'I felt like some latter day Newton who'd just had an Idaho potato caromed off his skull.'[1] That night, 'Visions of McDonald's restaurants dotting crossroads all over the country paraded through my brain.'[2] At that point, he was still thinking about the opportunity for selling milkshake mixers to this imaginary empire of McDonald's restaurants. But his devotion to the restaurant the brothers had created was real. Aged fifty-two, he had found his calling. He was a boosterish, ambitious man who had seen military action, played jazz piano, and chased fortune in Florida before driving back to a Chicago winter without a coat. Determined not to end up like his father, who had always been short of money, Kroc worked like a bee searching for nectar. Having come back from Florida with his tail between his legs, he spent more than a decade steadily working decent jobs. But Ray Kroc was not an organization man. He was convinced of his own ability, convinced with the instinct that poets and painters are convinced of themselves. Restlessness was inevitable. 'I was looking for work that offered something more than money, something I could really get involved in.'[3]

Kroc was never destined for a business career. He dropped out of school to drive ambulances in the First World War. Then he had a succession of sales jobs, playing piano on the side. Fast-food historians John Jakle and Keith Sculle say that with his combination of sales charisma and musical ability he could have been a dance band leader.[4] Kroc knew he was aiming at some sort of success, but his goal was vague.

Rather than planning his career, he concentrated on developing his talents, ready for opportunities that came along. That's how he went from piano player to real estate to paper cups to McDonald's. When he met the McDonald brothers he was fifty-two and trying to find a way of reviving the declining sales of his milkshake mixers. It speaks to his large and busy work ethic that he was able to see McDonald's as the opportunity to do something altogether more spectacular than sell milkshake machines.

This is more than a story of inefficient preparation. Kroc did display those qualities. But he is an example of something else. Ray Kroc was what economist David Galenson calls an 'experimental artist'.

•••

Many poets and painters, like Keats and Picasso, seem to arrive fully formed. This is a well-known type of creator. They know exactly what their artistic vision is, and they express it young – and brilliantly. Galenson calls them 'conceptual artists'. They tend to peak before they are thirty. Experimental artists are the opposite. They work incrementally, without an early vision, towards vague goals. They never feel they have quite succeeded. Through repetition, and trial and error, they discover what they are aiming for.[5] Their work becomes their research. Experimental artists peak in the second half of their careers. All of Picasso's most successful work – the paintings that sell for the most money today – was done in his twenties. Many experimental artists have not even started by then.

Kroc displays the incremental, inductive qualities of experimental artists. He had vague goals and had to work everything out as he went. He created his career in the same ways many artists create their visions: slowly, and with constant revision. He had the creativity not of great imagination but of careful attention to reality. What the art historians Jakob Rosenberg and Seymour Slive said of the painter Frans Hals is true of Kroc: 'Thrown upon the resources of his own imagination he must have been lost and unable to proceed.'[6]

Kroc's career shows constant development, aspiration and perfectionism, as you would expect of an ambitious artist. As William Carlos Williams said of Wallace Stevens (a late-blooming poet), 'It is a mark of genius when an accomplished man can go on continually developing, continually improving his technique.'[7] Like Hals, and many other artists of this sort, Kroc worked with diligent experimentation. He developed slowly and his success was late and unanticipated.

It might be difficult to think of Kroc as creative like an artist. He could not paint or dance. He was not a composer or a poet. He was a manager who built a global fast-food business. But consider this Warren Bennis quotation, which Xerox chief scientist Jack Goldman cut out of a newspaper and kept pinned above his desk: 'There are two ways of being creative. One can sing or dance. Or one can create an environment in which singers and dancers flourish.'[8] Kroc is creative in that second way. Advertising entrepreneur David Ogilvy (another late bloomer) said in his memoir, 'Copywriters, art directors, and television producers are easily come by, but the number of men who can preside over an agency's entire creative output – perhaps a hundred new campaigns every year – can be numbered on the fingers of one hand. Those rare trumpeter swans must be capable of inspiring.'[9] Kroc can be numbered on that hand: he created a business that was new in its field. And he inspired hundreds of people who worked for him.

For Galenson's experimental artists, each piece of work is a test, a discovery. Rather than seeing each painting as a finished execution of an idea or an instalment in a series of complete works, each is an experiment that gives results. These results accumulate and are taken into account in future works. In this way, experimental artists gradually accrue their vision and the techniques needed to achieve it. That's exactly how Ray Kroc created McDonald's.

•••

Kroc got into the mixer business while working as a paper cup salesman during the Great Depression, from 1927 to 1937. Why had a man with so much desperate energy and ambition stayed in a stable paper cup sales job for a decade? He quit during a row about pay once, but then went back. Otherwise it was a remarkably settled period. He was having 'so much fun selling' for his battles with the boss to bother him too much.[10] In fact, before 1927, Kroc's luck had been so up and down, it is unsurprising he decided to dedicate himself to that job. His career had been highly disjointed.

Kroc left school aged sixteen and sold coffee beans door-to-door before signing up to drive ambulances in the First World War. (He never made it to France as the Armistice was signed weeks later.) He then got a job selling ribbon novelties and claimed to be earning more than his father. He played piano on the side and inadvertently got a job in a bordello. Selling ribbons bored him, so he joined the Charleston boom playing piano in a band, complete with 'striped blazers and straw boaters'. He then got a job watching the ticker tape and writing up prices at the Chicago stock exchange. His parents moved to New York and he was obliged to go with them, leaving behind his girlfriend Ethel. He and Ethel had wanted to get married, and Kroc was now stuck without her, working as a cashier in New York. Eventually the firm folded and he raced back to Chicago and Ethel. He and Ethel had been shocked by the move to New York and now they were determined to get married.

Kroc's father insisted he get a real job. 'A few days later I went to work selling Lily brand paper cups.' As well as pounding the streets by day selling cups to soda fountains, Kroc was playing piano for a radio station in the evenings. It was uneven work, especially while Kroc learned the ropes, and paper cups were seasonal, so he did little business in the winter. In 1925, he decided to go to Florida and chase the real-estate boom. He got a good start but 'just when I was getting into the swing of selling those lots, the whole business vanished'. He had taken a leave of absence from Lily paper cups and rented some rooms in Florida. Now he was left without any work at all. Someone in his building heard him play the piano and got him a job.

He learned a big lesson from this experience: the bar where he played had a fixed-price drink menu and simple food service that 'left a lasting impression on me'. It's easy to look back and find these important moments in your life – but we shouldn't be entirely sceptical. Kroc spent his career in the burgeoning restaurant and food business. He played in bars, sold soda fountains, and visited kitchens. He was studying restaurants and becoming an expert in the emerging style of simple service.

Florida didn't work out. Kroc was playing in a bar that breached Prohibition laws and spent a night in jail when the bar was raided. Ethel was already lonely and miserable in Florida, longing to go home, and she was disturbed by this event. So Ethel went ahead to Chicago with their new child, and Kroc worked his two-week notice with the band. He drove home to Chicago, and Florida's economy tanked shortly afterwards.

Kroc was spooked by the way that the opportunities in Florida had fallen away like a rotten floor. With a child to support, he had to find something reliable. He gave up music and real estate, and dedicated himself to paper cups. Kroc was diverting into an opportunity where his different talents and interests would eventually be given the chance to converge.[11]

Experimental artists prefer the concrete, the real. That is Kroc, who always persisted in learning the details of his business – nothing was beneath his notice. While selling paper cups, he met Ralph Sullivan, who had invented a new method of making milkshakes that made them thicker and colder than the old style. The queues went round the block. Kroc started selling to Sullivan, pleased to have a customer who needed a lot of cups. But he also saw the potential in Sullivan's business, as he later would with McDonald's, and got his bosses to join with another client, Earl Prince, who ran an ice cream parlour, to go and see Sullivan. It was a significant opportunity for both ice cream and paper cup sellers. Earl Prince was inspired and started selling a new sort of milkshake, and Kroc started selling him many more paper cups, too. Prince then invented his own milkshake mixer – called the Multimixer – that was more efficient at handling the new, thicker drink. Kroc got his employer interested and they became the distributors.

Prince offered Kroc the chance to join him. Kroc was keen, but Ethel was furious that he would leave a steady job for a 'flyer' like that. It was the beginning of the end of their marriage. He faced further problems. His employer held the contract to distribute the mixers – and despite being uninterested in the business, refused to give it up to him. He cut a deal where he got the contract but his employer got 60 per cent of the business he was setting up. Kroc had to extend his mortgage to buy his employer out. The importance of structuring the business properly at the outset was a lesson he had to relearn with the McDonald brothers, but which became central to the way franchising worked.[12]

Kroc also learned to find the right people for the right job. His paper cup employers had been the wrong people to involve in the milkshake mixer plan. When he set up McDonald's, he did so with the talented finance director Fred Turner. Most importantly, the Multimixers taught him about kitchens: selling them took him into thousands of kitchens. 'I prided myself on being able to tell which operations would appeal to the public and which would fail.'[13] As was the case in Florida, where he paid attention to the simple service methods of the restaurants he played piano in, he had an eye for opportunity by looking at the details. Kroc was accumulating experiences that he could not anticipate would be so life-changing later on.

The mixers also brought him luck. It was only because they bought so many milkshake mixers that Kroc visited the McDonald brothers.

•••

Ray Kroc didn't invent McDonald's. Maurice and Richard McDonald did. Kroc brought scale to their operation. Without him, it would have remained a family business, unknown to the world. Or, if the two brothers had somehow grown the business, they would, in their own words, have 'wound up in some skyscraper somewhere with about four ulcers and eight tax attorneys trying to figure out how to pay all my income tax'.[14] With Kroc, though, the McDonald brothers' principles were rigorously turned into a global business. It's one thing to run a hamburger restaurant, quite another to create a global empire of consistent standards. The miniaturist and the muralist are both artists but of very different sorts.

The brothers invented the restaurant system that made McDonald's so efficient. It was their arrangement of the kitchen and their impeccably precise system that meant they could produce a hamburger and fries every fifty seconds. Ray Kroc's contribution was to work out how to franchise this business to make it work at scale, which the brothers had failed to do.

To many, this makes Kroc a plagiarist, or worse. He is sometimes presented as the man who stole McDonald's. 'The brothers lost out on a fortune and had their legacy all but erased for decades because of going into business with Ray Kroc. "I remember him saying once, when I was a teenager, 'That guy really got me,'" recalled Richard McDonald's grandson Jason French.'[15] It's not clear, though, how that fortune would have materialized for the brothers *without* Kroc. They had tried franchising the restaurant and it hadn't worked. Keeping track of the franchisees was too much: they were initially sceptical of working with Kroc for reason.

The McDonald brothers' nephew has claimed that Kroc reneged on a deal to pay the brothers 0.5 per cent of gross sales, an arrangement that would have made them much richer than they were. But the brothers disliked paying high rates of income tax and wanted simple lives without the complications wealth can bring. As Richard later said, 'Taxes were killing us. We weren't kids anymore. We had three homes and a garage full of Cadillacs, and we didn't owe a dime to anyone. I have no regrets. Yachts on the Riviera were not my style at all.'[16] They sold to Kroc for one million dollars each, after tax, payable in cash. This was a big demand to make of Kroc at that time, worth about ten million dollars today. And they too reneged on the deal, insisting on keeping the original restaurant, against the terms of the contract. To maintain the idea that Kroc conned the

McDonald brothers you have to pass very lightly over the fact that it was his brains and effort that took the restaurant global, not theirs. The *Daily Mail* describes it like this: 'After taking over McDonald's, Kroc oversaw a period of staggering expansion.'[17] 'Oversaw' is an understatement.

A recent biopic about Kroc, *The Founder*, takes the same view that many critics have, presenting Kroc as a rapacious businessman who outmanoeuvred the innocent, gentle McDonald brothers. Undoubtedly, Kroc was unpleasantly competitive. He had a relentless focus that took little account of personal feelings. If he felt you were dishonest, he was done with you. But the film tilts at windmills. A rapacious competitor stealing an idea is a movie trope. *The Social Network* told a similar story about the origins of Facebook, with Mark Zuckerberg presented as the man who stole the idea from the Winklevoss twins. This elides the idea and the making, as if there is not an important distinction. As Zuckerberg says at one point in the film, 'If you guys were the inventors of Facebook you would have invented Facebook.' That distinction makes all the difference. As the real Zuckerberg said, 'Writing code and then building a product and building a company is not a glamorous enough thing to make a movie about.'[18] Kroc's story is similar. The brothers invented the system; Kroc invented the business. There is no credible alternative history in which the brothers got rich without Kroc or someone else with his capabilities.

To see the two distinct contributions Kroc and the McDonald brothers made, we need to put them in the context of hamburger history.

•••

Like anything, hamburgers had to be invented and perfected. Walter Anderson, a grill cook from Wichita, Kansas, invented the modern method of cooking hamburgers. Before Anderson, hamburgers were loosely formed and held between slices of bread. Thanks to a combination of persistent tinkering and good luck, Anderson struck on the technique of pressing down on the burger patty with his spatula while cooking it on a hot grill. This gave the burger better shape and more uniform flavour. Anderson put these new hamburgers inside a bun. This made them mobile, perfect for the automobile age.[19] It was the time of Henry Ford, the assembly line, and mass-produced consumer goods. People *wanted* to find the same product in every branch. As White Castle, the chain where Anderson worked, said of their restaurants, 'The hamburger you eat is prepared in exactly the same way over a gas flame of the same intensity… the same standard of cleanliness protects your food. Even the men who serve you are guided by standards of precision which have been thought out from beginning to end.'[20]

The McDonald brothers perfected these standards of precision: they were building on an established model. There are many aspects of the hamburger process that they improved – but many are fundamental. It was one of Kroc's franchisees who discovered that gas cookers (rather than the electric fryers used by the McDonald brothers) were cheaper and produced a better French fry. This was so important to the McDonald's process that *cooking with gas* became an important phrase in their culture. 'When somebody was *cooking with gas* around our place it meant he was doing everything right.'[21] White Castle, unknown to McDonald's, had discovered that years earlier. White Castle also discovered that paper cups were easier to use than China ones before McDonald's did. White Castle expanded their market by targeting women, who traditionally saw diners as male places, just as McDonald's would later have a marketing breakthrough by targeting children.

The brothers, and Kroc, were part of a chain of innovators that created the modern fast-food restaurant. Fast food started with the addition of soda fountains to shops in the 1880s, which started selling sandwiches and soup. This spread to department stores and railway stations. During Prohibition, saloons converted into luncheonettes. In the 1920s, lunchrooms opened near streetcars and subways, to appeal to commuters. As cafeterias developed in the mid-century, assembly lines were introduced, with customers pushing their tray along a counter. This was especially popular in California, a hub of fast-food development. The cafeteria model allowed hot meals to be served as well, not just sandwiches.

Then came the diner, modelled on dining cars and sometimes built inside old railroad carriages. With automobiles came highway diners. Here the fundamental aspects of modern fast-food chains were developed: busy grill cooks and scuttling waitresses serving customers on the go-go. As drive-ins flourished, they hired car hops, pretty young women who took drivers' orders and brought them their food, often on roller skates. This model was slow, and the food was often cold. And it meant that teenage boys with no money loitered in the car parks to watch the car hops, putting off family trade and dropping litter.

By the time the post-war consumer boom began, fast-food restaurants were a well-evolved model, ready and waiting to be perfected by the McDonald brothers and Ray Kroc. The brothers did two things that made them successful: they installed the golden arches, so visible from a car they are universally recognizable to toddlers today, and they produced a burger, fries and shake every fifty seconds, with no need for car hops.[22] For years, McDonald's advertised a guarantee of hot food.

The McDonald brothers' redesign of the fast-food kitchen was so exact that they controlled the number of steps employees took between each item of equipment.[23] For something like that to scale, someone had to figure out how to make franchising work. This was the problem Ray Kroc solved. So successful was Kroc that, in 1980, the courts formally recognized the idea of business format franchising as distinct from product franchising – that is, a model in which a franchise licenses the whole way of doing business, not just the menus. It took Ray Kroc to find the right people to run the franchises and to instil the McDonald's way of doing business into them.

Walter Anderson had tried to profit from his insights about cooking hamburgers, but, like the brothers, he needed a business partner. He opened three restaurants but lacked capital. He partnered with Bill Ingram, a real-estate agent. They created the White Castle model. By 1931, they were the biggest chain of the time with 115 restaurants.[24] As Kroc later did, Ingram gave the operators instructions about *everything*, including 'how to dress, how to speak'. Still, it was difficult to maintain standards. Good operators were entrepreneurial, but the business relied on consistency. It is difficult to run a Henry Ford-style assembly line with so many different operators in different locations. White Castle used frozen burger patties as one attempt at standardization, a compromise on standards.[25] They never franchised, and still don't, which helped maintain control but limited growth.

White Castle was innovative, as McDonald's later was. Just as McDonald's franchisees invented menu items like the Big Mac and branding like the Ronald McDonald character,[26] so too a White Castle operator named Bob Wian created the first double-decker burger, known as Big Boy. Still, Ingram refused to franchise.[27] And so, until someone combined that exactitude and creativity with a workable franchising model, those sorts of innovations remained in small, not major, chains. The McDonald brothers were not the visionary types to achieve that: for their success to scale, they required Ray Kroc.

Kroc revolutionized the way franchising was arranged in restaurants. Rather than give out franchises to areas or regions, the usual practice at the time, Kroc franchised individual stores. In this way, McDonald's made much less money than it might have done. Territorial franchises pay more and pay quicker. But Kroc's approach gave him control. 'Once they sign, they are going to conform and we are going to hold to it they do conform.'[28] No one who failed to live up to Kroc's standards got a second franchise. That's how you create an environment in which singers and dancers flourish. And it worked: only one franchisee failed in the first thirty years of operation.

Kroc prioritized standards over money. He wanted to find the best talent, to create the strongest network of individuals in his business. That way, when growth came it would be reliable. He had an individual leadership style, learned from past experiences. He worked through inspiration, with dedicated followers. And he applied the methods of experimental artists. Galenson argues that experimental artists' ideas emerge from the work. Leonardo, for example, said: 'Those sciences are vain and full of error which are not born of experience.'[29] Kroc also worked with the experiential method:

> There is a certain kind of mind that conceives new ideas as complete systems with all of their parts functioning. I don't think in that 'grand design' pattern. I work from the part to the whole, and I don't move on to the large scale ideas until I have perfected the small details. To me this is a much more flexible approach… You must perfect every fundamental of your business if you expect it to perform well.[30]

The result of this mindset is that McDonald's was built on many attempts and many failures. As John Love says, 'The key ingredient of Kroc's management formula is a willingness to admit failure and to admit mistakes.'[31] This combination of perfecting small details and being willing to admit mistakes is exactly like Galenson's archetypal experimental artist, Paul Cézanne, who never placed a stroke of paint without thinking about it carefully but had something of a disregard for his own paintings.[32]

In the foreword to Kroc's memoir, the business professor Paul D. Paganucci described Kroc's life as 'a long apprenticeship'.[33] That is exactly what an experimental artist goes through – and it is the model for understanding the late blooming of Ray Kroc. Galenson's ideas are applicable beyond artists. It is a model for late blooming in all sorts of careers. Cézanne is the archetypal experimental artist, but his example can be followed by any late bloomer in any walk of life.

Cézanne did not even formulate the central problem of his career until he was in his mid-thirties. He then worked steadily at developing his solution to that problem – 'searching for a technique' – for more than three decades, and arrived at his most important contribution towards the end of his life.[34]

It was after this long experimental life, searching for a technique, that Cézanne transformed art, developing Post-Impressionism. He discovered what he was looking for one canvas at a time. He had to search for his artistic vision painting by painting. Once he discovered his big idea, it took constant work to make it real, to perfect it. You do not have to be Cézanne to follow Galenson's strategy. You can change the way an industry works using the experimental artists' technique, whether you are an artist or accountant, a painter or a programmer. As Cézanne practised on every canvas, trying to find the way to change Impressionism, you can practise in every job, every email you write, every meeting you attend, every project you complete. Galenson's insights apply so clearly and accurately to Kroc that we can see this as a general model of late blooming. Kroc changed fast food just as much as Cézanne changed painting: he was an experiential artist of the business world. Like Cézanne and other experimental artists, he took a long time to mature into a major new vision of the way things could be done. The fact that fast-food franchising is now ubiquitous can be largely credited to Ray Kroc, who never worked in fast food before he was fifty-two.

•••

The McDonald brothers were also late bloomers and had a long apprenticeship of their own. They moved to California from New Hampshire in 1930, when Maurice was twenty-eight and Richard was twenty-one. First, they worked as odd jobbers in the movies. When they realized no preferment was coming, they set up a movie theatre. It was the middle of the Great Depression; the theatre flopped. In 1937, now aged thirty-five and twenty-eight, they opened a food truck at a racetrack. The business was seasonal, and they eventually decided to open a restaurant. All the banks they went to refused them a loan because the brothers had no collateral. In 1940, one manager at Bank of America saw something in them and took a punt, saying he had 'a hunch that McDonald's is going to make it big'. And so they opened their first drive-in.

It was a hit, but people were waiting twenty minutes for their food. Car hops were expensive and inefficient. This wasn't a problem. Customers weren't complaining. 'But our intuition told us they would like speed.' This instinctive sense of what the customer wanted was a trait they had in common with Kroc. Their drive-in was a barbecue restaurant, but they realized that 80 per cent of sales were hamburgers. So, in 1948, aged forty-six and thirty-nine, eleven years after they started the food truck, they closed the restaurant down and reinvented the whole process.

Their efficiencies make White Castle's system look weak. Everything was custom designed. The grills were bigger and easier to clean and held the heat better. All kitchen items were bespoke. They visited candy companies, pretending to be writers, to find better machinery for cutting burger patties. Everything was focused on 'speed, lower prices, and volume'. In their own small, charming way, they were just as ruthless as Kroc. They wanted to be millionaires and nothing was left to chance. As well as cutting most items off the menu they added French fries and milkshakes. The new system became popular with families, especially children. Staff were told to be nice to kids, a marketing ploy McDonald's used throughout the twentieth century. The division of labour was intense: there were grill men, French fry men, milkshake men. Revenue jumped 40 per cent – and the old restaurant had already been successful.[35] By the mid 1950s, the brothers were making

$100,000 profit and driving new Cadillacs every year.[36] (The average car trade-in time was two years by 1960.)[37] That is something in the order of a million dollars in modern money. Their new system had worked. In their mid forties and early fifties, the brothers were starting to make the money they had dreamed of. Kroc was not to be their only imitator. People travelled to see this new restaurant and replicated it back home.

George Clark, founder of Burger Queen, once said, 'Our food was exactly the same as McDonald's. If I had looked at McDonald's and saw someone flipping hamburgers while he was hanging by his feet, I would have copied him.' Kroc was not a copycat. Essential to his work at McDonald's was a constant eye for marginal gains. Like Galenson's experimental artists, he saw everything he produced as a chance to improve. He had to make the McDonald's system work in non-desert climates and incorporate efficiencies discovered by franchisees. Where others copied the system, Kroc finessed, expanded and improved it with his relentless eye for detail. It was Ray Kroc whose background and personality equipped him to turn a lucky break with a small family business into one of the twentieth century's financial titans.

Kroc could have been one of those copycats. The brothers gave him an extraordinarily detailed tour of the kitchen. He knew their system inside out. Nothing was stopping him from setting up on his own. But he saw it all differently. 'The idea never crossed my mind. I saw it through the eyes of a salesman. Here was a complete package, and I could get out and talk up a storm about it.'[38] Kroc knew his ability. He was not the man to build a kitchen. And he knew his comparative advantage. The brothers were not the people to get out and talk up a storm about McDonald's. This was not just Kroc's learned ability in sales. He had an intensity about McDonald's that was quite unsettling. There was something evangelical about his devotion. As he wrote, 'The French fry would become almost sacrosanct for me.'[39]

Among the first things he noticed was that, unlike other drive-ins with their car hops and loitering teenagers, there was no litter in the

McDonald's parking lot. This mattered not just because Kroc was obsessive about cleanliness, but because he could see a new market in this fresh and friendly model. He once said: 'I've made up my mind that all hamburger joints had jukeboxes, telephones, and cigarette machines and that your wife wouldn't go to a place with leather-jacketed guys and smoke-filled rooms.'[40] For the man who had previously moved into the paper cup business because 'paper cups were part of the way America was heading', this was a moment of realization.[41] This was part of the way America was heading. He lost his temper over one item of litter in the car parks of early franchises. Small transgressions were 'gross affronts' to Kroc, as if he had found litter in a shrine. The reason for his anger was simple, it just wouldn't drive most people to the inordinate lengths of work and attention it drove him to: 'Perfection is very difficult to achieve, and perfection was what I wanted in McDonald's.'[42] He sounds like the artist Bridget Riley: 'My goal was to make the image perfect, not mechanical… but perfect in the sense of being exactly as I intended it.'[43]

The golden arches are often described as modern icons with their mesmerizing power. For Kroc, the whole enterprise had that quality. Even in retirement, he watched the local McDonald's through binoculars from his house and called the franchisee to give him hell when he saw standards slipping. He had learned on his first visit that the brothers 'lavished attention' on their French fries, and he continued to lavish attention on everything about the business whilever he was in charge.[44] What sounds fatiguing to most people was energizing to Kroc. 'For me, work was play.'[45]

Kroc's most important ability in building McDonald's was talent spotting. As a young man, when he had moonlighted as a radio pianist, one of his jobs was to find acts to fill airtime. He picked out a young comedy duo who later became one of the most famous comedy acts of their generation. This ability to spot talent served him well throughout his career. During his time as a salesman, he was focused on finding and nurturing the right people. He became famous at McDonald's for his demanding, insistent attitude. Top executives were issued with a small packet containing a nail file, comb and brushes. It wasn't just the parking lots. Everything had to be speckless.[46] That was the level of attention he paid to his people. Some leaders might tell you it's important to look smart. Ray Kroc bought you a nail file and a comb. Twenty years earlier, when he was selling paper cups, he had imbued the same spirit of neatness into his team: 'I stressed the importance of making a good appearance, wearing a nicely pressed suit, well-polished shoes, hair combed, and nails clean. "Look sharp and act sharp," I told them. "The first thing you have to sell is yourself."'[47] Kroc was an instinctive manager who knew that morale and unity are essential to a well-functioning team:

> I had about fifteen salesmen working for me then and we had a fine spirit of enthusiasm percolating among us. After work we would get together and talk shop, batting around ideas about how to sell more paper cups. That was fun. I loved to see one of those young fellows catch hold and grow in his job. It was the most rewarding thing I've ever experienced. I wasn't much older than any of them, and some were older than me. But I felt like a father to them.[48]

Supposedly, this is how he created so many disciples when he ran the McDonald's corporation. He wasn't an overbearing manager – he provided a well-defined atmosphere of ambition, enthusiasm, hard work, and purpose. Once he found the right people, and put them in the right conditions, he let them run. 'I believe that if you hire a man to do a job, you ought to get out of the way and let him do it.'[49] (He had several rows with his managers over the years, all of them at root caused by the fact that he felt like he was not given the freedom due to a high performer.) This was the spirit he brought to corporate headquarters but also to selecting the franchisees. Especially in the early years, it was Kroc's dedication to finding, nurturing, and then freeing the right talent that made McDonald's a success. In an echo of Henry James, who said the only recipe for writing a great novel was to care very much for the cooking, Kroc once told the *New York Times*, 'McDonald's people take the hamburger business just a little more seriously than anybody else.' He was looking for people who cared. 'We want someone who will get totally involved in the business. If his ambition is to reach the point where he can play golf four days a week or play gin rummy for a cent a point, instead of a tenth, we don't want him in a McDonald's restaurant.' That was the secret to his success. No matter that he was dealing with hamburgers, he persisted, insisted and progressed through his career with the intensity of slow-growing experimental artists. Ray Kroc took this so seriously that a sign hung above McDonald's executives' desks that read:

NOTHING IN THE WORLD CAN TAKE THE PLACE OF PERSISTENCE.

TALENT WILL NOT; NOTHING IS MORE COMMON THAN UNSUCCESSFUL MEN WITH TALENT.

GENIUS WILL NOT; UNREWARDED GENIUS IS ALMOST A PROVERB.

EDUCATION WILL NOT; THE WORLD IS FULL OF EDUCATED DERELICTS.

PERSISTENCE AND DETERMINATION ALONE ARE OMNIPOTENT.[50]

Supposedly, this is a quotation from Calvin Coolidge, but was often printed in newspapers anonymously as filler before Coolidge's time.[51] Of course, these homilies are not true. The world is full of failures. Ray Kroc got lucky. He found a restaurant that had perfected the efficient kitchen system and was ready to be expanded. But getting lucky doesn't mean having it easy. Without his personal qualities – his cleanliness, agonizing insistence on every detail, willingness to experiment, to do what it took to get things *exactly* right, to nurture future talent rather than chase profits; his instinct for what the public would go for; and his energy – Kroc's luck would have run out. Many other fast-food entrepreneurs had mixed backgrounds like he did. Dunkin' Donuts was founded by a door-to-door salesman; Wendy's by a busboy. Harland Sanders founded KFC very late in life after having been a farmworker, mule handler, railway fireman, unqualified lawyer and doctor, insurance salesman, tyre salesman, and gas station operative.[52] Something of the variety, the need to hustle, the way they had scrambled around to find their niche actually helped these people. This inefficient preparation, their approach to their careers as experimental artists, made them ready to seize their opportunity when it came along.

They were prepared for luck. And that really is something we can learn from Calvin Coolidge.

Part Two
When Fate Intervenes

'There's nothing you can do about where the pieces
are. It's only your next move that matters.'

Steve Jobs

4

Intentionally unplanned careers: being ready for luck

The sort of unplanned career Ray Kroc had can be more satisfying than the direct route to success. When the journalist Charles Duhigg went to a fifteen-year reunion of his MBA class he saw former classmates who were 'Wealthy, Successful, and Miserable'. 'Even among my more sanguine classmates,' he said, 'there was a lingering sense of professional disappointment.'[1] Duhigg noticed that the other group of people – the ones who were happy – had something unexpected in common. They had not done well on leaving business school. They didn't get a plum graduate job. Their great expectations were disappointed early. This forced them, at the start of their careers, to deal with trade-offs and to scramble for work. They were not, Duhigg thought, employed by the most enlightened companies, and had not learned anything special at Harvard. Rather, 'they had learned from their own setbacks. And often they wound up richer, more powerful and more content than everyone else.' The indirect route to success was more satisfying.

A study about the early career setbacks of junior scientists who applied for research funding came to similar conclusions. The researchers compared those scientists who narrowly missed out on their funding applications to those who narrowly succeeded. Being on one side of the line or the other made a significant difference to their future prospects. Both groups outperformed the average in terms of the success of their published research, gaining more citations than the baseline. In the first five years after the initial application, 13.3 per cent of papers published by the narrow-win group were a hit, compared to a 5 per cent baseline. For the narrow-miss group, it was 16.1 per cent. Over time, the narrow-miss group's advantage over the narrow-win group got bigger. In the next five-year window after application (i.e. five to ten years after being rejected), the narrow-miss researchers got 19.4 per cent more citations than the narrow-win ones. And in the five-year window after that (i.e. ten to fifteen years after being rejected), they got 12 per cent more citations. Despite the fact that the near-miss group got fewer grants overall, they produced just as many papers and got more citations. Part of this is accounted for by the fact that some of the people who narrowly miss out on funding leave their roles to work in other sectors.[2] More research needs to be done in this field, but it does seem that an early near-miss can teach you something important about how to succeed. The junior scientists seemed to learn from their setback in the way Duhigg's classmates had.

This sort of unplanned career is how Calvin Coolidge became the thirtieth President of the United States. When Coolidge graduated from Amherst College in 1895, there was a recession. He and his classmates were worried about not being able to find decent jobs. Charles Garman, an Amherst tutor, advised the class not to worry. You don't have to start successful to end that way. 'A career was like a body of water,' he told them. 'All that was required to move a career forward was to stay with events and stay with the mainstream.' If you did that and you kept going, a chance would come to you one day. In 1901, young Coolidge got a vivid demonstration of that principle in action. William McKinley was assassinated a few months into his second term and his Vice President, Theodore Roosevelt, became the youngest President of the United States. As Coolidge's biographer, Amity Shlaes, puts it, 'Fate had intervened. Because Roosevelt had been in the water, now he was president.'[3]

Twenty-two years later, in 1923, the same thing happened to Coolidge at the age of fifty-one. He was Vice President when Warren Harding had a heart attack, and automatically took over when Harding died. Coolidge had made little impact as Vice President and had been a surprise choice to join Harding's ticket. He had not got to that position through climbing the greasy pole. His elevation to the presidency was quite unanticipated. Being in the swim of events, keeping himself ready, did not make for an efficient or planned career. There were no targets, no deadlines. But it worked. Like the people at Duhigg's reunion, Coolidge might not have had such a successful or rewarding career had he been more deliberate about it. The Coolidge approach shows that you can build a successful career by not having a direct path to your goal.

This sort of career path relies on chance. For Coolidge to become President, the wheel of fortune had to turn. Had Harding survived, Coolidge would have left office at the next election. To make the Coolidge approach to a career work, you need luck. Think about Ray Kroc and Katharine Graham. Luck was essential to their success. But they prepared for their luck, even though they didn't know what they were preparing for.

This preparation takes many forms. The psychologist Richard Wiseman believes that lucky people are not blessed with better fortune: they make their own luck. Lucky people are more extroverted, engage in more social encounters, have body language that attracts people to talk to them – lucky people smile twice as much as unlucky people – and, most importantly, 'lucky people are effective at building secure, and long lasting, attachments with the people that they meet'.[4] Unlucky people are significantly more neurotic and much less open to new experiences.[5] One obvious problem with this is that you would expect lucky people to be happier. After all, they got lucky. These are correlational studies. And it is easier for people like Katharine Graham to get lucky because they have the privilege of education, networks, and status.

But as Paul Graham said, 'You need to make yourself a big target for luck.'[6] And chance events happen to everyone. Ray Kroc had no special privilege (other than the massive privilege of being born in America, of course), and he brought the talents that he had been developing all his life to the opportunity. He took his luck because he was ready and able to. Even as Kroc ground away at his ordinary job, he was practising and refining the skills that would be so fundamental to making the McDonald's corporation a global success. We saw Katharine Graham preparing the same way. Coolidge made a point of focusing on doing every job he had as well as it could be done, and not worrying about the next job up the ladder. In this way, excellence prepared him for luck. Inefficient preparation doesn't always know what it is aiming at, but it does know it is preparing for an opportunity.

Maya Angelou's life illustrates the role a chain of chance events can play. Angelou only realized her ambition to write in her thirties when she was working as a dancer in California. She heard that the writer John Killens was in town and she sent him samples of her work. He advised her to move to New York. There she joined the Harlem Writers Guild, a group that provided support and feedback on her writing. Some years later, her friend the novelist James Baldwin took her to dinner with Jules and Judy Feiffer. Judy Feiffer was a writer and editor. She persuaded Angelou that her incredible life story ought to be turned into a book and introduced her to an editor at Random House. It was in this way that Angelou wrote *I Know Why the Caged Bird Sings*, her first book, aged forty.[7] If Maya Angelou hadn't gone to the dinner party with James Baldwin, it's not obvious that another opportunity like that would have come along. But that wasn't random luck: she had spent years in the network, building relationships. And when she got to the dinner, she was able to dazzle with her story. Not everyone gets invitations to parties like that, but you are more likely to get them if you send your work out, take advice, join writers' groups, and so on.

We will see in Chapter 6 why network connections are so essential to success. But Angelou didn't only persist at networking until the right connection was made: she was able to make use of that connection. Although she got started late as a writer, it was through what Wiseman would call her 'network of luck' that she got published. We are not all going to become Maya Angelou and make friends with James Baldwin. But if you decline to participate, the world will decline to pay attention. 'Many complain of neglect who never tried to attract regard,' said Samuel Johnson.[8] This is not a cynical prescription. Maya Angelou did not go to that dinner party with the intention of selling her book. The best networking happens unintentionally. As Wiseman says, the lucky are relaxed, not anxious. They don't spend their life searching for their magic moment. Instead, 'Lucky people see what is there, rather than trying to find what they want to see. As a result, they are far more receptive to any opportunities that arise naturally.'[9] In an unplanned career, you must be ready to catch an opportunity as it goes past, rather than constantly hunt them out.

The word 'serendipity', which today is used to mean a happy accident, originally meant 'making discoveries, by accidents and sagacity'. This acknowledges the skill involved to be able to make accidental discoveries. Happy accidents aren't just random, like capricious gifts from the gods: they happen to people with the sagacity to spot them. In his book *Chase, Chance, and Creativity: The Lucky Art of Novelty*, the neurologist James Austin used this to illustrate his theory that 'exploratory behaviour' was crucial to finding good luck.[10] Austin describes four sorts of luck.

First is the pure chance of accident that happens to everyone.

The second sort of chance involves what Austin calls 'motion': you must keep looking if you want to discover something. 'If the researcher did not move until he was certain of progress he would accomplish very little.' Austin said that 'ill-defined, restless, driving' action has a place in helping to uncover opportunity.[11]

Next is the type of chance that requires the 'special receptivity' of the lucky person. This sort of chance, as Louis Pasteur said, favours the prepared mind. This is how Alexander Fleming discovered penicillin. It is well known that penicillin mould appeared on a Petri dish he neglected to clean. Fleming was prepared to take advantage of this because years earlier he had discovered lysozyme, which also kills bacteria, when a drop of his mucus fell onto a Petri dish. Having discovered a bacteria-killing substance once before, his mind was open to the chance next time.

Finally, Austin describes how we create our own luck through what we do and the sort of people we are. He illustrates this with Benjamin Disraeli's comment that 'we make our fortunes, and we call them fate'. The way you act changes the sorts of opportunities you are likely to encounter. Circumstances that would be lucky for one person are not for another. Austin compares this to the way mutations occur in plants. Some plants have rare but helpful genetic mutations that make them better adapted to adverse weather conditions. Only when the weather does get more extreme is the plant's ability to thrive revealed; without the change, that capability would have remained dormant.[12]

Throughout this book, we will see these different types of luck. Purely accidental luck is common. But so many of the people here are busy, like Ray Kroc who uncovered the McDonald's opportunity through his restlessness. Or they are somehow specially prepared for opportunity, like Margaret Thatcher and Katharine Graham. All of them are singular: their personalities create their circumstances to some extent. They are lucky, partly, simply because of who they are and how they act. When Alexander Fleming chose to train at St Mary's Hospital, London, a crucial decision on his meandering path to discovering penicillin, it was because St Mary's had an excellent swimming pool and Fleming enjoyed playing water polo.[13] On that hobby hinged an unforeseen stroke of fortune.

The unplanned career is more normal than it looks. Although each story you hear sounds unique, there is reason to believe that most people's careers are strongly affected by chance. Psychologists Robert Pryor and Jim Bright have developed the chaos theory of careers.[14] Chaos theory says that there is inherent uncertainty in all systems. The systems around us (family, economy, work, community) are complex and dynamic: they are made up of many parts, each open to influence, and they all change at different rates. Even people are complex dynamic systems. This is why life is unpredictable: it is a mix of so many systems, which are all subject to external changes. Your career is one of these complex, dynamic systems. No matter how carefully you plan your climb up the corporate ladder, there are too many factors involved for you to be able to predict how your career will progress. All sorts of things that might not seem relevant can affect the course of your career.[15]

So many things can influence a career that Pryor and Bright advise career counsellors not to look at a narrow set of 'relevant' factors when giving career advice, but instead get to know their advisees more broadly, to understand their families, childhoods, hobbies, reading habits, general concerns, key life events, and life tragedies. Career paths are so complex, and so liable to be affected by chaos, that you cannot draw a line from one set of circumstances to one set of outcomes. What results in one sort of career for one person can become a very different sort of career for someone else.

Careers are also what chaos theorists call nonlinear. In a linear system, things happen in a regular, expected, or predictable way – the numbers in a column add up to the total figure at the bottom. In a nonlinear system, small changes can have disproportionately large impacts. Pryor and Bright give the example of the final exasperating meeting that can become a 'breaking point' for an employee who quits. They contrast that with more significant changes like a workplace injury. The end result can be of the same sort of magnitude from both events – a significant change in your career trajectory – despite the fact that one event was seemingly more trivial. Careers can be very sensitive to small changes or very stable after large changes.

Importantly, chaos doesn't mean randomness. Nonlinear systems – where small changes make big differences – often create complicated and beautiful patterns, such as in the repetitive complexity of lungs and clouds and trees. The closer you look at those objects, the more you see the same or very similar shapes recurring, again and again. The smallest twigs create patterns that are quite similar to the largest branches. This intricate manner of extending a pattern is why something as small as a snowflake can be so complicated and something as large as the system of veins and arteries can fit inside your body. These patterns of repeating shapes are called fractals. They are nonlinear because the starting point of the pattern creates big differences in the ultimate shape. Hence every snowflake is unique, every cloud slightly different.

The chaos theory of careers incorporates this idea of fractal patterns. Rather than thinking of careers as lines that go up and down depending on success, we can think of them as fractals, where similar patterns repeat themselves but with increasing complexity, the way a tree goes from a sapling to a vast canopy. Once we see the sorts of patterns that people exhibit, we can think about them in this complex, emergent way, rather than simplifying their career to a trajectory. Again and again in this book, we will see stories like Graham's and Kroc's where fractal-type patterns repeat and become more complicated but are only evident in hindsight.

The past can be a prologue to the future – depending on how you look at the past. Seen as trajectories, Graham's and Kroc's careers are hard to predict or explain. Seen fractally, as a set of developing patterns that changed with their circumstances, they make much more sense. That is what makes the Coolidge approach so sensible: it factors in uncertainty while understanding that people emerge from what came before. You must expect chaos and prepare for it. 'What really ruins our character,' said Seneca, 'is the fact that none of us looks back over his life... any plans for the future are dependent on the past.'[16]

Taking the unplanned route means careers can go in many different directions depending on the changes people go through. It does not mean a career is random. Maya Angelou ended up at that dinner party through a series of small encounters that added up to a big difference. The people at Charles Duhigg's reunion were affected by nonlinear effects, too. Very often, careers are simply too complicated to draw straight lines between two different points or to make confident predictions about the future. This is why people who seem to lack direction can end up being successful – and why failure can lead to success. Chaos is inevitable, and therefore so is failure. As Pryor and Bright say, 'Failure should be a perpetual consideration even in the best planned and strictly controlled circumstances.' But order emerges from chaos: and from failure come new opportunities and learnings. Ed Land, the founder and CEO of Polaroid, used to keep a sign on his wall that said, 'A mistake is an event, the full benefit of which has not yet been turned to your advantage.'[17]

Many late bloomers accept that careers are nonlinear – in the case of Charles Duhigg's classmates they were forced to accept it – and end up on a less-planned path that gives them the opportunity to prepare for chance. They get used to the fact that careers are nonlinear and chaotic. Many people have expectations of linear careers: get a degree, go to a graduate programme, get promoted at a steady rate every year, reach partner by a target date. Even in a goal-oriented career, you will have to constantly adapt on your route to the target. Chaos theory shows us that the Coolidge approach can become an active and useful career strategy. In a system with inherent chaos, it can be sensible to take an unplanned route. The linear, corporate-ladder model of a career underrates the importance of chance and the fact that you can benefit from unplanned paths, which prepare you for your luck when it comes along.

Coolidge became president by *not* aiming to be president. Ray Kroc created McDonald's by *not* knowing what he was looking for. Maya Angelou found her publisher by *not* actively seeking out an editor. The benefit of indirect career paths and unplanned preparation is that they prepare you for chaos and teach you how to respond to it.

●●●

What unites the chaos theory of careers and Austin's theory of luck is the role of the individual. Chance events happen to us all. Chaos is unavoidable. Both theories show that we play an active role in our luck, and that we can take advantage of the fact that life is chaotic and nonlinear.

Think about Chris Gardner, the stockbroker from Chapter 2. Chaos theory explains his unplanned career. His career path was derailed and redirected by his upbringing, his qualifications, and his relationship and parenting challenges. Perhaps the moment that had the single greatest impact on his change to a stockbroking career was walking past a Ferrari one day. That was pure accidental luck, as it was that the man driving the Ferrari was happy to go to lunch, explain the job, and organize an introduction to his firm. Gardner also had moments of bad luck, such as starting a new job the day after the manager who recruited him was fired.

But Gardner's openness to opportunity was the sort of luck Austin says is the result of 'restless, driving' behaviour. His story is full of energy: he literally *never* gave up, *never* did less. It was by turning up to so many interviews, regardless of the fact that he was fresh out of jail and his partner had left with their son, that he finally struck the right opportunity. It was by making so many calls that he became the leading broker. It was by talking to so many people that he was able to find accommodation for him and his son.

Finally, Gardner had a 'special receptivity' – to that Ferrari, that driver, and that chance. To most people, the Ferrari was just a car on the street. To this ambitious man, looking for a new life, prepared to work hard to get there, it was transformational. He had wanted to be rich as a child and the lessons his mother taught him never left him. He didn't have a plan for his career, but he did make his own luck by talking to the Ferrari driver, being prepared for that moment. As he said, 'I made a decision, the second most important one I ever made in my life. I was going to become world class at whatever I did.'[18]

When Gardner started his own brokerage firm, it opened on one of the worst days in the history of the market:

> The day I launched my brokerage turned out to be October 19, 1987: Black Monday. The market crashed 508 points. It was not a good time to be raising capital. I showed up to meet a prospect 20 minutes late. He said, 'If I can't expect you to be on time, I can't expect you to do timely things with my money.'[19]

From then on, Gardner has worn two watches and is known for being 'aggressively early'. That's how personality interacts with luck.

There are limits to what we can know and what we can control. The chaos theory of careers, and Austin's theory of luck, say that we ought to expect uncertainty and prepare for it. By doing so, we will be more open to the transformational opportunities we encounter.

•••

One important element in this sort of unplanned preparation is a period of retreat. 'Daily we are on trial, to do a job, to make a marriage good, to find depth, serenity, and meaning in a world of politics, false values, and trivia,' said Audrey Sutherland in her memoir about her solo explorations of the Moloka'i coast, 'but rarely are we deeply challenged physically or alone.'[20] We will now see the benefit of time spent alone.

The political strategist Dominic Cummings spent three years in Russia after graduating from Oxford. He set up a failed airline before returning to Britain and making a failed attempt to study to be a barrister.[21] In his late twenties and early thirties, he joined Business for Sterling, the campaign against the euro, worked for the head of the Conservative Party for a mere eight months, ran a referendum against the North East Assembly, and set up a short-lived think tank. It's a patchwork quilt of success and failure with no clear direction. Then, aged thirty-three, he went home to Durham and spent three years living in a purpose-built bunker on his parents' farm, reading history and physics and trying to understand the world.[22] After that, he ran the *Spectator* website for a year before going to work for Michael Gove in the role that would make him infamous in British political life. From ages thirty-six to forty-three, Cummings was part of the drive to open thousands of new academies and free schools in Britain and to overhaul the curriculum. It was the largest set of changes to education policy since the 1950s.

When he left that job, Cummings published a massive research paper, which detailed his belief in the need for an 'Odyssean education'. Much of the thinking that was important to his view of Brexit and the policy agenda he tried to implement in government can be seen in this paper. More interestingly, perhaps, the paper shows his continuous and intensive education up until that point. He is essentially in full development until at least the age of forty and beyond. In order to properly understand the uncertainty of economic modelling, Cummings taught himself A-level and degree-level maths while working for Gove.[23] He rereads Tolstoy after every major campaign, drawing lessons about people and personality. While he was an advisor, he ran focus groups that showed him that voters don't fall neatly into the ideological lines of the Westminster political parties. According to Cummings's mother, this trait, having wide-ranging interests, was inherited from his father. 'He ran a canoe paddle factory, now he's a farmer, he can turn his hand to anything, he's a polymath – he and Dominic are both like that – interested in a lot of things and interested in learning new things.'[24]

All of this came to a head with Brexit. Cummings was persuaded to run the Vote Leave campaign, which wasn't just revolutionary because of the result of the vote, but also for its use of physicists to manage the advertising campaign. The use of data to inform marketing strategy was far ahead of other political campaigns. Nor is this just about Brexit. Cummings' wide-ranging experiences and education led him to believe that the British government was not fit for service. Without the interruption of the referendum, it's not clear whether his interests would have amounted to anything more than the transformations he had already sought in education. With that referendum, his strange and winding career path became an inefficient route to success.

•••

Sister Wendy Beckett became an international television star in her sixties after a lifetime as a nun. She spent the twenty-five years before her first broadcast living as a hermit in a trailer in the grounds of a Carmelite convent in Norfolk, England. Before she appeared on television, she had never watched any. She hadn't been to the movies since the Second World War. At a dinner given for the sixtieth anniversary of the BBC, in 1982, the first grand event she ever attended, she saw footage of major world events like the four-minute mile and England winning the World Cup for the first time.[25] When she lived in her trailer, she usually only saw one person a day, another nun who took Sister Wendy her post and milk in the mornings.

Sister Wendy knew she wanted to be a nun, she said, from when she was a baby. Her mother realized this and described her as an 'odd child'.[26]

She joined a convent aged seventeen with her mother's support. The convent sent her to Oxford, where she got a Congratulatory First in English Literature, talking to almost no one and making no friends during her time as a student, as she was bound by her vows as a nun. For more than twenty years she taught in convent schools in South Africa (the country of her birth – she grew up in Scotland). She became a hermit after she had three *grand mal* seizures, praying for seven hours a day, and subsisting on coffee for breakfast, Ryvita crackers for lunch, and a pint-and-a-half of skimmed milk for supper.

This life of withdrawal, focused on contemplating God, was everything she wanted. She described herself as having 'a very small human capacity', saying she was 'in some ways an inadequate woman'. 'I was so weak, I needed that orderly set-up. That's the sign of a vocation, that you *need* it.'[27] She only started studying art in 1980, when she was fifty. Perhaps most astonishing, she had never been to see any of the art she was passionate about until the television programmes she hosted took her there. The premise of her first show, *Sister Wendy's Odyssey*, was to follow this hermit as she saw her favourite works of art for the first time.[28] What is most remarkable about Sister Wendy in all her television appearances, especially interviews, is just how happy she is. This strange, restricted life suited her.

•••

Blake Scholl had no experience in aviation, and no technical experience in aeronautics, when he launched a start-up to bring back supersonic travel. He spent the first year reading textbooks, experimenting, and talking to experts:

> I started reading textbooks, and if one textbook didn't help me understand something, I'd throw it out and get another one and read that until things clicked. I took an airplane design class and built a spreadsheet model of an airplane, which showed how a few variables predict a plane's capabilities. It was just me by myself in my basement, puttering through these things.

Amazingly, although flying Mach 2 had been Scholl's ambition for over a decade, no progress had been made on the problem. He'd had a job, started a business, and become a father, assuming that someone would have created subsonic flight. 'I thought I would spend two weeks researching supersonic flight to understand why no one else was doing it and why it's a bad idea. But instead, what I found was that the space was full of stale conventional wisdom.' Scholl's start-up, Boom, has now got contracts with two major airlines (United and American) to supply them with supersonic jets for consumer flights. This is the first time such a thing has been possible since the Concorde was retired in 2003.

Scholl's story has interesting – if improbable – parallels with Sister Wendy's. Where she was deeply motivated by her Catholicism, he is an Objectivist. He adheres to a moral philosophy that emphasizes the importance of individual action and clarity of thinking, just as Sister Wendy's life as a hermit emphasized contemplation. 'You can just chew on a topic until it clicks, and you can actually learn a lot quickly, including things that weren't in your formal training,' says Scholl.[29] Neither of them was an accepted or credentialled expert in their field, and yet they brought energy and originality to their work after a period of retreat.

Dominic Cummings, Sister Wendy, and Blake Scholl were outsiders who spent time in deep learning before they got to the practical implementation stage. Sister Wendy had her trailer; Scholl worked in his basement; Cummings built the bunker on his parents' farm. It was in a period of retreat that they acquired the skills, knowledge, and perspective that would help them to achieve their goal – or discover what their goal was.

In all three cases, this period of retreat had to be joined with a change of luck – the Brexit debate, the chance encounter with a television producer, the fact that Scholl's father-in-law was an eighteen-hour flight away from his grandchildren and no one had yet solved the problem of supersonic travel.

•••

Blake Scholl is far from the only entrepreneur who came to his idea as an outsider, after a period of inefficient preparation, and with an unplanned career. Having a sense of calling that expresses itself in a meandering career path with slowly accumulated learning driven by failure characterizes many people who start businesses in middle age. Although stories of young entrepreneurs abound, there are many compelling examples of older business founders. Herbert Boyer was forty when he founded Genentech, later sold for $47 billion. David Duffield founded Workday aged sixty-four. It is now worth more than $43 billion.[30] Julian Robertson set up his own investment firm aged forty-eight. He had one of his best ever trading years in retirement, during the subprime credit default swap crisis of 2007–8.[31] Bill Franke was home-schooled before attending an American school in Brazil. After Stanford, and three years in the army, he became a lawyer. Through a contact he found a job working in mergers and acquisitions in a forest products company where he became CEO. He discovered he enjoyed business more than law. Aged fifty, after negotiating a merger with a Chicago firm, he quit and started his own investment firm. A few years later, he took over as CEO of the failing America West Airlines. In his sixties, he opened an investment firm focused on airlines. He invested in Wizz Air, Tiger Airways, Smart and other low-cost carriers, becoming a pioneer of the budget air travel industry.[32]

In all these cases, entrepreneurs have to accumulate a series of relevant skills and experiences that allow them to take advantage of opportunities when they come along. Through a process of learning through failing, they make their own luck and keep themselves in the swim like Coolidge.

Economists Pierre Azoulay, Benjamin F. Jones, J. Daniel Kim, and Javier Miranda looked at a sample of high-growth businesses started by 2.7 million founders in the United States between 2007 and 2014, and linked tax, census and patent data to estimate the average age of people who found '"growth-oriented" firms that can have large economic impacts and are often associated with driving an increasing standard of living'.[33]

They found that the average age of people whose business went on to hire at least one employee was 41.9. The average age of founders of the highest-growth businesses was forty-five. In this sample, the 1,700 fastest-growing new businesses (the top 0.1 per cent) were founded by people with an average age of forty-five.[34] Furthermore, a fifty-year-old founder is twice as likely to make a successful sale of their company than a thirty-year-old founder.[35] The results are even more counterintuitive about technology founders: 'Founders in high-tech employment sectors tend to be slightly older than the US-wide average, and founders of patenting firms are the oldest of all, with an average age of 44.3 in Silicon Valley.'[36] This is still consistent with the idea that the youngest founders can produce the businesses with the biggest impact – people like Bill Gates and Mark Zuckerberg, for example – but on average you are more likely to find high-growth businesses being started by the middle-aged than the young.

It is possible that the experience of failing, and learning from failing, is what makes the difference to older founders. A study of retail entrepreneurs found that people who have started more than one company have a higher success rate and a lower dropout rate. The skills they accumulate through experience contribute to the success of their later ventures.[37] This is how Michael Ramsey founded TiVo aged forty-seven. He moved to the United States in his twenties, worked for Hewlett-Packard (HP), and then took a stint away to work at a start-up: after a year back at HP, he realized he could no longer tolerate big company culture, and went back to working for a smaller company, SGI.

At HP he had met the colleagues with whom he would later found TiVo. They left HP with him to go to SGI. At SGI he started meeting people who worked in entertainment and got interested in how to apply computer technology to that area. One former HP colleague, Jim Barton, had gone to work elsewhere on a video-on-demand service. That turned out to be technically accomplished but soured Barton about working in the television industry. One day, Barton and Ramsey had lunch and shared experiences. They began developing the idea for TiVo. Initially, they struggled to get investment. Their idea was too complicated; it was through the trial and error of starting the company that they came to TiVo as we know it. Without their combined professional experience, they wouldn't have been able to found the company. Ramsey also needed to move to the United States to make him think like a founder. He had previously lived in the UK where the culture was 'much more subdued… more cautious'.[38] As we will see in the networks and culture sections, the people you associate with have a major influence on what you do.

It is a common belief among venture capitalists that young talent is more likely to succeed. This might be explained by the fact that young entrepreneurs are more likely to require funding. Venture capitalists may also get better returns investing in young people who sell their company earlier.[39] In one study, it was found that people in their early twenties are most enthusiastic to start a business, but least able: as they age, they acquire the skills necessary to start a company, but gradually lose their willingness. That study also found that your employment experience – such as experience of being self-employed – affects your chance of starting a business. Although willingness declines with age, opportunity is the main limiting factor. Getting funding increases the chance of starting a business, but experience can somewhat compensate for a lack of funding. Learning through experience remains a strong indicator of whether someone will start a company.[40] This is why so many entrepreneurs are older: there is often no quick way to get experience.

Older workers have accumulated networks as well as capital. In one study that used a large data set of people born in early March 1958 in the UK, the economists David Blanchflower and Andrew Oswald found that the more money someone inherits, the more likely they are to become an entrepreneur at a younger age. There was a cut-off point of inheriting £15,000, after which the likelihood of becoming an entrepreneur declined. They concluded: 'A gift or inheritance of £5,000 approximately doubles a typical individual's probability of setting up his or her own business.'[41] The year under study for starting businesses was 1981. £5,000 in 1981 would be worth approximately £17,000 today. Of course, someone in middle age is more likely to have accumulated the money needed to start a business, rather than needing to rely on an inheritance.

David Duffield is an interesting case study of how these principles work. Duffield first worked at IBM, leaving aged twenty-eight to start his own company. In his twenties and thirties, he founded four companies, and made several million dollars. But he had not properly absorbed the lessons on management from IBM. 'I didn't know how to keep bureaucracy or infighting or bad behavior out of a company,' he told *Forbes*. 'I either would start a new company, go off on my own and start again or bring somebody in to run it who had more management skills than I did.'[42] When he was forty-seven, he founded PeopleSoft, which went public when he was fifty-two. 'I always had in the back of my mind, when is bureaucracy going to set in here? When are we going to start fighting each other?' Duffield began to focus on corporate culture – on making sure the business could work properly at scale. Now that he looked back, he could see that was what had made IBM a success: keeping people happy while making a profit. In 2005, PeopleSoft was subject to a hostile takeover by Oracle. Duffield was sixty-five. He didn't retire: he founded a new company, starting with the values this time. He and his co-founder personally interviewed the first five hundred hires.[43] Today, Workday takes in about $5 billion in annual revenue. In 2014, Duffield stood down as CEO to become Chairman of Workday. In 2017, at the age of seventy-seven, he started a new company called Ridgeline, which sells cloud software for investment management. Duffield's experience is consistent with the research on serial entrepreneurs, who tend to found their first business younger than one-time entrepreneurs. Their businesses also don't last as long and they sell the companies slightly younger too.[44] This reflects a pattern of acquiring skills and capital to take into the next opportunity – which is exactly how Duffield worked.

•••

Entrepreneurs are able to make their own luck through long preparation – like Ray Kroc's long apprenticeship – and being ready to spot and seize opportunities that come up. The more they accumulate skills, networks, and capital, the more opportunities they can take advantage of. Politicians have to prepare for opportunities in similar ways, and often with a period of retreat, or a 'wilderness' period. But like we saw with Calvin Coolidge, in politics luck relies much more on the way the wheel of fortune turns.

Women first became a significant presence in the US House of Representatives through a process called widow's succession. Between 1917 and 2000, thirty-seven widows took over from their recently deceased congressmen husbands. This was only 14 per cent of the widows who *could* have taken over – a total of 298 congressmen with healthy wives died during the same time period. But it represents a large proportion of the women who have served in Congress. In 1962, 45 per cent of women representatives had first become congresswomen through widow's succession. These women were often elite. They were active in philanthropy, political committee work, education, and local community work. They had the important experience of having worked for their husbands as secretaries or campaign managers. They were well prepared for the job of congresswoman by virtue of their long apprenticeship – but it took the wheel of fortune to actually get them into Congress.[45]

Widow's succession is no longer a major mechanism in countries with women's suffrage, especially as far fewer congressmen now die in office, although as the average age of members of Congress keeps rising perhaps that will change. Women now have much more access to political careers in their own right, even if their husbands are also in politics (a dynamic that often restricted women's political activity in the past). The longer women's suffrage is in place, the less important family connections are for women to become politicians.[46]

As these changes have happened, more strategic and less privileged women have become congresswomen. One effect of this privileging was that only one of the widows who became congresswomen was African American. The wheel of fortune was not able to turn in favour of Black women who wanted political careers in this way. This shows us the other sort of luck late bloomers need – the luck of being in the right circumstances, which is discussed in Chapter 4.[47]

Widow's succession shows a particular instance of the way fortunes can change in politics. Fewer politicians die in office now, which means we see fewer instances of people suddenly assuming high office the way widows used to, or the way Coolidge and Roosevelt did. But politics is still an area where circumstances change unexpectedly, unpredictably. When they do, careers are made and lost. Many late-blooming political careers were formed fortuitously.

Being in the swim, preparing and working for a chance, without always trying to make careerist moves was how Andrew Bonar Law became the leader of the Conservative Party in Britain, a position which saw him become Deputy Prime Minister during the First World War and then Prime Minister in 1922, before ill health forced him to resign. Law had been an iron trader in Glasgow, making no attempt at a political career before he was forty.

Law was known for his exceptional memory, able to calculate his net position at the end of a day of trading without any notes. Those financial skills later enabled him to run the Treasury during the First World War and to make a decisive call on interest rates against expert opinion. He also worked effectively with John Maynard Keynes. In Parliament, he was an adept speaker on financial and economic issues, always in control of the details, a rare parliamentary skill then as now. When he ran the trading business in Glasgow, he always went to court when business gave him the opportunity. In this way, he honed his speaking skills. He had no university education, but he read Edward Gibbon's *The History of the Decline and Fall of the Roman Empire* three times before he was twenty-five. His descent from Ulster Presbyterians meant that the party took him seriously on the fraught and dangerous issue of Irish Home Rule, a crisis which nearly became a civil war in Britain before the First World War.

Law was a dour Canadian who had no idea what a pheasant looked like, in a party of aristocrats who spent their weekends shooting. He was nothing like a Conservative leader: the previous two leaders had been a marquis and his nephew. It was an era of dinner-table networking, but Law was teetotal and disliked entertaining or eating rich food. However, his advantage was that his predecessor Arthur Balfour (the marquis's nephew) was highly intelligent but ineffective. Law was a straight talker and after Balfour's convoluted circumlocutions that satisfied nobody, Law came across like a horn in the fog.

He was elected to Parliament in 1900, got a Shadow Cabinet position in 1906, and then became the astonishing choice for leader in 1911, after coming to politics aged forty-two, with no support base in the party. The two leadership candidates were ineffective and their rivalry threatened to split the party. The 1906 general election had resulted in one of the worst results ever for the Conservatives. The Liberals had trounced them, and the new Labour Party was starting to win seats. Law was unknown, but he was in the swim. When two other candidates quit the leadership race, worried about splitting the party, Law was chosen as a strange and unique Conservative leader.

Senator Samuel Hayakawa of California had a similarly unexpected rise to prominence. Hayakawa was an English professor who migrated to the United States from Canada to study his PhD in 1929. He didn't become a US citizen until 1954, aged forty-eight, because of wartime restrictions imposed by the Roosevelt administration on Japanese Americans. In 1968, aged sixty-two, as the newly appointed acting President of San Francisco State College, he opposed a student strike that had been inspired by the suspension of a Black lecturer, the lack of Black studies programmes, and a lack of student diversity. Hayakawa banned demonstrations and speeches. Hundreds of people were arrested. In December, a photograph of him went national in which he climbed 'up on a sound truck manned by campus radicals and jerked out the wires of the public address system'.[48] Without television, this act would have left him as a relatively anonymous professor. But in the age of the image, one simple action caught the public mood and changed his life.

As he entered the San Francisco campus that first day of his presidency, his head covered with a jaunty tam o' shanter, he tried to speak to a group of students but was drowned out by a loudspeaker. Mildly irritated, he pulled the speaker wiring out and continued his remarks. The television cameras caught the action. It hadn't seemed like a big deal to people at the scene, including Hayakawa. But to the national television audience he was a 5-foot, 5-inch 145-pounder who spat in the eye of the bullies and radicals.[49] He became 'the symbol of adult authority taking control of rebellious students'.[50] It was the media that made him a politician: 'One of the real successes of my administration was that I captured the media from radical students...'[51] He described his confrontations with students as 'the most exciting day since my 10th birthday'.

He was the man for the moment, the third person to become acting president of the college in a single year. During the confrontations with students, Hayakawa went from sleeping in and working late to getting up early. As a young man, he was told his Japanese heritage precluded many career options: now he was finding his niche, though he lacked the appearance of a senator – the *New York Times* describing him as 'a bouncy little man with a scraggly moustache'.[52] He was college president until 1973; he ran for the Senate in 1976, aged seventy, becoming a Republican for the first time. He gained the nomination with only 38 per cent of the vote because the two better-known candidates split the vote. Hayakawa's lack of political background was thus an advantage, as it had been for Andrew Bonar Law.[53] He served one term, abandoning his re-election campaign in 1982 partly because his reputation for napping in the Senate made him unpopular.[54] His age was also cited: 'He would be 76 at the start of a new term. It has been 13 years since he pulled the plug on the student radical sound system.'[55] A strange critique for a country whose President was then seventy-two. But the culture that had brought him to public attention was gone, and he was now known as 'Sleepin' Sam' rather than the man who stood up to student radicals. The wheel of fortune turned again and his political career was over.

This sort of chance happening is common in politics. It was the Second World War that made Harry Truman and Dwight Eisenhower late bloomers. If these two men had died aged fifty, they would be almost unknown today: one a local politician, the other a mid-ranking army officer of little consequence. Truman was so unknown that the first time his name was proposed for Vice-President, all Roosevelt said was that he didn't know much about him. He later came to think Truman would be the least bad candidate.[56] Eisenhower spent years learning war strategy under the guidance of senior generals who mentored him and nurtured his potential. He had no promotion for sixteen years. Without the outbreak of war, he would have retired quietly. In 1940, he told his son he would be forced to retire as a lieutenant colonel. 'In an emergency anything can happen,' he said, 'but we are talking about a career, John, not miracles.'[57]

What Truman and Eisenhower had in their favour was earnestness. They were self-taught, hardworking, strong-willed men. When Truman was in charge of having a new courthouse built in Kansas City, he drove around to dozens of other cities, saw their public buildings, and found the architect he wanted. In the Senate, in 1940, he drove ten thousand miles to inspect army camps. Eisenhower was so interested in mechanical warfare he and George Patton stripped tanks down to their constituent parts and reassembled them.[58] Truman's knowledge of procurement made his name in the Senate as Roosevelt built the arsenal of democracy. Eisenhower was later seen to be ahead of his time when tanks became integral to modern forms of battle, something denied by the top brass until the brutal necessities of the Second World War disrupted their dogmatism.

Coolidge had that sort of intensity. So did Sister Wendy and Blake Scholl. Many of the people profiled in this book are earnest. It marks them out from the people around them. Think of Ray Kroc, who *travelled across the country just to see a hamburger restaurant* because it had ordered more milkshake mixers than any of his other customers. There was something almost religious about Kroc's inspirational moment when he discovered McDonald's, and there is something more akin to the amateur scientist than the budding army officer in Eisenhower's willingness to strip a tank. Penelope Fitzgerald studied several European languages alongside her difficult teaching job. Vera Wang's frustration at being unable to find a suitable wedding dress became the basis of a business that would overturn the market for bridal wear.

This intensity can be difficult to see. Fitzgerald's friends noticed her unusual lifestyle and the state of her children – the intensity of her interest in languages and culture was less noticed. Kroc's wife simply couldn't understand why a relatively successful salesman would want to take a gamble on a hamburger business. The army was full of officers of Eisenhower's generation who anticipated another war: many of them left to make better money elsewhere. This is not about ambition, curiosity, or the unwillingness to give up – those are homilies of what it takes to be a success: they are necessary, not sufficient. To spot late-blooming talent, we must look also for the persistent interests, the willingness to give over precious time to peculiar interests – people for whom stripping a tank out of sheer curiosity doesn't seem unusual.

Persistence alone is not the key characteristic. *What* you persist at matters. Late bloomers often seem to be chasing phantom goals, or no goals at all. They might have a sense of some future success, however vague, and they're willing to let current opportunities pass them by in pursuit of the bigger goal – with really no guarantee of success at all. This is not just how late-life success is made. This is the cause of much failure and disappointment too. In short, late bloomers are often quite weird. And when fate intervenes, their weirdness pays off.

So many times in Margaret Thatcher's career, fate intervened. If it hadn't, she would not have become Mrs. Thatcher, the Iron Lady. As we have seen in this chapter, chance favours the prepared mind and Thatcher was always preparing. 'Time spent in reconnaissance is never wasted'[59] was one of her favourite sayings. To understand her success, we must look closely at what she persisted at, not just what persistently happened to her.

5
Margaret Thatcher: chance favours the prepared mind

You might baulk at the idea that Margaret Thatcher (1925–2013) was a late bloomer. She became leader of the British Conservative Party aged fifty, which is about the average age that people become party leader. But a few weeks before it happened, no one, including her, thought it *could* happen. As her biographer Charles Moore said to me, 'Few expected greatness of her until she was nearly fifty.' Even the few people who strongly believed in her abilities never imagined she might be Prime Minister, let alone a global stateswoman who would play a role in ending the Cold War. Although she was clearly capable, the actual nature of her talents was unforeseen, and she bloomed much later than many others of her generation. Far from being seen as the person who would become the most decisive and divisive figure in post-war British politics, she was assumed to be a failure in waiting. She confounded expectations.

The Principal of Somerville College, Oxford, where Thatcher was an undergraduate, remembered her as 'a perfectly good second-class chemist'.[1] After failing to get elected at Dartford in 1950 and 1951, she was rejected as a candidate for Orpington in 1954 and had to wait until the 1959 election, when she won the seat for Finchley aged thirty-four. It would be another fifteen years until she became leader of the Conservative Party. She had never dreamed of being Prime Minister as a child, and even in 1959, when she was elected as an MP, 'the possibility of one day being Prime Minister did not cross my mind – I just didn't think there would ever be a woman Prime Minister in my lifetime'.[2] Even when she was in the Cabinet as

Education Secretary, her highest ambition was to be the first woman Chancellor. She never indicated she wanted to be Prime Minister to her parliamentary colleagues.[3]

She was a politically active young woman, canvassing in the 1945 election and speaking at political meetings in Colchester in her early twenties. She was regarded as a 'winner' by the Dartford association who selected her in 1949. The former MP Lord Balfour of Inchrye said she was '[a] grand young candidate. Speaks well. Good looking. Keen, knows her subjects. Watch and Encourage'. After the 1951 election, the association described her as 'an amazing young woman with experience and knowledge far beyond her years' and recommended she 'not be lost sight of'. They couldn't reselect her, however, because she was getting married.[4]

But none of that adds up to a serious prediction of her later success. And she *was* lost sight of: she failed to get selected for Orpington in 1954. She then wrote to Conservative Central Office, 'I shall continue at the bar with no future thought of a Parliamentary career for many years.'[5] She asked to be put back on the candidates' list fifteen months later, but for 'safe Conservative-held seats only'. She had no appetite for more failure. The party promised only to 'bear your name in mind'.[6] Thatcher was not alone in this struggle. In 1952, several women MPs wrote to Conservative associations complaining that women candidates were given 'hopeless' seats to contest 'over and over again'.[7]

Thatcher was always described as a 'woman candidate', which tempered the praise she received. The Maidstone association doubted her ability to be an MP and a mother, despite her having a nanny.[8] When she was adopted for Finchley, objections to having a woman were strong enough to prevent the conventional unanimous vote by the committee after she won the ballot.[9] 'I am learning the hard way that an anti-woman prejudice can persist even after a successful adoption meeting,' she wrote. In the same letter she wrote that she wore the outfit Donald Kaberry, who ran the candidate list, had recommended.[10] Thatcher also told Kaberry, 'I seem to have done very little in thirty years.'[11] That wasn't true – she had been to Oxford, worked as a chemist in two companies, stood for Parliament twice, and qualified as a barrister. But she always expected more of herself. How else would she become Mrs Thatcher?

In these incidents, some of her later steel is evident. As one of the candidate reports said, 'The mere fact that she secured selection among 22 candidates interviewed by an association determined not to have a woman, speaks for itself.'[12] But she was not the Iron Lady; that would take many more trials. And once she was, she shrewdly understood that for a woman to retreat from dominance – a middle-class woman in an upper-class man's world, about whom so many people had mixed emotional, psychological and sexual feelings – for such a woman to retreat would impossibilitate her dominance in the future. Being a woman always palliated what people expected of her. In 1970, four years before she became leader of the Conservative Party, the *Sun* wrote: 'One day someone will achieve the unclimbed height of becoming Britain's first woman Chancellor of the Exchequer. It might not be too outrageous for Mrs Thatcher to wonder whether she could be the one who does it.'[13] Chancellor, maybe; but not Prime Minister.

Thatcher was underrated throughout her career. In 1972, the *Sun* called her the most unpopular woman in Britain because, as Education Secretary, she had ended free milk for school children. She was widely thought to have been named Education Secretary only because she was a woman. A 1975 biography of Thatcher says Edward Heath was 'more obliged to have a woman in his cabinet than if he had been a family man'.[14] Education was the sort of brief that a sexist institution could safely give an upstart woman. Heath originally thought about making Thatcher the 'statutory woman' in the shadow cabinet in 1966 but didn't because 'we'll never be able to get rid of her'.[15] (He was more right than he knew.) By some accounts, she 'refused Edward Heath's offer of shadow social security secretary because it was a job stereotypically reserved for women'.[16] That is difficult to verify, but Thatcher did make a detailed point to the *Finchley Times* in 1966 about the way women politicians were now experts not just in social and health policy – departments given to them for sexist reasons – but also on topics like finance and defence.[17]

Shortly after that, William J. Galloway, first secretary and political officer of the US embassy in Britain, chose Thatcher to receive a grant that enabled her to travel to Washington, DC. This was a rare instance of someone recognizing her talent. Galloway was impressed by Thatcher's 'very strong will', 'high standards of ethics and morals', 'tremendous self-confidence', and the fact that 'she didn't hesitate to express her views'. He thought of her as 'a politician who was not seeking support for her own personal advancement' and described her as 'the outstanding lady in the House of Commons' at that time.[18] He did not think of her as an intellectual, however. This is an example of Thatcher being what Alfred Sherman called 'not a person of ideas but a person of beliefs'. As Charles Moore told me, 'she was always thinking, thinking, thinking. "What's right here? What's the best? What's the problem? What's the solution?" But she didn't have the philosopher's sceptical mind or pure intellectualism. She wanted results.'[19] It was her strong will, iron morals, and belief in the importance of getting results that steered her to the leadership.

There is some support for the idea that great leaders are not the most educated, but the most decisive. The psychologist Dean Keith Simonton, looking at a data set from 1923, found that the more formal education a leader has, the lower their eminence.[20] This sounds counterintuitive, especially as the data is so old. But US Presidents Truman and Reagan didn't have much academic success and were highly eminent. It may not be a firm correlation but it is certainly true that you don't have to go to a top university to be a good leader. Thatcher had no formal political education, but she was a chemist and a barrister. (She was more proud of being the first science graduate

Prime Minister than of being the first woman Prime Minister.) However, she was an attentive and disciplined autodidact.

In 1971, there was a government proposal to change the way science funding was allocated. Various imperfections in matching pure science research to practical problems meant the government wanted to 'marketize' some research funding. This affected a small number of institutions, but became a political dispute. Thatcher was Education Secretary, with responsibility for science, and was part of the policy discussion. Initially, she took the line that the system should not be changed. The scientific establishment was concerned that a market in funding for a few small organizations would spread to other, larger scientific bodies, jeopardizing free, independent enquiry. During the discussions, Thatcher changed her position. The minutes record: 'The Agricultural Research Council, the Medical Research Council and the Natural Environment Research Council would become organisations primarily dealing with applied research [and therefore research shaped decisively by customer–contractor market language].'[21] The academic Jon Agar sees this as an 'early moment when Thatcher chose the market as an alternative to established models of resource allocation'.[22]

This exemplifies many important strands of Thatcher's character that would enable her later success. First, as Agar says, 'She viewed science as a source of wealth, and therefore as a justified expenditure from the public purse. Yet this elevation made science even more of a test case for her developing views on economic liberalism. If markets could work for science policy, they could work anywhere.'[23] This shows Thatcher's ability to think about the implementation of ideology; she was not a Friedman copycat or Hayekian mime. She approached problems individually. She was by no means the most 'Thatcherite' member of some of her cabinets. Second, her experience as a research scientist in a plastics company and at the food manufacturer J. Lyons & Co. honed her ability to marry the practical and the theoretical.

'It was precisely because Thatcher knew what scientific research was like that made her impervious to claims that science was a special case, with special features and incapable of being understood by outsiders.'[24] Her practical mind enabled her to learn the system – and learn how to change it.

There are many other examples of her autodidacticism. While Thatcher was Leader of the Opposition, Martin Gilbert was publishing Churchill's official biography, including large volumes of documents alongside the narrative volumes. Thatcher wrote to Gilbert about a footnote in one of the document volumes that said Churchill had prepared notes for a book about socialism in the late 1920s.[25] That sharp eye for small details characterized the way she worked as Prime Minister. Everyone who worked with her was impressed at her grasp of minutiae. Lord Carrington said that she 'actually listens' and had 'a very acute intelligence'.[26] Charles Moore told me: 'She's extremely unusual in politicians for a sustained interest, sustained over a very, very long period in her case, in office, in the content of what she was doing.'[27]

Thatcher governed through details by governing on paper. She was rigorous about reading and annotating the huge amounts of paperwork she received, with a system of underlinings and squiggles to denote approval or disapproval. She frequently challenged analysis, corrected messaging, demanded more information. She knew that she needed to make decisions to turn ideas into real-world change.[28] Monetarism, free markets, and individual liberty were important concepts, but having those ideas actually change the world required a decider, not an intellectual. It was through her paperwork, her decisions, and her public communications – through work – that she made these ideas real. As Charles Moore told me, she had 'a resourceful seriousness, which might not be intellectually original, but which was in a political sense, profound... There was simply nobody else in the first rank who was behaving and thinking that way.'[29]

Coolidge, Truman and Bonar Law had the same 'resourceful seriousness'. They were earnest. Coolidge was so dedicated to reducing the size of government that he had a weekly meeting with his budget director where they went through every line of the US federal budget looking for ways of reducing expenditure. In this, as in much of his work, Coolidge modelled himself on Abraham Lincoln, who proved himself a master administrator of the 'practical affairs of his day'.[30] Through things like cuts to telephone and transportation bills, the renegotiation of contracts for paper, and efficient logistics for the delivery of equipment, Coolidge found a $300,000 surplus in a budget of $3 billion.[31] The Soviet ambassador Averell Harriman said of Truman that 'you could go into [Truman's] office with a question and come out with a decision quicker than any man I have ever known'.[32] Similarly, Bonar Law was a workhorse during the First World War, his office strewn with papers as he managed the national finances and acted as Lloyd George's deputy, discussing the conduct of the war with him every morning. To be a leader, you must be able to look at the details and make a decision. You cannot govern with principles, only practicalities.[33]

The other shared characteristic of Bonar Law, Coolidge, Truman, and Thatcher's resourceful seriousness is moral earnestness. Bonar Law believed strongly in the union with Ireland because of his ancestry. Coolidge had a rock-like resistance to debt based on his family history. Truman's small-town morals were mocked as corny but acted as a cornerstone for the creation of the post-war world order.

Because of her upbringing in a small town, with a religious, business-owning family, Thatcher saw her mission as moral, not merely economic. She told her speechwriter Ferdinand Mount that her real task was to 'restore standards of conduct and responsibility'. Mount records that after a day of meetings full of 'haranguing visitors for hours' she would kick off her shoes, have a glass of scotch, and '"resume the harangue" with him "as though we had never met"'.[34] (Lynda Lee-Potter once said: 'She doesn't talk in sentences so much as entire chapters and she'd be brilliant at that party game where you mustn't reply "Yes" or "No" to anything.'[35]) Mount found her total lack of small talk unbelievable. She was 'indifferent to most of the tricks of paradox, ambiguity, understatement, and saying the opposite of what you mean, which pepper the talk of almost everyone in the country'.[36] No wonder Heath and Whitelaw had been so reluctant to have her in Cabinet; no wonder she was regarded wearily by her colleagues. But to achieve what Margaret Thatcher achieved you have to be a uniquely serious person, which often isn't simple or easy for others to deal with. She never let conformity distract or subdue her earnestness.

One common criticism of Thatcher, related to how seriously she took herself, is her slightly warped view of reality. Mount says that she remembered working with him twenty years before and recalled him as an energetic young man who had agreed with her when he was in fact rather idle and hadn't agreed with her at all. 'Successful politicians – perhaps people who are successful at anything – ', Mount writes, 'need to doctor the past if they are going to keep going.'[37] It was always a moral vision of the world that kept Thatcher going. Her distortions were made in service to that bigger belief.

Galloway was right to note Thatcher's non-educational qualities as her most important. The way Thatcher started studying political philosophy rather late, once she was on track to the top, is sometimes mocked, or noted as an example of her unsuitability to be leader. In fact, Thatcher's relative unsophistication as a political intellectual was an advantage. The *Finchley Times* said in 1966 that she was 'no blue-stocking', and 'as her appearances on "Any questions" and her down-to-earth approach to politics confirm, she is no hide-bound academician'.[38]

Galloway got to know the Thatchers relatively well, going to dinner with them and becoming friendly with Denis as well as Margaret. He later recalled that in the mid-1960s 'she was then the same woman who later became Prime Minister; in other words she would not hesitate to voice her views to anyone whomever. She was different from other women in the House of Commons. She was not particularly liked by her colleagues because of her personality and her kind of aggressiveness.' Galloway recalled that Jim Prior was an early admirer – though they would later be at odds in Cabinet. According to Galloway, Prior 'persuaded Heath, against his will, to take her in the Shadow Cabinet. According to Jim, she was not shy about joining in the deliberations. She irritated Heath repeatedly, and Jim had to intervene with him frequently to save her neck.' Most people judged Thatcher on appearances, on whether she irritated them; they let their prejudices get the better of them. For that reason, they didn't see her coming.

She didn't see herself coming either. Galloway congratulated her when she became Leader of the Opposition and she wrote back: 'I still do not know quite how it all happened! Six months ago I should have said it would be impossible.' Despite his enthusiasm, even Galloway didn't quite realize who she was. 'I have to confess, although I liked her very much, I never in the world thought she would become prime minister.'[39]

Being able to get things done was part of Thatcher's pitch to be Conservative Party leader. In a television interview a few days before polling, she said of her career, 'I've gone on at each stage, first a member, then a parliamentary secretary, then a minister tackling each job and I think getting on top of it.' When she was asked why it should be her challenging Heath and not a more senior MP, she made a virtue of her quick decision-making: 'The interesting thing was, I didn't hesitate, I took the decision quickly and I've never had any doubt about it, that it was the right decision and I never faltered and

I'm in no doubt now.' She also made a pitch of her beliefs rather than her ideas. 'I don't like Opposition very much, I much prefer to have the chance to put one's beliefs into action.' She made it clear that her core beliefs about the role of the state were formed before she was seventeen or eighteen.[40]

Being a woman made her easy to overlook, but the men around her were also overlooking one of her key political advantages. Her position as a middle-England housewife, who said she had delayed her political career when she had small children, was a favourable one that she used to some effect.

Her first two elections were 1950 and 1951. Britain had been through five years of more intensive rationing than during the war. According to one academic, 'The index of food rations shows that rations of fats, meat and other sources of animal protein were lower and more volatile after 1945 than during the war.'[41] The only cheese available was consistently substandard, sometimes called Government Cheddar. At least one woman used it to light fires.[42] Food rationing was a major political issue, consistently among the highest concerns of the general public in opinion surveys in the late 1940s. Even in 1949, 75 per cent of the public still thought their diet was worse than before the war.[43] Rationing became a political issue again in 1951 when the meat ration fell to a new low.[44]

Rationing became a central issue for the Conservatives.[45] It was especially important to housewives, who had to work out how to feed their family. They were the ones to stand in the queues, and were often treated badly by shopkeepers. This is why Churchill used to describe socialism as 'queuetopia'.[46] Although the swing from Labour to the Conservatives was smaller among women than men, it was larger among middle-class women.[47]

The 1951 election, called by some 'the housewives election', saw a larger number of women candidates. The journalist Ruth Adam wrote, 'No woman member of any kind, at this period, dared to forget to describe herself as a "housewife".'[48] Margaret Thatcher didn't call herself a housewife because she wasn't one in 1951. But the importance of housewife rhetoric, a Tory staple since the Great Depression, was not lost on her. In her 1950 election address she said, 'I ask every housewife, does she want her sugar to increase in price and go down in quality?'[49] In 1966 she told the *Finchley Times* that women 'have a wider understanding [than men] of problems affecting the family, and of matters such as health and welfare'.[50] In her 1970 election address she said, 'Inflation, the worst for twenty years, is with us again. Pensioners and housewives are helpless as they watch the extra shillings eaten up by price rises.'[51] She also used to talk about giving up politics in the 1950s, when her children were young, to signal her credibility to mothers and housewives.[52]

When she was Leader of the Opposition, her publicist Gordon Reece was careful to put her on radio programmes like the Jimmy Young show and in magazines that appealed to Labour-voting housewives.[53] In 1978, the Conservatives ran a poster set out as a *Cosmo* quiz. It asked who was more likely to know what it was like to do the family shopping: a) James Callaghan [Thatcher's opponent], b) Your husband, or c) Margaret Thatcher.[54] In 1979, she countered press accusations that she hoarded food by saying, 'Well, you call it stockpiling, but I call it being a prudent housewife.'[55] Remarkably, she gave that interview to a magazine called *Pre-Retirement Choice*, three months before she stood for the leadership. She said that with Denis turning sixty (she was nearly fifty), she was buying items like sheets and towels that she would need in ten years' time, as a hedge against inflation.[56] Although she said she hoped to keep working for another fifteen or twenty years, those are hardly the words of a woman who expected to be Leader of the Opposition in six months.

Interestingly, in that interview she talked about how as a minister, when she had to make an appointment to committee, she looked to people who were retiring. Those choices often faced prejudice:

> I would suggest the names of people who have just retired from industry or commerce. These are the people with invaluable experience.
>
> But often when you put down their names the reaction would come back – well, don't you think they are too old? This is a terrible dilemma and I said unless we are going to use some of the talent and skill and experience of some of these people we are going to deprive ourselves of the advice they can give.[57]

So Margaret Thatcher was an advocate for late bloomers.

Her housewife rhetoric shows how Thatcher's electability came from her core beliefs and experiences, some of them rooted in her experience as a working mother who felt, as she told one journalist, like she went around the house on roller skates.[58] Analogies and rhetoric drawn from her experience and identity as a working mother gave her an advantage over the men she was competing with. This was all part of the practical learning she acquired over the course of her unplanned career.

These core beliefs were not just beneficial to Thatcher in the crude sense of winning votes. They underpinned her approach to problems such as how to tackle inflation, whether to make mortgage payments tax deductible, and how to end the Cold War. Part of what enabled her to succeed when no one thought she could was the fact that she was not a fashionable thinker. To have been able to talent-spot Margaret Thatcher, this is what you would have needed to see. Not her Hayekian credentials, not her technocratic policy platform, but her beliefs, her experiences, and (as William J. Galloway saw) her ethics, energy, decisiveness, and indifference to popularity.

Almost no one did talent-spot her... Ladbrokes had her at fifty-to-one against for being next Conservative leader in October 1974 – four months before she won. At that time, only Keith Joseph was thought of as a possible replacement for Ted Heath.[59] The 1975 biography says she was almost entirely unknown before the leadership election.[60] This was certainly true abroad. When she visited the United States in 1967 and 1969, 'official Washington did not consider her sufficiently significant to put itself out for her'.[61]

Even Airey Neave, who ran her leadership campaign, only backed her because Edward du Cann decided not to stand. Neave wrote in his diary that Thatcher had a 'good chance' but was a difficult 'sell'. Two months before the leadership election, he wrote that there was 'no unanimity' about Thatcher and that Heath's stock was rising among MPs.[62] Neave had admired Thatcher as a fellow scientist but showed some reluctance to back her. Even to her supporters, her talents were not obvious.[63]

Indeed, hardly anyone thought a woman could be Prime Minister. The former Scottish Labour MP Jean Mann wrote in 1962 that there was very little chance of a woman even becoming Chancellor or Foreign Secretary. (There still has not been a woman Chancellor in the UK.) Mann was impressed with Thatcher's determination, accomplishments and businesslike attitude – Thatcher's maiden speech was also the introductory speech for a Private Members' Bill – and forecast that the young MP might be capable of the Foreign Office.[64] One person who realized Thatcher was a viable candidate was the *Times* journalist Bernard Levin, who wrote that there had already been women leaders of Sri Lanka, India and Israel, the first two of which were 'countries even more male dominated than Britain'.[65] Thatcher, he said, had a 'vivid and challenging public image', would be able to use her sex to her advantage, was clever, had stamina, and 'will not be easy to ignore'.[66] Despite this prescient insight, Levin said he would still vote first for Edward Heath.

He wasn't alone. Heath led a poll of party members in the *Daily Express* and the National Union. The peers and grandees supported Lord Carrington.[67] Thatcher herself supported Keith Joseph. Even in early November 1974, three months before she became leader, she said, 'The party isn't ready for a woman and the press would crucify me.'[68] It was only on 20th November, when Keith Joseph dropped out of the race after making a controversial speech, that Thatcher decided to stand. Fate intervened.

Only a month earlier, Airey Neave had written in his diary, 'We could find nothing but objections to possible candidates e.g. Whitelaw, K. Joseph, Carr, Margaret Thatcher.'[69] *The Economist* described her as 'precisely the sort of candidate who ought to be able to stand, and lose, harmlessly'.[70] Edward du Cann took weeks to decide if he would stand, so support was hovering around him. This went on into 1975. Thatcher was not just unknown but, in the words of her publicist, 'was not at this stage good at either communicating with people, or on television'.[71] Many factors contributed to her win, not least Airey Neave telling MPs that if they didn't vote for her they would be stuck with the deeply unpopular Heath. Neave inflated Heath's support to the *Evening Standard* to scare MPs. 'Faced with the prospect of yet more Heath, several men with no time for Mrs Thatcher voted for her.'[72]

There was one lone Tory grandee who predicted Thatcher would be the next leader. In 1972, Lord Margadale told lunch party guests that Thatcher would replace Heath, three years before she did. It's not clear how serious his prediction was. Thatcher had been described as a future Prime Minister as early as 1958, when she was selected to be the candidate for Finchley. This was a prediction that she would be Prime Minister 'of England'.[73] This use of England instead of Britain was quite normal for Tories at the time, and was often how Thatcher spoke. But it suggests windy rhetoric rather than inspired prognostication. How many association members must have predicted that they were selecting a future Prime Minister! Despite this prediction, Thatcher was only selected for Finchley because the chairman rigged the count. He 'lost' two of her opponent's votes, thinking his privilege would secure him another seat. (It didn't.) Whether or not Margadale was more reliable than the Finchley bar-stool seer, the idea of Thatcher as leader was regarded by his lunch guests as 'very extraordinary'.[74] She required Fate to intervene in Finchley, in Keith Joseph's withdrawal from the race, and with the help of Airey Neave.

The reason she hadn't quite won in Finchley in 1958 was that many association members did not want a woman candidate. (Many of those who opposed her were the association wives.) Not much had changed in fourteen years, when the idea of a woman leader was as unlikely as had been a woman MP. As Bernard Levin said in 1974, in an article written before he realized Thatcher was a serious possibility, 'The male chauvinism of the people of this country, particularly the women, is still dreadful, and her sex would be a severe handicap.'[75] Even Norman Tebbit, later one of her most loyal supporters, didn't think of her as a potential leader. Many people, he said, thought she was 'fortunate to get into Ted Heath's cabinet'.[76] Thatcher herself thought there were limits to what she could do as a mother. She told Miriam Stoppard in 1985 that she'd been lucky to get a London seat. If she'd had a Yorkshire seat, she said, she wouldn't have wanted to leave her family for long periods of time.[77]

When she was elected it was only the start of her challenges. The speechwriter Ronald Miller's 'reaction was partly chauvinistic and partly, to my surprise, a sort of residual loyalty to the strange man [Ted Heath]'.[78] The MP Ken Clarke recalled after Thatcher died, 'I can remember old boys on the back benches saying, "Oh it's alright down here in London but in the North they won't vote for a woman as Prime Minister".'[79] Harold Wilson, the Prime Minister, condescended to Thatcher by calling her 'my dear' during parliamentary debates. 'He underestimated her terribly,' recalled the MP Shirley Summerskill.[80]

In 1977, after two years as Leader of the Opposition, she did not have the confidence of many members of the Shadow Cabinet. Lord Hailsham, the distinguished lawyer, and Lord Carrington, the aristocrat, had a meeting where they discussed their lack of confidence in Thatcher. They were worried the party was becoming right-wing, and believed that she was 'politically unaware'; they lamented that while there were several men who would do a better job it was not possible to have another leadership election.[81] Both men would later serve in Thatcher's government – before she won a historic landslide victory in 1983.

Carrington never quite got over his ambivalent feelings about Thatcher, telling a colleague in the early 1980s, when he was Foreign Secretary, 'if I have any more trouble from this fucking stupid, petit bourgeoise woman, I'm going to go'.[82] This sort of criticism had long dogged Thatcher: in 1974, Enoch Powell dismissed her chances to be leader by saying, 'They wouldn't put up with those hats and that accent'.[83] He had a point, but didn't realize how effectively she would be able to alter both her appearance and her voice. And snobbishness cut both ways. When she decided to stand for the leadership, Thatcher went to Edward du Cann's house with Denis, so du Cann could assess her as a candidate. He described Margaret and Denis sitting on the sofa together as being like a butler and housekeeper seeking employment.[84]

In 1978, George Younger, who later served in all her cabinets, wrote about Thatcher's mood during shadow cabinet discussions: 'Once more I doubt Mrs. T's coolness. She rattles on, arguing everything & is a bad chairman.' Notice the phrase 'Once more I doubt…'. Younger had faith in his leader. But he was quick to see her flaws, and knew that she relied on the changing political conditions of the country to succeed: 'There has been a fundamental shift of attitude over the past 3 years, and I believe the people want a change.'[85] This is the same analysis Jim Callaghan made shortly before Thatcher won the 1979 election. As David Cannadine said, 'The majority of her senior colleagues had remained his [Heath's] loyal supporters until the end, and only one of them, Joseph, had voted for her. So despite her victory in the leadership election, Thatcher was in a weak position.'[86] Until she was elected, few people attributed much of Thatcher's success to her.

To prove herself, and to make herself into a credible candidate for Prime Minister, Thatcher worked hard. Much is made of her makeover, with the Barbara Castle hairstyle and a voice coach from the National Theatre to lower her tone. Gordon Reece played a Henry Higgins role to modify her accent.[87] (Reece was something of a late bloomer himself, starting his PR career aged forty.)[88] This was an inevitable consequence of being a woman; no one remembered what her male predecessors wore. Women politicians were obliged to be more attentive than their male colleagues about their appearance for Thatcher's whole career. Jean Mann wrote that women MPs always dressed well when giving speeches because even a short speech by a woman would be reported, and 'nothing can escape the male eye'.[89]

The way Thatcher understood the importance of appearance to politics was more important than the details of her hairstyle and voice pitch. She understood television better than other leaders – she was 'very conscious of being accurate'. Her presentation and appearance were part of a complete package with her strong convictions and grasp of details.[90] In this respect, she resembled Barbara Castle in more than appearance. Castle, too, was a hard worker, who spent long hours absorbing statistics and official reports while her male colleagues took long lunches. 'Battling Barbara' was surely an influence. They both knew the importance of housewife rhetoric – Castle was photographed for the 1945 election darning her husband's socks. They both liked loud hats. They both continued to do domestic duties while maintaining hectic work schedules. They even shared the same preference for a light breakfast, yoghurt and fruit in Castle's case, coffee and fruit for Thatcher.[91] If you want to outpace your entitled male rivals, it doesn't help to have a heavy stomach.

Equally important were Thatcher's visits to countries across Europe, the Middle East, Asia, and the USA, where she first met Ronald Reagan in 1975. And her development as a leader of her own party, which was by no means accepting of her monetary and fiscal beliefs when she became leader. By 1978, when the famous winter of discontent started, when strikes left Britain without refuse collectors or grave diggers, and inflation topped 13 per cent, Thatcher was able to take advantage of the crisis. This was only the latest in a series of problems of this nature that politicians of all parties had failed to solve for a decade.

And she became a flourishing orator. In 1970, her recorded election broadcast had been deemed unsatisfactory by party headquarters. Ronald Miller thought she had little idea of the impact of television and came 'over as stilted and self-conscious with a tendency to over-elocute'. By the time she became Prime Minister, Miller says, 'she was a practised performer prepared to take on all comers'.[92] One of the ways she garnered credibility was by outperforming the Labour Chancellor Denis Healey in the House of Commons. On one occasion, when he mocked her supposed privilege and made sexist references, she retorted, "Some Chancellors are macroeconomic. Some are fiscal. This one is just plain cheap." Lord Gowrie, a member of the shadow Treasury, remembered Thatcher as 'the only person who was really knocking him about in the House of Commons'. The Tories were demoralized. They had lost two elections; Heath was a weak leader; and the candidates to replace him were lacklustre. Suddenly they 'saw one of their members looking tremendous, brilliantly briefed, and knocking a very able Chancellor for six in the House. And they were rather dazed by this.' Gowrie believed that this display of energy and purpose 'revitalised the backbenches'. Characteristically, 'she knew more, she'd done her homework'.[93] Thatcher's long apprenticeship, her work habits and grasp of the details, had made her ready to make the most of this unexpected opportunity.

She impressed MPs of all parties with her strongly argued, well-informed, logical arguments about taxation, spending, and inflation – an echo of the way Bonar Law made his reputation. She wasn't afraid to link detailed policy arguments to philosophical arguments about freedom. She was finding her voice, and it was making her more popular. You didn't (and don't) have to agree with her to find her compelling. As the biographer John Campbell said, 'it was not her convictions that they voted for, but her conviction'.[94]

This conviction became stronger and better articulated. Her oratory had many facets: her ability to make an audience laugh, despite being almost a-humorous sometimes; her capacity for aphorism; her capability to distinguish between, and combine, the moral and the practical; her use of detail; her forthright defence of her position; her instinctive timing; her serious, deadpan expression. All of these qualities come into view after 1975. Her career was then punctuated by defining moments of rhetoric: 'the iron lady of the western world'; 'you turn if you want to, the lady's not for turning'; 'there is no alternative'; 'all attempts to destroy democracy by terrorism will fail'; 'we have not successfully rolled back the frontiers of the state at home only to see them reimposed at the European level'; 'if you want something said ask a man; if you want something done ask a woman'; 'when people are free to choose they choose freedom'; and perhaps most famously, in response to the idea of the European Commission, 'No. No. No.' These lines were written by speechwriters: they were delivered in the singular, unforgettable tones of Margaret Thatcher.

Truman and Eisenhower needed the war for their talents to flourish; Coolidge needed the death of Harding; and Law needed the fractious, failing state of his party. Thatcher needed a leadership vaccum in the Conservative Party and the inflation and the economic collapse of the late 1970s for her talents to become evident, as well as the lack of a credible alternative for leader. Later on, she would also benefit from the Falklands invasion.

But Thatcher was ready when fate intervened. Who else could offer her combination of energy, decisiveness, experience as a housewife, and gift for communicating to become one of the most enduring political leaders of the twentieth century? How else would she get the chance to use these qualities other than in a leadership election when none of the men could decide to run and where the obviously failed leader refused to talk to the people who were voting?

Who else would have been so resilient? Thatcher turned adversity to advantage. She was surrounded by people who wanted to duck the fight or quit the course. She was the political energy behind the 1981 budget. She was the determination behind the Falklands War. She was the spirit that opposed the Miners' Strike. She was the visionary who darted around Whitehall chanting 'every earner an owner'. She was the libertarian refusenik who stood firm against what she thought of as evil, winning Nelson Mandela's praise for advocating for his freedom, and Mikhail Gorbachev and Ronald Reagan's admiration for her Cold War-ending diplomacy. She was the one prepared to tell the EU to focus on expanding western freedom to eastern Europe at a time when Jacques Delors was advocating the Commission should originate 80 per cent of legislation for member states. She was the one who secured the British rebate, a policy much derided but never reversed. She was the one who insisted on visiting the Gdansk shipyards on a visit to Poland, despite being banned by the Polish government. (Her visit spurred talks between the union and the government that were part of a process of liberalization. Radek Sikorski, the Polish MEP, has said, 'For those behind the Iron Curtain, she was a member of the anti-communist "Holy Trinity" – consisting of John Paul II, Ronald Reagan and herself – who altered the fate of the West, and consequently the fate of those outside it.')[95]

She was, in William J. Galloway's words, the one who 'restored the nation's stature and became a force to be reckoned with in international affairs'. He called it, 'one of the most striking turnarounds in a nation's affairs ever'. Galloway also saw more clearly than many parochial British commentators that Thatcher's important role in world affairs started in the Falklands, which 'went a long way toward reminding the world that, although there was no longer an empire, the UK still held a seat in the top international council. British arms, once more, proved their worth'.[96]

There is a lot of disagreement about her reforms. Where she was determined, she was contentious. Britain was a disputatious country before she arrived, and remained so throughout her tenure. Although her policies were mostly unchallenged by the governments that followed, to be called a Thatcherite is rarely a compliment in British politics. But amid this discord, Thatcher's personality is not in dispute. The character who made all of this possible, for better and for worse, is not contentious. She is a symbol of the inexhaustible. She was famous for her stamina and her stubborn determination.

This, too, had to be learned. In 1971, when she ended free school milk, Thatcher went from being a relatively anonymous politician to being known as 'Mrs Thatcher, Milksnatcher'. She was nearly sacked. She was hounded by a misogynistic press. It was draining. People who knew her said she was always tired. She considered quitting politics. The *Daily Mail* columnist Jean Rook wrote: 'Show some spunk, Margaret. Remember flaming Barbara Castle who came back at critics like a blow-lamp.' This was a trial that, as Moore says, 'she did not pass easily'.[97] But she did pass. It was milk that made Mrs Thatcher indefatigable.

There were other important moments in the early 1970s that forged the resolve of the woman who would become famous for riding in a tank. She was advised to stop wearing her pearls in 1972, on the basis that they did nothing for her image as a prickly, out-of-touch, upper-middle-class woman, who was being mocked in the press. She thought for a moment and then shot back, '*No*! I'm damned if I will! They were a wedding present from my husband and if I want to wear them I'm going to!' Ronald Miller recalled, 'Her voice was rather high-pitched and her fair hair bobbed furiously but there was no mistaking her contempt for such personal attacks or her resolve not to bow to them.'[98] She was hardening from the woman candidate who had taken fashion advice from Conservative Head Office into Mrs Thatcher, the Iron Lady.

In 1971, a group of students had chanted 'Thatcher out, socialism in!' 'Thatcher is here to stay!' she told them. She had to face several unpleasant demonstrations that year, requiring police protection. In 1985, she said facing those protests was 'just about the very best training a Prime Minister could have'.[99] In a 1989 interview, she said she worked in a more concentrated way than she had in the past, which was something she had learned to do over the years.[100] The pearls distracted her critics from the way Mrs Thatcher was disciplining her inner steel.

Other important aspects of Thatcher's success – her 'enormous powers of concentration', her ability to get by on less sleep than other people – were noted early, by a school friend.[101] Although Moore writes 'she was not as invincible as she believed' and often showed signs of tiredness, her ability to work hard on minimal sleep was well observed.[102] Ian Gow, her Parliamentary Private Secretary, said on the news in 1982, 'I don't know whether she needs less sleep. She certainly gets less sleep. But I think it's really a triumph of the spirit over the flesh.'[103]

Is there a better phrase to describe the role of tenacity in her success than 'the triumph of the spirit over the flesh'? This comes from the Methodism of her childhood, with its emphasis on duty and conscientiousness. 'We were brought up to work,' she told Kelvin MacKenzie. 'It was a sin not to work.'[104] It was the same for Bonar Law and Coolidge and Truman and Eisenhower. They had the chance to go an easier way. Their lives did not always reward their efforts. They did not have to persist. In a sense, it was strange that they did. Eisenhower could have left the military for a well-paying private sector job. Before the Senate, Truman assumed he would retire to a sinecure. Law sought the leadership because of fortuitous circumstances; he never looked for fortunate ones. He declined the chance to be Prime Minister twice, putting country before ambition.

A combination of endurance, learning, ideas, energy and decisiveness was how a woman whom few people expected anything of, with no senior Cabinet experience and a very small support base, became a great world leader, out of nowhere, aged fifty. She was lucky, but not passive. Lord Carrington said, 'She used the luck and she's been determined and courageous.'[105] As Mrs Thatcher said, when asked about the potential male contenders for the leadership, 'I didn't hesitate, I took the decision quickly and I've never had any doubt about it, that it was the right decision and I never faltered and I'm in no doubt now.' This ability to decide had been evident in her earlier career. It was what William J. Galloway noticed about her. And again and again, decisiveness would mean Margaret Thatcher was almost constantly underrated for the ten years she stayed in office. As John Campbell said, 'She made her own luck; she seized chances from which others shrank, and she exploited their hesitation with ruthless certainty.'[106]

Every time fate intervened, she was ready.

Part Three
Right People – Networks and Influence

'The sense of worth derived from creative work depends upon "recognition" by others, which is never automatic. As a result, the path of self-realization, even when it is the only open one, is taken with reluctance. Men of talent have to be goaded to engage in creative work. The groans and laments of even the most gifted and prolific echo through the ages.'

Eric Hoffer, *Notebooks*

6

The importance of *influential* connections

Margaret Thatcher had one more advantage – her network. Without Airey Neave, Thatcher would not have been able to sell herself to the MPs voting in the leadership election. It was Neave who went around the tearooms and corridors of Westminster, warning MPs they would be stuck with Ted Heath, exaggerating the number of votes he had secured, reassuring people that Thatcher was a good candidate. Heath was a poor leader but he had the support of the Establishment. It took Neave's networking to tip the balance in favour of Thatcher.

This was one of three shock leadership changes in the Conservative Party during the twentieth century. In 1940, Churchill took over having been widely dismissed as washed-up and untrustable. And, as we saw in Chapter 4, in 1906, Andrew Bonar Law became leader when no other candidate could be found. Like Thatcher, both were outsiders. Churchill had a reputation for opposing appeasement. Law was taken seriously because of his acuity with financial rhetoric. Thatcher, as a women, had no such advantage. She was much more reliant on Neave's network.

Thatcher had made a position for herself in the network of right-wing MPs, but she and Neave were not close. His diary entries, quoted by Moore, suggest he accepted her as a candidate: he had no preference for her. But Neave had three qualities that network theory would identify as reasons why he succeeded in selling Thatcher to the Conservative Party.

First, he and Thatcher were what sociologists called weak ties. They knew each other through Edward McAlpine. A decade apart, they had both been pupils to the same barrister, Frederick Lawton. Second, he was not an establishment figure. Neave had not been promoted, but was a respected war hero, which meant he sat at the edge of several networks within the Conservative Party. Finally, Neave was a crucially influential person among MPs. He had persuaded Sir Keith Joseph, William Whitelaw and Edward du Cann to stand against Heath before he got to Thatcher. He knew the party and was able to influence people within it because of his reputation as a war hero with integrity. Importantly, Neave had a background in intelligence.

While Jim Prior, who was organizing Heath's campaign, was aware that MPs from all sections of the party were going to Neave's office – a clear sign that Neave was able to move between different networks within the party, something insular Heath was unable to do – he didn't know why. Neave's biographer attributes this to his past as a spy and his ability to use 'disinformation, manipulation and misrepresentation'. Neave's unique position in the party – at the edge of many networks, not at the centre of any one of them – meant he was perfectly positioned to gather inform Whips' Office ation about voting intentions. It is thought he knew more than the whips office.[1] He had the best information network in Westminster. He persuaded Thatcher to be strategically ambiguous about her beliefs – playing down her pro-hanging, pro-Europe policies – so she became seen as someone who would *listen* as a leader, the opposite of Heath's intransigence. Neave knew who the potential voters were and exactly what they wanted to hear. Without that vital connection, Thatcher might not have won.

The three principles that made Neave so effective as Thatcher's campaign manager – a weak tie who can move between different groups with influence – are critical to the way networks operate. Networks are often talked about as if having connections is what matters. But it is this set of factors that makes the difference. What makes the most difference is not having connections, but having *influence*.

It is this influence that makes the difference to late bloomers trying to break into new domains.

•••

Influence is often essential to great political movements. The first serious attempt to create an anti-slavery movement in Britain was largely ineffective because the leader, Granville Sharp, was bad at influencing people. Partly, Sharp's efforts came at a bad time politically: there was too much else going on for his campaign to be noticed. But Sharp was a poor leader of a movement – so poor, he actually refused to be the leader of the organization dedicated to his ideas. He was too pious for most people, spent too much time trying to persuade the episcopate of the Church of England to change its mind, and didn't have enough of a clear message for what could be changed. He was also concerned with crown power and the American Revolutionary War. He was too diffuse, too obscure, too insistent, and too impractical to influence others.[2] But he was part of a chain of ideas and a growing culture that considered the moral aspect of slavery which would influence later, successful reformers.

The historian Niall Ferguson has shown the importance of networks to key historical events like the American Revolution, the Reformation and the Industrial Revolution. It was the connections between members of different parts of society that enabled Paul Revere's famous message that 'the British are coming' to spread efficiently. Protestant networks were so large they survived even when centrally important members were executed. James Watt's development of the steam engine depended on connections to professors in Glasgow and the Lunar Society in Birmingham. Being able to pass information between people and to cross class and social barriers allows for influences to spread further.

The physicist Geoffrey West switched to studying cities in his seventies and discovered a fundamental law. When a city doubles in size, every measure of economic activity increases by 15 per cent per person. West told the *New York Times*, 'This remarkable equation is why people move to the big city. Because you can take the same person, and if you just move them to a city that's twice as big, then all of a sudden they'll do 15 percent more of everything that we can measure.'[4] Perhaps one thing potential late bloomers ought to do is move to bigger cities.

These networks rely on the weak ties alluded to earlier – people in your acquaintance or your wider network who are not especially close to you. Weak ties are associates and acquaintances, not relatives and partners. Think of the party members who persuaded all those widows to take over when their husbands died in office, or the dinner party Maya Angelou went to. The connections who make the most difference are not the best friends or spouses – they are the weak ties.

We get our jobs through the weaker ties in our network, not the strongest. Interestingly, someone you have ten mutual connections with is twice as likely to get you a job as someone with only one mutual connection – but someone with twenty-five connections is useless. This varies by industry. But the general finding is consistent. When you need to make a change, you will do so through people you do not know very well.

The reason is simple: information. You and your strong ties already know each other, and have other strong ties in common. Weak ties are able to provide much more new information, connect and match you with opportunities otherwise unknown to you, compared to another strong tie. You, too, are new information for your weak ties. And the good news is that you have many, many more weak ties than strong ones.[5]

It is through these weak ties that scientific knowledge was spread so usefully in the seventeenth century. The founding of the Royal Society meant that Dutch scientist Antonie van Leeuwenhoek's letters were able to become part of a large network of knowledge exchange. The information he sent wasn't just received by members of the Society, it was also passed on to their weak ties. In this way, Van Leeuwenhoek's remedy for gout (among other innovations) reached a broad audience. Other scientists associated with the Society were able to gather information from many countries to inform their work.[6] These sorts of networks would later be essential to Charles Darwin, who collected much of the information he needed for *On the Origin of Species* through letters.

Antonie van Leeuwenhoek is a case study in how accessing the right influences and networks can spur a late-blooming transformation. Age sixteen, Van Leeuwenhoek was apprenticed to the cloth trade, where he used thread counters to assess cloth quality. Age twenty-eight he started experimenting with lenses. Age thirty-six he visited England, where he studied rocks. Age forty-one he unveiled his microscopes. At this time, Van Leeuwenhoek was unknown to the science establishment. It took eight months for his first letter to *Philosophical Transactions* to be published. Then Hooke, an English forerunner in microscope technology, repeated Van Leeuwenhoek's work, and it was accepted: Van Leeuwenhoek now became a major contributor to *Philosophical Transactions*.

Now began Van Leeuwenhoek's second act. He had started out looking through small lenses to check cloth quality and had ended up creating microscopes that were at least 266× magnification, more powerful than anything before. Much of what he saw through them was unknown and unnamed.

And so, aged forty-two, he looked at a drop of water from a lake and saw 'an abundance of little animals'. This was the foundation of microbiology. Two years later, he discovered bacteria, describing them as 'so small in my eye, that I judged, that if 100 of them lay one by another, they would not equal the length of a grain of sand'. As the authors of a recent biographical study write: 'Van Leeuwenhoek possessed excellent powers of observation. He calculated the size of what he saw through his lenses by comparison with the sizes of sand grains, millet and the width of his hair through the same lens.' The articulate network responded to these discoveries. He was bombarded with requests for more information to verify his claims. He discovered spermatozoa and saw in close detail blood, a cow's gallbladder, animal dung, frogs' intestines, his own diarrhoea and dental plaque.[7]

What's notable about Van Leeuwenhoek is that he started slowly, discovering ideas on his own and experimenting. Without the right culture, mentors, peers or influences, his initial advance took a long time. Then, when he was accepted into the relevant network, he was able to put his invention to hugely productive use. This was the position Neave had to Thatcher. He was associated with her. They had connections in common. But they were not close-knit before he helped her win the leadership. This was important because she needed someone on the edge of many networks, not in the middle of one.

•••

To succeed, where should you be in a network – close to the centre or on the edge? To succeed in many fields in the UK, the best bet is to go to London and become part of the *milieu*. Networking is an important part of becoming a creative person, whether artist or scientist, engineer or pastry chef. It is not just that being in the network will influence your ideas, but it will provide feedback about what work is important. We are all capable of producing something creative at home – it is not until that work is tested in the complex real-world environment that we know if it is really original or interesting. Networks coordinate information. As the psychologist Mihaly Csikszentmihalyi says, 'Creativity cannot bring forth anything new unless it can enlist the support of peers.'[8] The same was true of Neave: he couldn't bring forth Margaret Thatcher until he enlisted the support of their peers; nor could Van Leeuwenhoek bring forth microbiology without exposing his ideas to the scientific network.

Csikszentmihalyi realized the importance of recognition to creative work during a long-term study of art students. He and his collaborators realized that '10 years after graduation, the students we thought had the greatest creative potential were no more likely to have continued in an artistic career than their peers whose performance in school had suggested a lack of creative potential'.[9] What they thought of as creative potential wasn't a very reliable indicator. 'For artistic creativity to exist,' Csikszentmihalyi says, 'one must have an appropriate audience.' It is not enough to be right: you must also be influential.

Creativity is the result of an interaction. 'If you cannot persuade the world you had a creative idea,' says Csikszentmihalyi, 'how do we know you actually had it?'[10] This effect is so strong that one study has found that the artists who start their career by exhibiting work in a gallery in the top 20 per cent of rankings have a far more successful career than those who don't. Nearly 60 per cent of those artists remained high-prestige throughout their career; only 0.2 per cent of them ended up exhibiting in a bottom 40 per cent gallery.[11] The quality of your work has a lot to do with the quality of your network. This study suggests that the route to success is at the centre: peripheral artists do not make it to the centre of the network.

In fact, there are advantages to both. Being in the core brings credibility support for your work. The closer you are to the best galleries, the more successful your paintings are. However, being on the edge of the network means you have connections to other types of networks, and can mix different influences. The people at the centre of a network are very similar to each other; being on the margin gives you a differentiating perspective.

The price of being peripheral is that you often lack recognition: that is, peripheral members of networks might be creative, but they are also likely to be late bloomers. As Randall Collins says, 'a peripheral position condemns one to coming too late into the sophisticated center of the action; the most successful rebels are those who most quickly capitalize on the opportunities for new combinations that are visible at the center.'[12] But the effect of working with people who are not from your discipline can be profound. DNA was discovered by a biologist, James Watson, and a physicist, Francis Crick, working together; Rosalind Franklin, whose work they relied on, was a chemist. Walt Disney was never the best animator: he collaborated with others to make his ideas work. These peripheral collaborations reinforced initiative and self-direction.

Often the best place to be in a network is neither the limit nor the centre, but somewhere in between.[13] Albert Einstein was building on the work of several other physicists, recombining the ideas of thinkers like Ernst Mach, Max Planck, Hendrick Lorentz, Henri Poincaré – as one sociologist said, those others were '*too* familiar with, and too committed to, what had come before to see how Einstein's new combination could be something greater than the sum of its parts'.[14] Einstein was sufficiently detached to make the insight. He was familiar with the ideas but still willing to reinvent them. Had he been right at the core, he might have been too attached to the prevailing consensus.

Many late bloomers are in this position. Think of Ava DuVernay, a publicist in a film studio. It was her in-between position – neither core to the film production, nor so far away from it – that meant she was open to the realization that she too could make movies, only picking up her first camera in her thirties. She was close enough to be influenced, detached enough to be different. 'Being so close to really great filmmakers and watching them direct on set and the experiences that I did have, although different from film school, were still super valuable. I learned just from being around. I coupled that with some very intentional study and practice.'[15] Katalin Karikó, one of the inventors of the COVID vaccine, was an expert in her field who wasn't believed in until she made the right connections: these partnerships kept her just close enough to the core. This enabled her to keep conducting research until the critical moment when she went to the core of another network: biotech start-ups.

Similarly, Airey Neave was never promoted enough to become an establishment politician under Heath. He was never in the core of the governing group that supported Heath and so was able to make use of his peripheral position to move between different sections of the party. That's why Jim Prior saw so many MPs from so many different ideological groups going to Neave's office. It's why Neave knew so much that the whips did not know. And it's how he knew to position Thatcher's politics strategically. Had he been at the elite centre of the party, he would have been of much less use to her.

•••

In *The Tipping Point*, Malcolm Gladwell identified people he called Connectors: people who enjoy knowing people and connecting them with other people, places or ideas.[16] What seems like a chore to most of us is no problem for the Connector. They keep in touch with many, many more people than the average person. This means that, wherever they go, if they find something or someone interesting, they can tell *someone* in their network about it.

This concept is based on an experiment conducted by Stanley Milgram. Milgram sent letters to a random sample of people in Kansas and Nebraska. The letters explained that the recipients were part of an experiment and they were asked to send the letter to a named divinity student in Cambridge, Massachusetts, or a stockbroker in neighbouring Boston. No addresses were given. So the sample had to either forward the letters directly if they happened to know either person or to send them to someone else who might know. A third of the letters arrived at their destination, none having been through more than ten people.

This demonstrates the famous six degrees of separation rule. The rule works through weak ties. The people at the start of the chain do not know the people at the end. Those ties are weaker than the ties between close friends or family. As we saw earlier, to use your network effectively, you must leverage these weak ties.

But not all weak ties are equal. A recent follow-up study replicated Milgram's original experiment, with 24,000 emails instead of letters. Only 3,084 emails reached the target. That's a significantly lower success rate. The experiment didn't fail because of lack of connections. Only 1 per cent of those who didn't forward the email said they couldn't think of anyone to send it to. More likely, they were not interested, couldn't be bothered, were too busy, forgot, the email went to spam … all the usual things that get in the way.

While this experiment somewhat confirms the six degrees of separation idea it also illustrates that it's hard to make your network work for you. It takes persistence. Knowing who to connect with is not the same as having the time, energy or inclination to make the connection. You need to find the right people and ask them the right thing at the right time. They need to *want* to help and be influential in the right way.

It is probably true that we are all connected by six degrees of separation – but not everyone that we are connected to is going to do us a favour. It's a small world, but a busy one. The people you know might connect you to opportunities, but it's not guaranteed. And those opportunities might not be very significant.

In the email experiment that tried to replicate Milgram's findings, Connectors were significantly less important. Whereas many of Milgram's letters passed through a small number of 'hubs' – hyperconnected people, similar to Gladwell's Connectors – less than 5 per cent of the emails did. Think of the Connectors you know. They give you far more recommendations than you take. If you went to every restaurant, watched every show, met every person, and visited every place recommended to you, you would find yourself doing little else. Connectors are real, but they often lack influence. And they are no longer the hubs of connectivity they once were. We are all taking more recommendations from strangers on the internet, whose reliability on the particular topic we are interested in at that moment is usually quite easy to find out through ratings, followings or sampling.

What can make a difference is a small increase in the likelihood of being able to reach the eventual target. If I ask you to get an email to a member of a remote Indigenous people who do not speak English, you probably won't know where to start. If I ask you to connect to someone demographically more similar to you, it will be much easier to think of someone to forward the email to. Watts found that one of his targets received a much higher proportion of emails than the others. This target was a professor – and the majority of people participating in the study were college educated. It is possible that it just seemed much easier for a college graduate to think of someone to email when the target is a professor than when it is a Norwegian army veteran or an Estonian archival inspector.[17] Connectors might be at their most useful when they are more similar to the final target. It is not connections we should be interested in, but influence. You need to find Connectors who have the right degree of influence over the people you want to be put in touch with.

Social scientists Nicholas Christakis and James H. Fowler have found that while networks do have six degrees of separation, they have only three degrees of influence. Friends influence friends. They also influence friends of friends. And they can influence friends of friends of friends. You have some influence over your sibling. They might pass on something to a friend, based on your reliability. That friend might then pass it on. But the link back to you has become weaker. The extent to which this information is trusted has diminished. Christakis and Fowler found that as information moves along a network it becomes more unreliable, somewhat as it does in children's whispering games. It is also the case that your network is much more stable within three degrees. Your friends and family don't change that much. As you move beyond that, people come and go. The churn is higher. You lose contact, people die, or move, or change jobs, and thus your network changes. Unstable connections have much less influence. It is thought that we evolved in groups of three degrees of connection and that it is difficult for most people to get beyond that.[18]

So, although weak connections are more likely to be useful, they are less likely to be able to reliably influence people who are four degrees or more of separation away. That's the paradox of networking. And it's why, even though you are technically six degrees away from the major hubs of wealth and power in the world, you never get invited to their parties. Your degrees of separation are all there, but you lack the appropriate influence.

Airey Neave was perfectly positioned in this regard, able as a war hero and respected MP to get a hearing among other MPs. There is churn among MPs, but at that time the Conservative Party was a reasonably stable body with large numbers of non-landed middle-class figures like Neave. And he was well established enough to have influence on several other figures to consider running for the leadership.

These principles apply across domains, not just in politics. We saw earlier that art networks often work by drawing people to the centre, not through peripheral figures. But in the case of Grandma Moses, one of the best-known late bloomers, it was an influential person on the periphery of a network that made all the difference.

•••

Not everyone has the time to put life aside and pursue their passion. But you can take control quite late in life. As we saw in the chapter about inefficiency, your calling might not be clear to you until later on. Some people know their passion from a young age and are derailed in following it; others find their interest emerging later in life. Once that interest emerges, finding the right network connections is essential to success. Anna Mary Robertson Moses (1860–1961), known as Grandma Moses, began painting aged seventy-eight. She became internationally famous for her art – because the right person happened to find her work one day. What drove her to start painting was not pure artistic vocation but what her curator, Otto Kallir, called 'the compelling urge of an old woman never to remain idle after having worked all her life'.[19] Born in 1860, Moses had started work aged twelve, as a house helper. She called this work 'a good education for me, in cooking, housekeeping, in moralizing and mingling with the outside world'.[20] She became a farmer's wife, had ten children, five of whom died young, and spent most of her life in rural New York. (Moses lived so long, at least three other of her children died before her; her obituary suggests she outlived them all.)[21] In 1927, her husband died and her eldest son and his wife took over the farm. Moses was left unoccupied: 'I had to do something, so I took up painting.'[22] A few early signs of this interest can be found: she drew as a child, on paper her father brought home ('it cost a cent a sheet and lasted longer than candy'), and had decorated furniture at the farm. In two of those pieces, a table and fireboard from 1918 and 1920, when Moses was about sixty, Kallir saw 'painterly technique rarely found in the work of self-taught artists'.[23]

Although Moses lacked a peer group, and was lucky to have abilities that seem rare in the self-taught, she now benefited from the intervention of three people. Two of them known to her, one of them not. To begin with, in her late sixties, she made yarn pictures, which she would later see as much the same thing as painted pictures. Her sister saw them and encouraged her to paint. Arthritis was making it hard for Moses to hold a needle, so she took up a brush. When she did, her family was impressed with the results, and so her son and daughter-in-law took the paintings to be displayed in the Women's Exchange in a local drugstore. (Women's Exchanges were a way for women to sell homemade goods and make money without working outside the home.) The work was discovered in the drugstore one day by Louis Caldor, who was passing through. It was a lucky break. Caldor was an engineer who worked for the New York City Department of Water Supply – and he collected art.[24] The art was on display among jellies and rugs Moses had made.[25] Caldor had only gone into the drugstore because he had a stomach ache. The paintings cost $3 and $5.[26] He found out who the artist was from the drugstore owner, went to visit Moses, and bought ten more paintings.[27]

Caldor spent a year promoting Moses' work in the art world in New York City, to no avail. He nearly gave up. Just before he did, he heard of a show at the Museum of Modern Art (MoMA) for unknown painters. Caldor took Moses' work to the curator, Sidney Janis, who agreed to display three paintings. Janis was also a collector, with a business background, who had collected other artists of a similar 'primitive' or 'naive' style to Moses, such as Patrick J. Sullivan, William Doriani, and Morris Hirshfield. He later collected Moses' work also.[28]

Caldor had finally found the right person to understand Moses' art. Janis had the credibility Moses needed: he was on the advisory board of MoMA in recognition of his collection of modern art. In the years that followed he defended the 'primitivist' or 'self-taught' art movement against its critics.[29] With this boost, Caldor continued encouraging Moses and kept looking for outlets for her work until he heard of Otto Kallir, who had opened a new gallery that was interested in folk art. Caldor and Kallir met one evening when Caldor showed Kallir the paintings in the back of his car with a torch, having been unable to meet during working hours. Kallir agreed to a solo show on condition that he could choose which paintings to display.[30] Moses didn't attend that first show, saying she knew all the paintings already, but she did go to her second show – she took her homemade preserves with her, remembering that they had won prizes at local fairs years ago while her paintings had been overlooked.[31]

Moses is a perfect example of someone who found the right person in the network. When her jams got more attention than her painting, it was because her work was not on display to the right people. The locals at the fair were all outside the art world network. Similarly, had she gone right into the heart of the New York art establishment, not only would she have been utterly lost, but she would also have been rebuffed as unfashionable. Caldor was in the ideal middle ground: he was not in the core, but he knew enough about the New York art world to be able to find the right people and pitch the work in the right way. He knew not to give up, how to find out about the right sort of shows, and importantly, as a collector, he would have had some influence in persuading people to take the work seriously. Without Caldor, Moses would have struggled to get noticed by Kallir and Janis, the people in the right part of the core network who gave her credibility and accelerated her fame. Although she wasn't enthusiastic about the spotlight, or New York City which she always disliked, Moses enjoyed the attention her fame brought, and Kallir sees this as a turning point: 'a new conception seems to have emerged, as though the artists' eyes had been opened to broad vistas of nature.'[32] She had been working on her art, though embroidery and paints, for over ten years by now, and was starting to work repeatedly on the same topics, as we will see Frank Lloyd Wright do in Chapter 11. Her practice continued. Popularity brought requests for certain scenes from potential buyers, which she disliked, although she felt obliged to comply.[33] Each time, she varied the compositions. Being opened to the network of the market was a force for improving and popularizing her work.

Luck isn't everything. Moses made the most of her opportunity by working hard. Aged a hundred, she was still getting up at six-thirty and painting till noon, after a small breakfast and with a coffee break at ten. She ate a large lunch, painted some more, napped for a couple of hours and then, if there were no visitors, painted until 5.30. After supper she enjoyed the radio and television and had to be persuaded to go to bed at

9 P.M. by her son.[34] She often worked on several paintings at once, so as not to waste the colours she mixed.[35] She produced twenty-five pictures after she turned one hundred.[36] Her influence continues to live on. In 2008, the *New York Times* reported on an exhibition called 'A Long Way Home: Elder Artists in the Neighborhoods of New York'. The exhibition featured artwork created by people from twenty senior homes in New York. The work was included in a study into the benefits of remaining creative into old age, which found that cultural activity improves health and morale in the elderly. The *Times* titled its report 'Grandma Moses's Descendants'.[37] Moses would have approved. When she turned ninety-five, the *Times* reported her thinking, 'Anyone can paint if he tries hard enough.'[38]

7

Samuel Johnson's years of obscurity

In his early letters, we do not see English writer and lexicographer Samuel Johnson (1709–84) preparing for greatness. The man who would be drawn in cartoons, mocked in gossip columns, celebrated in drawing rooms, sought out by enthusiasts – the man at the centre of a famous club of thinkers, writers, politicians, and scholars, who was generally regarded with the bemused awe and wonder owed to a celebrity intellectual – appears in the letters of his late twenties and early thirties as a hack and a failure, scraping around for money like a hen scratching in the dirt for corn. Far from being 'Dictionary Johnson', living on a government pension, the legend who would inspire Jane Austen, the massive multifarious subject of one of the most comprehensive and original biographies ever written, he is a nobody, leaving no hint that he is charting a trajectory to anything other than his next badly paid article. These toils told on the young Johnson; like pebbles being dropped into a jug of water, accumulated disappointments slowly displaced his energies. 'Sorrow,' he would later write, 'is a kind of rust of the soul.'[1]

Had he died at forty, he would have left behind a few poems and some journalism, read only by specialists. And it would have been difficult to see how he could have become anything greater. Before he was famous, he was a failure.

For his whole life, he resented the poverty he lived in when he was young in London. He had to save his one clean shirt for the day in the week when he made house visits. Before London, he founded and ran a failed school, losing most of his wife's money in the process. After that his play *Irene*, which he hoped would be the great tragedy of the age, was a moderate success – but was never revived. It was about then that he took to hanging out with the reprobate Richard Savage, drinking and roaming the streets of London at night. He was in his early thirties, living away from his wife. That friendship later led to the *Life of Savage*, one of the first great literary biographies in English.

Years later, Boswell described Johnson's mind as a gladiator in the Colosseum fighting off lions of despair:

> His mind resembled the vast amphitheatre, the Colisæum at Rome. In the centre stood his judgement, which like a mighty gladiator, combated those apprehensions that, like the wild beasts of the *Arena*, were all around in cells, ready to be let out upon him. After a conflict, he drives them back into their dens; but not killing them, they were still assailing him.[2]

Johnson maintained an attitude of stout defiance throughout his life. He told a friend about his final illness in 1784, 'I will be conquered; I will not capitulate.'[3] His life was what Leo Damrosch called 'His resolute fight to *become* Samuel Johnson'.[4]

Two things need more attention in the way we think about Samuel Johnson: the networks he developed in the struggle of an uncertain commercial career that helped to make him great, and his stout denial that everyone suffers mental decline as they age.

Johnson got his first break as a writer at the *Gentleman's Magazine*, edited by Edward Cave. Johnson first wrote to Cave in 1734, aged twenty-five. It was, to say the least, a presumptuous letter. Johnson, an unknown man from the provinces, offered to 'undertake on reasonable terms sometimes to fill a column'. He asked Cave to confirm by return of post. We have no further record of any contact between them for the next three years. Whether or not this is because Johnson opened by telling Cave he could 'improve' the 'defects' of the current poetry column, we can't say.[5] A year later, Johnson wrote to a university friend saying that friends who haven't spoken for a while give each other 'an account of that interval of life which has passed since their last interview'. Johnson doesn't do this, however, 'as little has happened to me'. His time, he says, 'was not always very agreeably spent'. Instead, he tells his friend about his 'Scheme of Life' – his plans to open a school. Johnson was going to teach 'in a method somewhat more rational than those commonly practised'.[6] The school didn't appear for at least another six months, attracted very few pupils, and eventually folded, taking a large portion of his wife's inheritance with it.

His wife is a silent figure in these early letters, but she seems to have been the first significant turning point for young Johnson. Before he wrote to Cave, Johnson had been idling his time away. Aged twenty-five, with no degree, Johnson had been an unhappy school master (a job he was lucky to get without a BA). He had no serious prospect of a literary career. His poor eyesight, convulsions, ineptitude in business, a tendency to melancholy and sloth, and a superior attitude about the work he should do meant he had few prospects.

But then he fell in love with Elizabeth – 'Tetty' – Porter, an older woman, but perhaps the only woman who ever loved him back. Suddenly he was writing to find work and setting up his own school. A good marriage was the making of young Johnson. It jolted him out of indolence. His first serious literary work, a few years before, was the translation of a Portuguese Jesuit's travels to Abyssinia. He was so slow and unwilling to work, he ended up dictating his translation to a friend from his bed. Johnson scholar James Clifford says the basic tone and form of Johnson's style emerges in the Preface of that book, but much more initiative, industry and energy were required for Johnson to make anything of himself.[7] His next project was a proposal to edit the complete Latin poems of the Renaissance scholar Politian (Agnolo Ambrogini). A lack of subscriptions meant the project was abandoned. Before he got married, he was adrift. Who knows what would have happened to Sam without Tetty...

By 1737, his school had failed. Johnson travelled to London looking for work. He was seeking fame. Why else do writers walk to London? He wrote to Edward Cave again, noting Cave's 'uncommon offers of encouragement to Men of Letters', and saying he was a 'stranger in London'. He offered to translate a History of the Council of Trent. Nothing came of this. In 1738, aged twenty-nine, he had his first important poem published in Cave's magazine. *London* is based on a satire by Juvenal. It's excellent, but Johnson was not a poet at heart, and this is not among the works on which his reputation really rests. His poetry was powerful: Harold Bloom thought he could have been Pope's successor. But his real genius was for moral judgement.

Around this time, Johnson was prevented from getting a job at a grammar school because he had left Oxford without taking his BA, due to a shortage of money. No wonder he wrote in *London*, 'SLOW RISES WORTH, BY POVERTY DEPREST'. What's interesting, though, is that he was still looking for work as a schoolmaster. He wanted to start a legal career, also impossible because he didn't have his BA. Although his writing career was getting started, it wasn't his first choice. According to Lawrence Lipking, 'Johnson became an author against his will.'[8] Johnson's acquaintance William Shaw said, 'He never would work, but in order to eat... composition had no charms for him.'[9] Shaw didn't know Johnson as well as others, and seems to have been ambivalent about him. But it certainly took Johnson a long time to settle into the profession life chose for him. It wasn't for another decade, in 1748, that his name appeared on his work, in the aptly titled poem *The Vanity of Human Wishes*.

That Johnson did not want to be a writer seems extraordinary – but there are hints of this later on. In 1778, Johnson met a friend from Oxford he had not seen for fifty years. This friend said to Boswell, 'Dr. Johnson should have been of a profession.' Johnson agreed. 'I ought to have been a lawyer.' Boswell says this was a thought that haunted Johnson who 'often speculated' on the way he might have been honoured by the state in another profession. Boswell relates a story when another acquaintance told Johnson he might have been the Lord Chancellor 'and attained the dignity of a peerage' if he'd become a lawyer. The poor man hit a nerve. 'Johnson, upon this, seemed much agitated; and, in an angry tone, exclaimed, "Why will you vex me by suggesting this, when it is too late?"'[10] Johnson wrote as early as 1750, 'Converse with almost any man, grown old in a profession, and you will find him regretting that he did not enter into some other course, to which he too late finds his genius better adapted, or in which he discovers that wealth and honour are more easily attained.' Such is life. He cannot have been seriously unhappy in his choice. Genius can only be produced 'by collision with a proper subject', like getting sparks out of a flint, he said. He surely did collide with his proper subject. His purpose, he wrote in his twice-weekly periodical *The Rambler*, was to 'consider the moral discipline of the mind, and to promote the increase of virtue'.[11] Hardly attainable as a lawyer.

Johnson always had what Boswell called 'a noble ambition floating in his mind'.[12] This drove him to achieve fame through literature when other paths were closed to him. 'Every man,' as he said, 'is to take existence on the terms on which it is given to him.' Melancholy, poverty, lack of qualifications, and what Lipking calls 'a defensive pride' all prevented Johnson from being successful in a profession. William Shaw said that 'Johnson's temper was ill calculated for supplicating favours from inferiors'. Johnson's inability to 'hang about a manger' or 'cultivate with spouters' was part of why his play *Irene* was less successful than he hoped.[13] He was bad at networking.

But he applied himself to life as best he could. He made the most of the terms of his existence. And he knew that we are not born to do one thing. 'The true Genius,' he wrote in the *Life of Cowley*, 'is a mind of large general powers, accidentally determined to some particular direction.'[14] He could have been – and probably was – writing about himself.

Lipking says, 'The wonder is not that his triumph came so late but that it came at all.'[15] But Johnson's early struggles in London made him the man he was: they made him commercial, enabled him to acquire much of his massive reading, and, importantly, they gave him a knowledge of life. He could not have become the writer he did without seeing so much of London. His years of obscurity were not purposeless. In one conversation with Boswell about the effect of living on an island, or in a 'narrow place', Johnson claimed that if he'd lived on an island between fifteen and twenty-five he would still be the man he had become. After all, he would have been able to read well enough. But if he had lived there from twenty-five to thirty-five – without the exposure to London's teeming variety – he would have been very different. 'I own, Sir, the spirits which I have in London make me do every thing with more readiness and vigour. I can talk twice as much in London as any where else.'[16] This was not just the stimulation of the great and the good. Johnson thought all of life could be found at Charing Cross. He said to know London you had to know the alleys and side streets, not just the magnificent places. He once picked up a destitute prostitute in the street and carried her on his back to his house where she stayed for some weeks to recover her health. He loved few things better than a tavern. 'It is wonderful, Sir, what is to be found in London,' he told Boswell, 'the most literary conversation that I ever enjoyed, was at the table of Jack Ellis, a money scrivener behind the Royal Exchange.'[17] 'A great city,' he believed, was 'the school for studying life'.[18] It was by studying life, as much as from his scholarly reading, that Johnson became the writer he did.

In 1754, the year before the *Dictionary* was published, Johnson visited Oxford. During his visit, he went to see an old college friend, the Reverend Mr Meeke. 'I used to think Meeke had excellent parts,' he told Boswell, 'when we were boys together at the College: but alas!

"Lost in a convent's solitary gloom."'[19] His old friend who had shown such promise as an undergraduate was now an obscure academic. And what had once been a disappointment to Johnson was now seen as an opportunity. 'About the same time of life, Meeke was left behind at Oxford to feed on a Fellowship, and I went to London to get my living: now, Sir, see the difference of our literary characters.'[20] Memory elides. It was not quite 'the same time of life' – Johnson didn't make it to London until he was twenty-eight. Still, he did throw himself on the demands of commercial life in London. In that way, he slowly gained a reputation among literary professionals, which led to the consortium of booksellers commissioning Johnson to write the *Dictionary*. It was not an easy or comfortable life, but commercial London matched him to an opportunity he wouldn't have got if he'd been lost in a convent's solitary gloom.

Johnson's comment about his old friend might be the most important fact of his own life. It's not among his famous sayings, but it explains him better than anything else. To young Johnson, Oxford was all. To become a fellow would have meant status, security, and position. But it would also have forced his talents to run in a narrow channel. It would have reduced the opportunities for his abilities to collide with their proper subject and produce sparks. London put Johnson under a different and better set of influences. Like the late boomers at Charles Duhigg's reunion, Johnson missed out on the certainty of corporate life when he was young, but eventually benefited from the early scrambles and compromises of hack writing. By adapting to London's commercial culture, Johnson developed as a writer for an audience, not a closeted academic, without losing his scholarly edge. In the convent's solitary gloom, he could never have written *The Rambler* or become Dictionary Johnson. London allowed his talents to be recognized. Dodsley, the bookseller who organized the *Dictionary* project, was in exactly the right position to help – he was a weak tie within three degrees of influence. In Oxford, the connection would have been too weak, he would have been too far from the printers; London would have found another writer, another project. He had to be in the swim. This is an example of what Steve Jobs called 'connecting the dots backwards'. By moving from the hierarchies and strictures of Oxford to the opportunities, demands, and spontaneities of London, Johnson acquired influences, culture, knowledge and connections – all those conversations, all that writing, all those bookshops – that made his career feasible in a way it never could have been somewhere else. Leaving Oxford felt like a desperate failure. But change begets change, as Charles Dickens wrote, and it turned out to be perhaps the best thing that happened to him. Johnson embraced the chaotic elements of his career and benefited from taking an unplanned approach.

But being in London was not enough. Johnson also needed to find the people who would influence him in the right way. Hugo M. Reichard sees Johnson's life as a 'pattern of dependence', noting that 'most of Johnson's published works are conceived, or carried through, or mutated, or delivered in association with others'. Reichard catalogues the way Johnson's remarks are often reactions to other people's, that he never travels unless he is taken anywhere, and that he is very often silent until spoken to. And Johnson acknowledges, 'I am in the habit of getting others to do things for me.' It is 'thanks to the initiative of others', Reichard believes, that 'Johnson not only produces and performs, he prospers'.[21] This is exaggerated – Johnson founded a school, took himself to London, wrote *Irene* and *London* without any prompting, and acquired his encyclopaedic knowledge alone – but it has some insight.

Johnson was dependent on others to make him more commercially successful and to bring him appropriate projects. So it is with many people. But Johnson became a sorry case. Shortly before the *Dictionary* project, the friend who had once predicted Johnson would be a great tragedian wrote to David Garrick saying, 'When you see

Mr. Johnson, pray my compliments, and tell him I esteem him a great genius – quite lost both to himself and to the world.'[22] He was more than a hack: he wrote with real quality. But he was not well adapted to matching himself with success. He needed partnerships for that.

It was not until middle age that Johnson got the opportunities he needed. But there was more to his selection as the author of the *Dictionary* than luck. Johnson became commercially minded. He was the son of a bookseller and was forced to make his living as a writer when he failed to get his degree and the prospect of a cosy Oxford fellowship faded away. He was the first biographer to pay proper attention to the arrangements poets made with their publishers. This is one of the things that distinguishes his *Lives of the Poets* as an innovative work.[23] The *Dictionary* was a commercial project as much as a scholarly one, conceived of by a group of booksellers who approached Johnson knowing he had the extraordinary capacity required.

Johnson was well known as a talented writer in the small network of Grub Street literati. But he was no more than that. None of his major projects had got beyond the proposal stage. He mostly wrote anonymously. He got the chance to write the *Dictionary* through his network.

The *Dictionary* was a booksellers' project. And Johnson was friends with the bookseller and publisher Robert Dodsley, who was well connected with other booksellers. Dodsley had the entrepreneurial spirit Johnson lacked: when he first suggested the idea, Johnson said it was a good one, but went on to say, 'I believe I shan't undertake it.'[24] Dodsley knew Johnson. He had bought *London* from him. He knew how to cajole the idle, bookish writer into taking on the project. As Harry M. Solomon said, 'In his bookshop, Dodsley saw Johnson omnivorously foraging among books from disparate fields and recognized an opportunity.'[25] Dodsley persuaded other booksellers to invest in the project. He was, in some ways, like Johnson's agent as well as his publisher. Johnson called him his patron.

Dodsley's career was also one of useful and lucky connections: he moved to London from Nottinghamshire and got a job in Charles Dartiquenave's house. Dartiquenave was a well-connected member of literary London. Dodsley was a poet and through Dartiquenave he met Alexander Pope, the great poet of his generation. Pope helped Dodsley get a play performed and then helped him learn the bookselling trade. Dodsley published many big names of the period, and was always coming up with ideas for new collections of plays and poetry. He published Johnson's poem *The Vanity of Human Wishes* and his play *Irene*. By the time he published the *Dictionary*, he was one of the pre-eminent booksellers in London.[26]

This was the connection that Johnson's brilliant but somewhat idling talent required. And Johnson had the capacity to make Dodsley's vision real. Who else in London could have written such a thing? Johnson was one of the most knowledgeable people of his time. It was an age of infovores – people were hungry for newspapers, books, sermons, directories, dictionaries. It was the era of the codification of knowledge. Twenty years before Johnson's *Dictionary*, Carl Linnaeus created his system of taxonomy for all plants and animals. The following decade, James Cook's first voyage brought back over a thousand plant specimens, along with hundreds of minerals, animals, birds and fish.[27] It was common for gentlemen to collect everything: eggs and shells, architectural fragments and art, fossils and sculpture. So widespread was this culture of organizing knowledge that scrapbooks for collecting prints and specimens became popular.[28] Johnson called it 'this age of dictionaries' and encouraged and supported proposals for a geographical dictionary and a scientific dictionary.[29]

All the members of The Club, a dining club that Sir Joshua Reynolds put together for Johnson in 1764, were engaged in intellectual work. Edmund Burke was an orator and political philosopher who set out the principles of modern conservatism; Adam Smith was the father of economics; Charles Burney wrote a book about music in Italy and France; Reynolds revolutionized the teaching of art and founded the Royal Academy; Joseph Banks was a famous botanist and president of the Royal Society. At meetings of The Club, Johnson 'talked for victory'. Such was the breadth of his knowledge, he could hold his own among all these men. (Although Johnson was not especially interested in botany, Banks's book was an inspiration for Johnson's *Tour of the Hebrides*.)[30]

What makes Johnson stand out is his ability to work alone. He had a small number of literary assistants (amanuenses) who helped with the cutting, organizing and pasting of quotations. But it was Johnson who read the source material, selected the quotations and wrote the definitions. In doing so, he gave English an orderly reference that had never quite existed before. It was Johnson who created the layout of arranging variations of a word under the headword, 'to exemplify graduated senses of a term, a procedure', according to the scholar Pat Rogers, 'which redirected the course of English lexicography'.[31] His selection of quotations, 16,000 in total, became an anthology of moral and literary wisdom, helping to define the canon of English writing. All of this from one mind. The *Dictionnaire de l'Académie française* had taken fifty-five years to his nine and forty workers to his six. Similarly, When Diderot edited the *Encyclopédie* he had material from one hundred and forty writers. When Henry Murray worked on the *Oxford English Dictionary* in the 1880s, 750 people were involved.[32]

The same thing that made him the centre of The Club made him Dictionary Johnson: his vast reading. 'You can never be wise,' he wrote to his servant Francis Barber, 'unless you love reading.'[33] From a young age, he read across a great range of books. He had read books people at Oxford had not: 'When I came to Oxford, Dr. Adams, now master of Pembroke College, told me that I was the best qualified for the University that he had ever known come there.'[34] On his first night in Oxford, he quoted from the obscure Latin author Macrobius. Dr Adams later told Boswell, 'they wondered that a schoolboy should know Macrobius.'[35]

Johnson said more than once that young people should read extensively. 'A young man should read five hours in a day, and so may acquire a great deal of knowledge.'[36] So it was for the young Sam. 'In my early years I read very hard. It is a sad reflection, but a true one, that I knew almost as much at eighteen as I do now.'[37] He did not attach too special an importance to youth, however. When he was seventy, he said, 'It is a man's own fault, it is from want of use, if his mind grows torpid in old age.' He agreed with Solon, quoted in Plutarch: 'I grow in learning as I grow in years.'[38] Knowledge was to be acquired for its own sake. This was not careerism. For one thing, Johnson found it impossible to stick to any plan of study. 'I myself have never persisted in any plan for two days together.'[39] Rather, knowledge was sought for its ability to improve our character: 'A man always makes himself greater as he increases his knowledge.'[40]

The range of subjects Johnson knew about is extraordinary. In 1734, he translated *The Voyage to Abyssinia*. In the 1740s, he offered to write a play about Charles XII of Sweden and produce a history of the British Parliament.[41] In 1743, he contributed to a medical dictionary. He could explain the process of making enamel lining for pots out of bones. In 1755, he wrote two pamphlets to promote Zachariah Williams's theories of longitude. He frequently gave James Boswell detailed legal opinions. He often wrote other people's sermons for them, knowing much theology, and earned money in this way. He once had the idea of writing a *History of Memory*.[42] Boswell lists an extraordinary number of projects Johnson had ideas for, across translation, philosophy, geography, histories of knights and Venice, anthologies of letters and proverbs, dictionaries of ancient history.[43] Johnson paid close attention to all sorts of details, even his belly. 'I mind my belly very studiously, and very carefully; for I look upon it, that he who does not mind his belly will hardly mind anything else.' This wasn't mere gluttony. Boswell reports that 'he was, or affected to be, a man of very nice discernment in the science of cooking'.[44] When his friend Hill Boothby had a problem with her bowels, he recommended his own concoction made of orange peel, with various instructions about what it could and could not be taken with (hot port was all right but sugar was not, unless perhaps it was the syrup of quinces, 'but even that I do not like.') He had come to this recipe, he said, as he had 'thought much on medicine'.[45] In a few surviving letters from the period when he wrote the dictionary, he requested to borrow (or have returned) the following books: *A Treatise on Opium*; *A Serious Call to Devout and Holy Life*; *A Course of Lectures on Natural Philosophy*; *Angliae Notitiae, or the Present State of England*; Clarendon's *History of the Rebellion*; and the catalogue of the library of 'historian, diplomat, churchman, and bibliophile Jacques-Auguste De Thou'.[46] And he was skilled in arithmetic, which he used to do in his head when he was in a disturbed mental state. Hester Piozzi, one of his closest friends, once asked him what he had done when his mental health kept him in his room all day. He showed her a calculation that worked out what size of sphere could be made from the amount of silver's worth of the British national debt. He also talked to Piozzi about whether numbers can be infinite and wrote a dissertation on the number sixteen.[47]

Johnson learned wherever he went. On a visit to an army camp in 1778, when he was nearly sixty, he enquired about many aspects of military practice, including the weight of musket balls, and the range at which they could be effective. He displayed a good knowledge of gunpowder, talked on a range of military topics, and sat up late watching a court martial.[48] The inventor Richard Arkwright said that Johnson was the only person who, on first view, 'understood the principle and powers of his most complicated piece of machinery'.[49]

He had been advised by his cousin Cornelius Ford, with whom he spent some formative months as a young man, 'to obtain some general principles of every science'. A man who can only talk about one subject, Ford said, 'is seldom wanted'. Whereas, 'a man of general knowledge… always pleases'.[50]

And Johnson had mental abilities only a few people can claim. He was supposed to be able to read a page by little more than looking at it and could then give the gist of it. Yet he was unmethodical. He claimed never to have finished a book or a poem. He never read the whole *Odyssey* in Greek. When he made a plan for the systematic study of all branches of knowledge he abandoned it.[51] He was an erratic, unsystematic worker, who sometimes struggled to concentrate. Boswell records an evening when Johnson 'read in a variety of books: suddenly throwing down one, and taking up another'.[52] But Adam Smith thought Johnson the best read man he knew. And he read intensely. His memory was prodigious. Joshua Reynolds's sister thought he rarely needed to read something twice to repeat it nearly verbatim.[53] Aged twenty-five he was temporarily a tutor in a local gentleman's house. He went with the family to church on Sundays and on the walk home would repeat 'the greater part of the sermon, with criticisms, additions, and improvements'.[54] No wonder the novelist Fanny Burney was amazed at his 'universal readiness on all subjects'.[55]

He started his broad, immersive learning young. Johnson grew up in a bookshop where his father stocked books on all subjects, and published books on subjects ranging from medicine and zoology to grammar and religion.[56] The customers of Michael Johnson's shop were used to seeing the awkward, gluttonous boy sitting in the shop, a book held close to his good eye, and his ungainly body shifting and shunting from one cramped position to another. The swaying, shambling reader was often immersed in histories, travel books, romances. Instead of going to church on Sunday, where he would be gawped at and talked about, with his scarred and pockmarked face, he went to the local fields where he walked and read. Throughout his life, he kept a small book in his pocket. Although he could be an idle boy, completing his schoolwork at the last minute, he was bright. His parents tried to make him perform Latin conjugations to show off to their friends and neighbours – a practice that left him impatient of performing children for the rest of his life. Despite this, no one seems to have predicted that his talents would take him as far as they did. How could they know where all this accumulated knowledge would take him? The only sign that someone saw his potential was at Stourbridge School, which he went to aged sixteen, where they preserved his schoolwork.[57] When he left Lichfield, a local gentleman wrote on his behalf to recommend him to people in London, describing him as a 'very good scholar and poet, and I have great hope he will turn out a great tragedy writer'. It was not to be. *Irene*, the tragedy he worked on for years, had a decent run when it finally appeared, but it was never revived. Tom Davies, the bookseller and actor who introduced Boswell to Johnson, said, '*Irene* was not treated with the candour which its merit deserved.'[58] A generous statement from an old friend.

It is the range of Johnson's knowledge that makes the *Dictionary* so astonishing. Although it is a very literary work, Boswell praises 'the perspicacity with which he has expressed abstract scientific notions'.[59] There are over 116,000 quotations in the full dictionary. It was often used for general education as well as a reference work.[60] Johnson was, as Thomas Carlyle said, 'a man of facts and truths'.[61] It was the *Dictionary*'s 'clearness of definition' as well as its 'solidity, honesty, insights, and successful method' that made Carlyle say, even if it was the only part of Johnson's work to survive, 'one might have traced there a great intellect, a genuine man'.[62] In the *Dictionary*, Johnson combined deep scholarship, sharp stylistic writing, a strong moral code and his vast reading across many disciplines to create a unique, inventive, useful, serious and entertaining book. It made him famous, justly so, and gave him an enduring reputation as the great celebrity of his age.

But success was not what it might have been. Johnson spent most of the money he was paid for the *Dictionary* paying his amanuenses – literary assistants who helped compile the dictionary. To pay for living expenses while he compiled the *Dictionary*, Johnson wrote *The Rambler*, a twice-weekly essay on subjects moral, philosophical, literary, and religious. *The Rambler* has since come to be seen as one of his great accomplishments; by the end of his life, it was part of what made him famous. It was not always so popular with early readers. Johnson was an incredibly earnest person. He wrote seriously about serious things. As James Clifford said, 'His difficulty was in providing enough light entertainment to satisfy ordinary readers.'[63] Despite the fact that *The Rambler* didn't sell brilliantly, it was regularly pirated by country newspapers. There was a recognition of Johnson's superb achievement among the elite. As his wife said to him: 'I thought very well of you before, but I did not imagine you could have written anything equal to this.'[64] However, it was all too clear to many readers that the author of *The Rambler* was a dictionary maker. The Marchioness Grey complained, 'Every paper is full of so many hard words as really break my teeth to speak them.'[65] Adam Smith is supposed to have found it unreadable.[66]

Johnson had waited and waited for his success. Aged forty he was an unsuccessful poet and dramatist who made his money as a hack. True, he had written the *Life of Savage*, one of the great literary biographies in English. And *London* would be anthologized. But it was a small, anonymous record. At that point he was two years into his work on the *Dictionary* and had to redesign his entire scheme of work. Before he finished writing the *Dictionary* his wife died and then his mentor Edward Cave. Shortly after he finished the work, he spent the night in debtors' jail. He had planned a summer of excursions. Instead, he had to go back to grubbing for money.

Johnson was always nervous about the possibility of mental collapse. In 1754, his friend the poet William Collins was confined to a madhouse. Writing about this to a mutual friend two years later, Johnson said, 'The moralists all talk about the uncertainty of fortune, and the transitoriness of beauty; but it is yet more dreadful to consider that the powers of the mind are equally liable to change, that understanding may make its appearance and depart, that it may blaze and expire.'[67] A few years later, the character Imlac said something similar in Johnson's philosophical novella *Rasselas*. This was his great productive period, the time when he produced many major works – the *Dictionary*, *The Rambler*, *The Vanity of Human Wishes*. Three canonical works, each in a different mode: reference, journalism, poetry. He then worked on his edition of Shakespeare, *The Idler* and *Rasselas*. It was an extraordinary fifteen years. And throughout, he was nervous that his mind might blaze and expire.

By 1762, the fifty-three-year-old Johnson had finally done his work. He was famous, but not as famous as he had hoped, with *The Rambler* looking old-fashioned as soon as it was published. And he was anxious about his idleness. Scared that he had wasted his God-given talents, before he died he was sometimes literally terrified of going to hell. That is why, aged sixty-eight, he accepted a commission from three publishers to write *The Lives of the Poets*. He wrote in his book of prayers and meditations, the year he started *Lives*, that he resolved for 'more efficacy of resolution' after his 'barren waste of time' in the last year. In a poem written at the same time, idleness leads to 'phantoms of the brain' and 'vain opinions'. Work would keep him sane.

He was assiduous during his work on *Lives*, reading carefully through manuscripts and letters. He was a thorough researcher and careful note-taker. Far from being erratic, in this job he was, according to Harriet Kirkley, 'slogging away at the job of evaluating old material and accumulating new material'.[68] But his early years of immersive learning seem to have been important to him as well.

(His bookshop childhood played a role here, too, more than fifty years later. Clifford points out that Johnson would have heard much literary gossip in the shop: 'It is impossible to estimate how much of this intimate knowledge of seventeenth century authors came from merely keeping his ears open during his early years.'[69])

He was a firm believer that getting older didn't have to mean getting less intelligent. His retirement project would show the world that he was still the great doctor. Writing *The Lives of the Poets* was a way to demonstrate that his powers were not in decline. Boswell reports a conversation about this topic two years after Johnson started writing *Lives*:

> We talked of old age. Johnson (now in his seventieth year) said, 'It is a man's own fault, it is from want of use, if his mind grows torpid in old age.' The Bishop asked, if an old man does not lose faster than he gets. JOHNSON. 'I think not, my Lord, if he exerts himself.' One of the company rashly observed, that he thought it was happy for an old man that insensibility comes upon him. JOHNSON. (with a noble elevation and disdain,) 'No Sir, I should never be happy by being less rational.' BISHOP OF ST ASAPH 'Your wish then, Sir, is "I grow in learning as I grow in years."' JOHNSON. 'Yes my Lord.'[70]

In other conversations, Johnson was more condemnatory about the idea of mental decline. The Dean of Derry made the mistake of telling Johnson a man never improves after forty-five. Johnson was appalled at this defeatism and laxity. 'That is not true, Sir,' said Johnson. 'You, who perhaps are forty-eight, may still improve if you will try; I wish you set about it; and I am afraid,' he added, 'there is great room for it.'[71] There was never any excuse, for Johnson, to settle for what we are or to stop trying. Contentment, he believed, was an illusion. Even someone who was content in general would never be content with the present, 'he always has some new scheme, some new plantation, something which is future'.[72] There were benefits to this: 'Employments... prevent melancholy.'[73]

This idea came into the *Life of Waller*. Prompted perhaps as much by his own as well as Waller's (a poet who carried on writing well into old age), Johnson wrote, 'That natural jealousy which makes every man unwilling to allow much excellence in another, always produces a disposition to believe that the mind grows old with the body; and that he, whom we are now forced to confess superior, is hastening daily to a level with ourselves.' Johnson takes on another critic, who proclaimed that Waller's genius 'passed the zenith' when Waller was fifty-five. Johnson was having none of it:

> This is to allot the mind but a small portion. Intellectual decay is doubtless not uncommon; but it seems not to be universal. Newton was in his eighty-fifth year improving his chronology, a few days before his death; and Waller appears not, in my opinion, to have lost at eighty-two any part of his poetical power.[74]

Lives was also a way of working on his character and what we would call his mental health. For the new year in 1777 he wrote, 'Grant, O Lord, that as my days are multiplied, my good resolutions may be strengthened.' On 6 April that year, he wrote that he wanted to rise at eight, keep a journal, read the whole Bible, and worship more frequently in public. At Easter that year, just about the time when he signed the contract for *Lives*, he recorded, 'I was for some time distressed, but at last obtained, I hope from the god of peace, more quiet than I have enjoyed for a long time.'[75]

His resolutions were often so similar because a good resolution will help us make progress but never be complete. Wisdom is the work of a lifetime. He wasn't just trying to be a great writer; he was working to be a good man, to have a calm state of mind, to be at peace with himself. And work, as we see here, was the mechanism that helped him to live up to his resolutions. It was his view that no really good literary biography had been written. This was his chance to change that and to try to change himself.

He had failed before – had been lazy, he hadn't lived up to his own expectations. But you can always start again. This topic was on his mind throughout *Lives*. He wrote in the *Life of Pope*:

> The distance is commonly very great between actual performances and speculative possibility. It is natural to suppose, that as much as has been done to-day may be done to-morrow; but on the morrow some difficulty emerges, or some external impediment obstructs. Indolence, interruption, business, and pleasure, all take their turns of retardation; and every long work is lengthened by a thousand causes that can, and ten thousand that cannot, be recounted. Perhaps no extensive and multifarious performance was ever effected within the term originally fixed in the undertaker's mind. He that runs against Time, has an antagonist not subject to casualties.[76]

Every long work is lengthened by a thousand causes – that could be a motto for Johnson and for so many late bloomers. This is Johnson's real legacy. He is a moralist as quotable as the Bible. He spent his whole life dedicated to learning and practising good morals. As Lawrence Lipking said, 'He was a sage and adviser, a moralist whose mind was free from cant, a great man who cared about the daily problems of common people.'[77] As a biographer, Johnson was not concerned with 'vulgar greatness' but with 'the minute details of daily life'.[78] 'The heroes of literary as well as civil history,' he wrote in the *Life of Savage*, 'have been very often no less remarkable for what they have suffered than for what they have achieved,'[79] The same is true of Johnson; it is his constant resolution to *become* Samuel Johnson that is most important.

His letters are full of moral advice to improve life in small ways and big. To a friend starting at Oxford, he says record all strong impressions of new experiences while they are fresh 'before custom has reconciled you to the scene before you'.[80] To a friend who hadn't spoken to his sister in years, he advises reconciliation. If the friend is to blame, 'it is your duty first to seek a renewal of kindness' and, if the sister is to blame, then reconciliation is 'an opportunity to exercise the virtue of forgiveness'.[81] His sense of moral purpose informed his literary criticism. He believed 'the end of writing is to instruct'. Shakespeare was praised for 'practical axioms and domestic wisdom'. Shakespeare did not distort; he knew that 'love is only one of many passions'. He shows usurpers and murderers 'not only odious but despicable'.[82] The whole design of *The Rambler* is to impart practical and philosophical wisdom. 'Not only in the slumber of sloth but in the dissipation of ill-directed industry, is the shortness of life generally forgotten.' 'It cannot be thought reasonable not to gain happiness for fear of losing it.' Of the new form of realistic fiction that represents people as they really are he worried 'many characters ought never to be drawn' – by making them 'splendidly wicked' we 'lose abhorrence of their faults'.[83]

This is what makes Boswell's biography so splendid. It is full of Johnson's practical wisdom. As Boswell said, 'Johnson loved business, loved to have his wisdom actually operate on real life.' Johnson was known for his near obsession with truthfulness. Even the smallest slips should be regretted. 'You do not know where deviation from truth will end.' He had much to say on the regulation of mood: 'Vivacity is much an art and depends greatly on habit.' And on the regulation of your own character, he said: 'There is in human nature a general inclination to make people stare; and every wise man has himself to cure of it, and does cure himself.' His moral advice deals with almost anything, unified by the idea, as he wrote to Boswell, that 'of the short life we have' we ought to 'make the best use for yourself and your friends'. Johnson was not a mere philosopher, regurgitating ancient wisdom; he was, as Boswell said, 'well informed in the common affairs of life, and loved to illustrate them'.[84]

Johnson had an insight especially important to late bloomers. Being a genius is not enough: you have to work. 'Nothing will supply the want of prudence, and that negligence and irregularity long continued will make knowledge useless, wit ridiculous, and genius contemptible.' There are no shortcuts. Our lives, if they are well lived, are long works. Take Samuel Johnson's advice. Resolve, work, fail and resolve again. We should do this not just for ambition, for 'hope of a better fortune', but because 'the time comes at last, in which life has no more to promise' and all we can do then is remember our lives; and 'virtue will be all that we can recollect with pleasure'.[85] We should keep working and keep trying, keep expanding our perspectives and horizons, our stock of knowledge and our range of experiences, not just for aspiration, but so we will know at the end of our lives that we did.

Part Four
Right Place – Changing and Ageing

'Many of life's failures are people who did not realize how close they were to success when they gave up.'

Thomas Edison

8

Change your circumstances to change yourself

Apart from the role of networks, there are two lessons we can draw from Johnson's life. First, the culture we live in has a huge influence on our work: our circumstances change who we become. Second, our mental powers do not inevitably decline as we age: the more work we produce, the more likely we are to be successful. This chapter is about the way we change as our circumstances change. Mental decline is dealt with in Chapter 10.

•••

Samuel Johnson took himself to London and changed slowly. The life of a freelance writer taught him commercial necessity, grew his network, and put him in touch with audience demand. He became Samuel Johnson by developing in this environment rather than the sheltered culture of Oxford. Many late bloomers lack the cultural milieu that is essential to success. It matters who you surround yourself with and what circumstances you put yourself in. Influence builds up over time.

The lesson of influence is that, if you want to change your work or your life, you need to change the people you associate with. 'Tell me who you spend time with,' said Goethe, 'and I will tell you who you are.' There are two ways to categorize this influence: the way peers affect each other, and the way surrounding culture affects an individual's development. What we will see from these two forms of influence is that we are able to transform ourselves. We can become different by changing our circumstances.

•••

Painters and poets often form groups where they col
encourage each other. Without these groups, they can st
And a group is no guarantee of success. But when the rig
form a group, the effects are powerful. The sociologist Michael P.
Farrell believes these artistic groups rise out of social networks, last
for about ten or fifteen years, combine friendship and work, and
create 'a shared vision that guides their work'. Each member has an
expected role in the group and the interpersonal dynamics are just as
important as the exchange of ideas and feedback. The groups create
new cultures. The groups rely on shared goals, a common vision and
a set of assumptions about their discipline. For artists, the shared
assumptions might be about a style; for scientists, about a new
method or model. Farrell is clear this is not like having a mentor.
Mentors are older and more experienced, and they guide people into
a profession: collaborative circles are formed among peers.

These groups can be seen in many endeavours: the Impressionists and
the Inklings are two artistic examples.[1] Such groups exist in other
areas, too, such as the Manhattan Project or the 1992 Clinton election.
Those last two examples might not fit exactly the criteria Farrell laid
out. The Manhattan Project had all the aspects of his definition –
shared goals among peers who relied on friendship dynamics. But
the Clinton campaign (and other examples like Walt Disney Studios)
suggests that group dynamics are essential to high achievement even
when those groups become larger.[2] To get started, and to become
innovative, though, there has to be a small core of people who set out
to change the world together.

According to Farrell, although these groups 'usually form among
persons in their twenties or early thirties',[3] there is no why reason
why this has to be the case. Notable exceptions include J. R. R.
Tolkien who was in his forties when the Inklings started meeting and
Joseph Conrad who didn't start writing fiction until he was in his
late thirties. In his early forties, Conrad joined a collaborative circle

in Rye, on the south coast of England. The two other members were Ford Madox Ford, aged twenty-six, and Henry James, aged fifty-five. What made the group work, despite their disparate ages, was that all three writers were trying to establish themselves. Conrad and Ford were starting their careers; James was looking to re-establish himself after some professional setbacks. So, for different reasons, this group had two late bloomers.[4] There were two other members: H. G. Wells, thirty-three, and Stephen Crane, twenty-eight, the only one who was a success at that stage. The group read and critiqued each other's work, and formed a vision of how the novel could evolve beyond Victorian moralizing. Wells was inspired to polish his style by James; James wanted to write fantastical stories like Wells. Ford imitated Conrad and James. Several of them wrote stories from the perspective of a seemingly peripheral character rather than an omniscient narrator, an innovation of James's.

Despite these influences, the group could not hold. Successful groups need a peacemaker. The Rye circle lacked such a person. The group never gelled. While they never got to the stage of the Impressionists, who revolutionized art with their breakaway 1874 exhibition, they influenced each other and changed each other's careers. Over a decade, there were meetings where they read work, discussed literature and collaborated. Their work shows this influence with its shared use of 'psychological "horrors" and… moral dilemmas, the narrator within the narrative structure, the time-shifts of narration, the progressive intensification of effects, as well as the plots and settings of their stories'. Mixed ages was a problem for the wider group – but it created a fruitful dynamic between Conrad and Ford. 'During all those years,' Ford said, '[I] wrote every word that [I] wrote, with the idea of reading it aloud to Conrad.'[5] And Conrad emerged from this partnership with novels like *Lord Jim* and *Heart of Darkness*: it was his most productive decade. Collaborations between people of different ages but with similar aspirations and at similar career stages can be highly productive.

There is no reason why Conrad and Ford cannot be examples for other late bloomers. As Michael Farrell told me:

> I have always thought that late bloomers can form a productive collaborative circle so long as they all are peers... In most late-forming circles I have examined, or even been part of, the group is more a coalition of consultants, each with their separate expertise, each adding a piece to the product. Like a crew making a movie. Or an architect and the builders.[6]

As life expectancy gets longer, people make more career changes, and women move back into the workforce after caring for children, there will be more opportunities for collaborative groups to play a role in people pursuing new personal and professional interests. It is common for people of retirement age to form clubs dedicated to physical and cultural hobbies – why not also to the production, invention or creation of new ideas and products? If these groups were able to introduce people of other ages, as happened at Rye, the combination of experience and energy could be impressive.

•••

Some influences within a culture are more subtle. The way people behave sends a signal to the people around them. Influence at work can be unavoidable. Companies can harness these signals for better or worse. Daniel Coyle gives the example of Pixar, where every employee is shown early versions of the movies and asked for feedback. Coyle reports that suggestions are taken by the directors from anyone, if they are good.[7] Psychologist Amy Edmondson would call this 'psychological safety', the feeling that this is a place where you can offer ideas without being mocked or silenced. She says, 'Psychological safety enables candor and openness and, therefore, thrives in an environment of mutual respect.' This is not to say everything must be friendly and calm all the time. Coyle says, 'The feeling of being in a great culture isn't smoothness – it's the feeling of *solving hard problems with people you admire*.'[8]

Culture is also important in a much broader sense. Investor and essayist Paul Graham once asked, 'What happened to the Milanese Leonardo?' Milan in the fifteenth century was as big as Florence. But while Florence produced a Renaissance, including Leonardo, Brunelleschi, Michelangelo, Donatello, and many others, Milan did not. If this difference was just about genetics, you would expect hundreds of Leonardos in the modern USA, a vastly bigger population than Florence ever managed. But where are they? Graham says:

> Nothing is more powerful than a community of talented people working on related problems. Genes count for little by comparison: being a genetic Leonardo was not enough to compensate for having been born near Milan instead of Florence. Today we move around more, but great work still comes disproportionately from a few hotspots: the Bauhaus, the Manhattan Project, the *New Yorker*, Lockheed's Skunk Works, Xerox Parc.[9]

The people you work with have a significant impact on you. Culture matters. But sometimes it is difficult to draw firm conclusions from the studies about this topic. There is a study showing that when Tiger Woods is absent from tournaments, for example, his competitors perform better – the idea being that they are uninhibited by the superstar's presence. But it's not clear whether the finding is robust, and generalizing from that study would be a risk.

One study found that when academic superstars die prematurely, their collaborators' publication rate drops 5–8 per cent.[10] Their non-collaborating colleagues, however, see an 8 per cent *increase* in productivity. While a star academic colleague can increase the production of those closest to them, people slightly removed feel unable to challenge the star's position. Indeed, although the star's death can encourage people to come forward with more avant-garde ideas, this is only possible if there is not a group of the star's former colleagues preserving the star's legacy and keeping their influence alive. By keeping the star's influence alive, these former colleagues still discourage the emergence of new ideas.[11] So the influence of academic stars can be very different depending on who you are.

Sometimes, your best choice is simply to avoid working with bad influences. A large study of toxic workers found that they induce their colleagues to become toxic and increase turnover costs. The impact of toxic workers is so large that firms would 'be better off by replacing a toxic worker with an average worker by more than two-to-one'. Indeed, avoiding toxic workers is better for firms than hiring top 1 per cent superstars.[12]

Psychologists Therese Amabile and Stephen Kramer have studied the effect of workplace culture on productivity. Amabile and Kramer analysed 12,000 diary entries made by workers. They found that when people have positive inner emotional states, they are more productive. Being in cultures where your work is inhibited creates negative feedback loops, whereas positive cultures create positive feedback loops. The sort of managers who swoop in and derail projects or who disrupt people's ability to make small steps of progress every day encourage the negative inner emotional states that lead to lower productivity.[13]

Collaboration improves productivity for academics. According to a study that looked at tens of millions of research papers published since 1950, in the humanities, teams of authors have always produced more than solo contributors. In the sciences, individuals produced the more successful papers until the last twenty years, when it became decisively a question of teams outperforming. The most successful patents are also the result of teams, not individuals.[14]

Nor does this influence have to be as direct as a collaboration. A study of the acknowledgements sections of nearly 5,000 research papers accounts for the interactions of about 15,000 academics working in financial economics. We saw earlier that your position in a network could make you more productive: being closer to a star improves your output. Something similar is true of social networks – social networks being the informal relationships that mean you end up in the acknowledgements section rather than as a co-author. Your position in a social network doesn't predict your productivity. But, papers that get feedback from well-connected academics have a higher impact than those that don't. People more able to influence their peers are more likely to publish in the best journals. This isn't causal, but it does show that influence is part of productivity.[15] A recent study found that Black school students randomly assigned to have a Black teacher in their early school years were more likely to graduate from high school and enrol in college, showing quite a lasting influence.[16] The study authors suggest a similar effect might be possible outside of classrooms through mentorship.

While we might not take every result literally, we can see it really matters who you work with. This isn't just peer pressure: who you associate with affects what information you get about the world. The people you know don't just influence you with their opinions, but also help you sample the world differently. If you don't know anyone who works in advertising, you might think it's a boring profession. If you meet people in the industry and gradually become friends, you might change your mind. You could even consider a career change. Meeting those people gave you a bigger sample – by knowing more people, you knew more about advertising. This is not the direct influence of peer pressure but the indirect influence of sampling the world via your network.[17]

These peer effects can be strong. Economists who study peer effects, for example, have found that when students live with other students who do the same major as them, the student is more likely to persist in that major, and when one of the roommates changes major, the others are more likely to change.[18] A study from 2001, based on a survey sent to twenty-three Computer Science and Biology departments in Virginia, found that departments with predominantly male students had more women drop out. Female students who do not have other women to study with end up in an unfriendly male culture. A higher proportion of the people studying biology were women, partly because the faculty was more gender balanced.[19] It has also been found that having a roommate who drinks alcohol – and who drank alcohol at school before going to university – can decrease a student's average grades. What's important about that finding is that for some people the effect is small or non-existent while for others it is very large.[20] These are not the sorts of effects that operate in a uniform, predictable way. They show us trends and possibilities, not an inevitable chain reaction.

Raj Chetty and other economists have found that being good at school and coming from a rich family can predict whether a child is likely to become an inventor or innovator. Another major predictor is whether children are exposed to innovators. They say: '[I]f girls were as exposed to female inventors as boys are to male inventors, the gender gap in innovation would fall by half.' People from lower-income families or from minorities are less likely to be exposed to innovators and inventors, thus lowering their rate of invention. This leads to what they call 'lost Einsteins': 'Given our finding that innovation ability does not vary substantially across these groups, this result implies there are many "lost Einsteins" – people who would have had high-impact inventions had they become inventors – among the underrepresented groups.'[21] Raj Chetty has also found that, when children from low-income families are friends with children from high-income families, they are more likely to have higher incomes later in life. Those children get information about possible careers and universities, their aspirations and beliefs are shaped differently, and they may even be connected to opportunities.[22]

We are subject to more influences than we realize. This is perhaps more obvious when we look at history. This is an observation that goes back to Aristotle, who said in *Poetics* that humans were the most imitative of living creatures. As John Stuart Mill said, the main lesson of history is 'the extraordinary susceptibility of human nature to external influences'.[23]

People of accomplishment tend to work together, in a culture of high achievement, and in a chain of teaching. Donatello taught Bertoldo di Giovanni who taught Michelangelo; Socrates taught Plato who taught Aristotle. Historian and sociologist of philosophy Randall Collins writes: 'Creativity is not random among individuals; it builds up in intergenerational chains.'[24] Gerty and Carl Cori taught six future Nobel laureates in their biology lab in Missouri. Nobel prize winners often collaborate before they win their prizes, and are highly selective about their teachers and mentors; they also have the same chains of teaching that create great philosophers. (While this looks compelling, and is undoubtedly an important factor in the development of many future laureates, it's also important to note that many laureates don't have such connections. Network connections are beneficial, not the exclusive path.[25] Entrepreneur Patrick Collison, one of the founding voices in the new Progress Studies movement, believes this is an essential part of scientific success. 'The research culture set by specific people and the tacit knowledge transmitted through direct experience,' he says, when trying to explain why greatness happens in some times and places but not others, 'is probably the number-one thing.'[26]

The ability of peers and cultures to influence us is why Johnson benefited so much from being in London, rather than Oxford.

•••

Imagine that, rather than slowly acclimatizing to a culture, the way Johnson did, you were dropped suddenly into a new life, like Katharine Graham. What would happen to you? The Second World War provides a natural experiment in the way that picking someone up and dropping them into a more beneficial environment can transform their life, first through a sudden change, then through a slow process.

Many young men who were conscripted in the 1940s' United States came from disadvantaged backgrounds. They lacked the benefit of stable homes and good schools. Those environments are known to increase the chance of living stable and successful lives.[27] These men were on track to lead a different sort of life. The system had failed them. But once they joined the army, they were in environments with the discipline, leadership, structure, teamwork, cooperation, responsibility, and purpose they had previously lacked. They were given travel opportunities and new experiences. Of course, there were great dangers involved and this is not an argument in favour of military conscription or war. But it does give us the chance to see what happens to someone who, late in their education, with limited prospects and a poor track record, experiences a new culture and has a transitional experience. One key feature of the army is equality of rank: previous differences between these men and their peers, perceived inadequacies, were no longer pertinent.

Looking at a sample of men born during the Great Depression who served throughout the Second World War and the Korean War, one sociologist found that men from disadvantaged backgrounds became more socially competent and had improved psychological health after military service. They also improved their occupation outcomes as a result of skills training in the army. As well as going to college on the G.I. Bill, many army veterans completed high school and undertook craft or vocational training. The army was a bridge from one sort of life to another, often coming at a time when their prospects seemed settled. They went from being school leavers with poor prospects to veterans with the chance of a decent life. It had seemed too late to change, but it wasn't.

For men already established in jobs and families – who were usually older than twenty-two – the military was more likely to be disruptive. But for those who were on the route to a disappointing life, military service improved their trajectory. There were many negative impacts of army service: mobilized men were more likely to divorce, especially those who saw battle action and were in their thirties. But this goes to show the same thing: changing your life path is possible, whatever your age or current experiences. The more you change your circumstances, the more you can change yourself. In the United States, delinquent men who were given overseas service, for example, were much more likely to use training opportunities provided by the 1944 G.I. Bill. As one pair of sociologists said, 'Overseas duty, which embodies radical change, provides a unique stepping stone to eventual turn-around among those stigmatized with a criminal conviction.'[28] It changed the way people thought of them and changed the way they thought about themselves.

The timing of such interventions also matters. Fifteen per cent of delinquents who didn't serve in the military got skilled or professional jobs compared to 21 per cent who served but didn't use the G.I. Bill: it rises to 54 per cent for those who used the Bill to get training, and 78 per cent for those who used the Bill and had joined before eighteen. Although the intervention was more effective for younger veterans, there is a huge difference between delinquents who didn't join the army and those who did and then took training opportunities.[29] The general principle is clear: 'All life choices are contingent on the opportunities and constraints of social structure and culture,' as sociologist Glen Elder said.[30] Change your circumstances and your surroundings, and you might change your life prospects.

Similarly, it was by being in France, experiencing the food in restaurants, going to local markets, finding a French cookery school, that Julia Child turned her love of eating into a love of cooking and writing about food. She wasn't shipped off to France by the military but by her husband's diplomatic job. This simple, single transition was momentous, putting her on a path of becoming an entirely different sort of person, one who presented television cookery shows into her nineties. Like Katharine Graham, Child had been slightly stifled by her rich and privileged upbringing. She was a very social person in her twenties, but not a very focused one. Being in France and needing something to do gave structure and opportunity to inner motivation.

Your circumstances can be determinative even if you don't go abroad. Fathers who struggled financially during the Great Depression, for example, were more likely to be explosive and become worse parents and spouses. The current generation of teenagers, known as Gen Z, are widely noted as being more financially prudent than the generation before them, probably as a result of growing up in the after-effects of the 2008 financial crisis. The cumulative effects of your environment are significant, but they can be altered. It takes several years of army service to change your life track, just as Julia Child lived and studied in France for many years before going back to the States. Many women experienced this during the Second World War. Oxford University, for example, was left without many male philosophers, which made space for the development of four of the most prominent women philosophers of their generation: Philippa Foot, Iris Murdoch, Elizabeth Anscombe and Mary Midgley. Their lives were put on a different course by those events. Putting yourself in new contexts and situations can mean that your daily life accumulates into something very different over time. Finding transitional moments is essential to becoming a different person.[31]

This is what happened to Carl Bernstein. Now famous as one of the reporters who broke the Watergate scandal, the year before he started working on the story Bernstein was at risk of being fired. He could be careless about details and lax about deadlines. He was working on the 'Metro' section – reporting local Washington, DC, stories – and getting bored. He asked to transfer to 'Style'. His reputation was declining. His overtime and expense account was twice as much as anyone else's in his department. He rented cars to go on long wayward reporting jobs and racked up huge bills while the cars sat in car parks. In 1971, things came to a head when he failed to file a story he'd worked on for months. He was called in to see editor Harry Rosenfeld who said he could either become a productive reporter or leave the *Post*. He was shaken and said he'd reform. A year later he began working on Watergate 'and the tiger changed his stripes'. If he had been fired – Rosenfeld said the 'legal groundwork had been laid' – or transferred to 'Style', Bernstein would never have become the reporter he later became. Someone else would have got Watergate. As it was, 'Carl discovered his better self on Watergate. His talents of imagination and shrewdness flourished.' Bernstein still occasionally irritated his colleagues but with the transformative moment when he was told to get his act together, and then a slow process of change as he worked on Watergate, he had become a different sort of reporter on a different career trajectory.[32]

We go through many transitions: getting married, having or not having children, changing jobs, menopause, mental health problems, moving to a new area, redundancy, retirement. These can all be opportunities for change. They won't be exclusively good or bad experiences for everyone. But they can change the way your motivation is expressed. The same event will affect different individuals in strikingly different ways. Psychologist Jay Belsky and his collaborators have created the theory of 'differential susceptibility' which states that some people are more plastic than others, more susceptible to the influences of their environment. The stresses of a difficult childhood, for example, will affect some people very badly and others hardly at all. This is another example of average results concealing massive variations. As we saw with the men drafted into the army in the Second World War, the experience shaped some people much more strongly than others. Every parent knows that the same environment affects each child in a different way. This is only to be expected: the logic of evolution states that there will be almost infinite variation within a species. This is not a question of some people being susceptible to influences and others impermeable. Different people are influenced by different things. Some people are more strongly influenced by their parents but not by their peers, and vice versa. Some people are going to be strongly susceptible to the influence of music but not painting. Many people are what Belsky calls a 'mosaic' – rather than fitting a neat pattern, we are influenced by different things in different ways. One study found that 7 per cent of children are highly influenced by both parents and peers, 10 per cent were not much influenced by either, 15 per cent were highly susceptible to peers but not parents, and 19 per cent the opposite. Another study found that 6.5 per cent of children were susceptible to early-life adversity but not susceptible in adolescence, and another 6.7 per cent were the reverse. Some people are highly susceptible to their environments, others are not, and many sit in between, susceptible to different sorts of influences at different times.[33] That is why key transitional moments in life affect us differently. Just as the war affected the young delinquents in various ways, so will retirement, children, redundancy and other moments of change affect people. The average effect of these transitions tells us very little about the different ways in which people are susceptible to change.

Becoming a different person might begin with a single moment of change – but transformation is a process. Often, transformation begins by chance. When Julia Child sat down to lunch at La Couronne in Rouen and discovered a love of French cuisine, aged thirty-seven, she was there by chance. It was under the influence of her friends Simone Beck and Louisette Bertholle that she started to think of food as something she could pursue professionally, and she attended Cordon Bleu cooking school with them. They later spent a decade working on the best-selling *Mastering the Art of French Cooking*.[34]

Without that moment of inspiration, Child would never have changed from independent-minded socialite and wife doing government work to chef, best-selling writer of a definitive guide to French cuisine, and global television celebrity, who worked tirelessly from her midlife transformation until her death. She couldn't force what that change would be like, though, and often when we decide we want to be different, we don't know what that new reality will be like. We have to take a leap of faith.

The philosopher L. A. Paul calls this the 'Vampire Problem'. Imagine you had the choice to become a vampire – that is to become a glamorous and immortal lord of the night. This is an elegant and tempting opportunity. It involves great power but requires drinking blood and avoiding sunlight. You will be immortal, but also undead. It isn't possible to know what you need to know to make this decision. Until you are a vampire, you cannot really know what it is like: drinking blood sounds vile as a human but will be delicious as a vampire. Many life choices are Vampire Problems. They are, as Paul says, decisions about 'experiences that teach us things we cannot know about from any other source than the experience itself'.[35] The only way to learn what a new life will be like is to live it.

Many decisions, however, are not Vampire Problems: they can be reversed or adjusted. There are also many people who don't experience change as a Vampire Problem. For someone who lives in a large family and sees their older siblings have children, the change to parenthood might not be seen as a big transformation. They have been acclimatized to the new reality. This is probably what happened to Katharine Graham. In 1991, she interviewed one of the former *Washington Post* editors as part of the research for her autobiography. She told him she had taken on the job of running the *Post* knowing 'nothing, nothing, nothing'. Not so, he told her. She'd had an 'inside look' at the paper's challenges from her father and Phil. She agreed that this did give her a sort of 'indirect knowledge'.[36] Still, she knew very little compared to the people who worked for her, was often anxious about her inability to slip easily into the life of her newspapers, and spent much time learning in an almost neurotic state. 'There was nothing to do but feel my way. Gradually I put things into place.' Graham kept 'nibbling around the edges' piecing together what she had to learn.[37]

This way of approaching change, what philosopher Agnes Callard calls 'self-cultivation', is open to us all. [38] Cultivating a taste for something – vigorous exercise, unfamiliar music, learning to code – is different from deciding to be a vampire. Through sampling, you can see what these new things would be like. You can get a sense of what it would be like to go to the gym, listen to rap, or write in Python. Sampling can be based in existing preferences. It doesn't necessarily involve a big step into the unknown.

Once our lives are settled, we become increasingly unwilling to take risks in new areas. Taking a risk on a new career is one thing for a twenty-one-year-old with limited skills and experience – it's a lot more difficult for the same person twenty years later when they are an experienced expert, unwilling to revert to apprenticeship. It is hard to become good at something – once we have become accomplished, we can feel reluctant to go back to being bad at something new. This is the opposite of a Vampire Problem: we know what it was like to struggle last time, and we don't want to do it again.

Behavioural scientists Jerker Denrell and Gaël Le Mens call this the competency trap.[39] Being good at one thing can stop us from becoming good at something else. Once you have committed to a career and become expert, it gets harder to revert to a period of being bad at something new while you learn. Once we are competent we know how unpleasant it is to feel incompetent and we avoid it. When faced with big changes, whether Vampire Problems or not, we are more cautious once we have some experience. We know what failure is like – we don't want to go through it again. This is also known as the 'hot stove effect', named after a Mark Twain observation:

> We should be careful to get out of an experience only the wisdom that is in it and stop there; lest we be like the cat that sits down on a hot stove lid. She will never sit down on a hot stove lid again – and that is well; but also she will never sit down on a cold one.[40]

The editor Katharine Graham interviewed, Harry Rosenfeld, had an experience when hiring for the *Post* that illustrates the hot stove problem. Rosenfeld hired a PhD graduate who was smart and hardworking but unable to get on with the fast pace of newspaper work, and went back to academia within a few weeks. Later on, another PhD turned up for interview, who Rosenfeld didn't hire. 'He seemed to be a viable candidate,' Rosenfeld, said, 'but – like Mark Twain's cat… I could not bring myself to take a chance on another PhD. Big mistake. This second candidate was Richard Bernstein, who went onto a brilliant journalistic career.'[41]

When choosing what path to follow, we can also be hindered by not knowing what we will be best at. Let's say you have three choices: learn to be a chef, study physics or become a plumber. You think that your best option is to be a plumber. After some time at plumbing school, you find that you are good but not great at plumbing, unable to improve, and you are bored. You don't need to try the other options to know that this one won't work out.

So you switch to chef school. This goes well: you get better and you enjoy the work. But you cannot know whether chef school is your *best* option unless you also try physics. The challenge is that physics might start off much harder, requiring longer to be proficient, but in the long run you might be much much better at physics than cooking. In this case, you are more likely to go with cooking, which went well quickly, even though physics would have been a better option overall.

In the three choices set out above, there is less chance you will try out physics as well as cookery *because* you already tried plumbing. You failed once; you don't want to have to struggle again. But the best approach might be to try both.

It is difficult to realize that something that doesn't go well at first might be your best option in the long run. This is true of choosing what projects to prioritize, what technologies to invest in, and what career path to follow. Doing something you are comparatively less good at in the short run might not seem like the best idea, but it can be. Not knowing what sort of practice will pay off is one of the biggest challenges we face when making these decisions.

What matters is that we don't let this indecision become the default. We should aim to be comfortable at being incompetent when we try new things. The more we branch out, the more we can discover what we are really good at. We had to be incompetent for a long time while we developed our current expertise, and sometimes we should be willing to be incompetent again. Think of Ray Kroc, who went through years of challenge to build McDonald's. He went back to a period of learning, of mistakes, of trial and error – it had all the intensity of his early career. He could have stayed in his competency trap. But once he had his sudden moment of inspiration in the car park of the first McDonald's, he began a long process of cultivation.

Nuns make a good case study of transformation and of how significant change happens first quickly and then slowly. Writer Isabel Losada interviewed twelve nuns in their twenties and thirties in her book *New Habits* to understand how and why they joined convents. Many of them reported a moment of inspiration, when they found their vocation. Once they realized their vocation, however, it often took a long time for them to become nuns. Even the woman who described her transformation as being like a whirlwind romance with God spent months before deciding to join a community and then went back on her decision before finally committing. It takes seven years of being a novice and then living under vows before you are allowed to take 'life vows' and commit for ever. Inspiration is sudden and often intense; but the path to being a full nun is longer and slower and often not easy.[42]

The Vampire Problem of not knowing what it is like to spend your life in a convent is solved with the long and increasingly committed process of training. One of the nuns left her convent for a more contemplative community, but was unhappy at being unable to see her family, so gave up being a nun altogether. After a break, she went back to the less isolated community and became a nun under life vows. These are not binary choices that cannot be undone. Transformation is often a messy process even if it starts with a simple and self-defining realization or decision. For many of us, the changes we are considering will be significantly less significant than becoming a nun, and offer more opportunities to sample.

•••

Late bloomers spend a lot of time cultivating themselves. They often experience life as a long, organic process, where decisions emerge out of previous experience. They are always becoming themselves. Some people's lives change in a big way at a big moment: inspiration strikes, the wheel of fortune turns. Some people evolve slowly, perhaps erratically, but consciously, deliberately. For most, change involves both sudden inspiration and slow transformation.

You don't have to wait for your luck to change. Audrey Sutherland became a hero and a pioneer of women's solo adventuring. She had an extraordinary capacity to put herself into unfamiliar situations, such as solo kayaking 800 kilometres through Alaska in her sixties, seventies and early eighties. She was her own inspiration. She did it with one simple motto: 'Go simple. Go solo. Go now.'

9
Audrey Sutherland: live immediately

In 1957, aged thirty-six, recently divorced and raising four children on her own, while working full-time as a school counsellor, Audrey Sutherland (1921–2015) flew over the Hawaiian island of Moloka'i. 'Looking down on it wasn't enough,' she said, 'I had to be there.' There is no access to the part of the Moloka'i coastline she wanted to visit, except by sea. Because she couldn't afford to hire a boat, Sutherland decided to swim.[1] After an unsuccessful attempt in 1958, it took her until 1962, when she was aged forty-two, to get there. It was a ridiculous journey to undertake. She went in the summer, in the hope – by no means guaranteed – of calm waters. 'In three hours the sea can change from a liquid lapping among the rocks to an eight-foot shore break.'[2] This was no ordinary swim, and Audrey Sutherland was no ordinary explorer. For one thing, she was 'inexperienced in aquatic journeys' when she decided to undertake this adventure. She was, however, a proficient swimmer, having learned at college. She had also worked as a swimming instructor. 'Water came to be my element.' For three years she had gone out on a commercial fishing boat with her ex-husband, 'a hard, nasty, satisfying life'. And as a child following her father she learned to love the wilderness and solitude.[3] Now she was taking all those parts of her life and recombining them after the transition of her divorce. She was becoming a pioneering solo explorer.

This was far from the last time Sutherland did something so daring. In 1980, aged fifty-nine, she quit her job and solo kayaked 800 kilometres of the Alaska and British Columbia coast, her first time in such cold waters, a stark contrast to Hawaii. For that adventure too, she was inspired to take off by looking down from an airplane window.[4] She continued going to Alaska and British Columbia for two decades. In 2001, aged eighty, she took a kayaking trip along the Vézère River in France; the following year she paddled sixty-five miles in Alaska.[5]

The origins of Sutherland's explorer spirit are easy to find in her childhood. As she said, 'preparation had been going on for a long time without my realizing that it would lead to Moloka'i'.[6] She spent much time alone as a child in a summer cabin, exploring forests. Her father died when she was five, but her mother remained committed to the outdoor life. 'My mother taught school, and right after the last hour of the last day of school was done we were on our way up to the mountains where we had a cabin. It had a wood stove and no electricity.'[7] Sutherland was raised as the sort of person who could catch her own food and subsist in bare conditions. The instinct to get away ran deep. 'Once when I was 14 years old I went from our cabin to the top of San Gorgonio Mountain fourteen miles away.' This is perhaps why two of her friends took the view that 'Audrey was no late bloomer. She was singular her entire life'.[8]

As we saw in the previous chapter, people change after transitional moments, and then slowly over a long period they cultivate something new in themselves. Audrey's divorce was her transitional moment. That was when she moved her family to the north shore of O'ahu island. It was a few years after that, when her children were old enough to take care of themselves for a week, that she started going on more significant explorations. She had always hiked and swum: now she was drawn to wild places. This spirit continued to animate her as she took expeditions to Alaska in her eighties. Age was never an impediment. 'I don't think any of us had the sense of "you're too old to be doing that,"' her daughter told the *New York Times*. 'If she was still doing it, then she wasn't too old to be doing it.'[9] Her son Jock recalled to me that, while she had always had the adventurous spirit, none of them had ever anticipated that Audrey would end up exploring the coast of Alaska and British Columbia into her eighties.[10]

She started life, as many do, as an outdoors person, and ended it as a late-blooming explorer, encountering bears, orcas, and wolves during solitary trips in unknown terrain.

It's true that to some extent Sutherland's adventures are a natural emergence of her personality. Her friend Sanford Lung recalled:

> As a single parent she was a leader, good at planning, practical and solution oriented… She would stop her vehicle to retrieve objects dropped by other cars or trucks, lengths of rope or construction materials to use around her house for repairs or other projects probably saving hundreds that would otherwise have come out of the household budget. Her kids do the same to this day.[11]

The hot tub on the deck of her house had once been an army cooking pot.[12] Audrey was resourceful in all things, even making her own wines from Hawaiian fruit. And she had an acuity for adventure. Lung recalls the instinctive way she could navigate difficult situations, as if she was adapted to the environment. Paddling with her on Moloka'i through three-foot chop Lung saw that Audrey 'was as agile navigating her landing as the indigenous rock crabs that live in that rolling landscape'.[13]

She was singular all her life and showed signs of her adventuring spirit early on. No doubt, marriage and life as a commercial fisherman's wife put some limits on her activities. Although you might call that sort of life an early example of her explorations. But it is not everyone of her temperament who ends up exploring an isolated coast reachable only by swimming, persisting for several years. Still fewer make it to Alaska in their sixties, as an impressed reviewer noted when *Paddling North* was published in 2012.[14] For her trips to Moloka'i, Audrey used a map made in 1924. None other was available. It took her years of climbing mountains, getting ill from dirty water, flying on the single-engine mail plane to a leprosy colony, staying in a cave where an isolated philosopher lived – she did all this in preparation for Moloka'i. By

1962, she was ready, and opted to hike the steep cliffs, only swimming when necessary. After four years of exploring other parts of Hawaii in preparation, she went to Moloka'i.

Her first attempt went badly wrong. She had only three days off work, forgot her watch, was unable to eat one night as she couldn't find fresh water, and the pack that floated behind her as she swam had leaked, making her clothes and camera damp.[15] Made reckless by dehydration, she tried to scale a sixty-foot wall. Ten feet from the top, she ran out of footholds. Stuck, unable to go back down, she threw her pack towards a ledge fifty feet below. It broke open and her equipment scattered into the sea. 'Desperately, I coiled and sprang outwards.' She missed the ledge by inches, plunging into the water. After she gathered her belongings, she blacked out on shore. She was rescued by a passing boat and didn't go back for three years.[16]

Audrey Sutherland was singular, but she was not yet the explorer she would later become. In old age she said that 'I learned very young what I could and couldn't do and what dangers were out there', but on these early expeditions to Moloka'i Audrey was still learning her limits, still preparing for what she would become. At the end of *Paddling My Own Canoe*, Audrey's memoir about her expeditions in Moloka'i, she compared herself to other adventurers. She was wondering if her book would be too specialized. There were others like her, but how different it was to swim and paddle the warm waters of Hawaii than to kayak the rivers of Idaho. That was 'a different set of skills'. Not to mention Betty Carey, who had paddled dugout canoes through the inside passage of British Columbia. True, that was also kayaking, Audrey wrote, 'but they have icy water and seven-foot tides'.[17] A decade later, Audrey went into cold waters for the first time.

In 1980, aged sixty, Audrey flew over Alaska and had the same sort of epiphany she'd had with Moloka'i more than twenty years earlier. 'For years, I had searched for a combination of mountains, wilderness, and sea, and here it was.'[18] She asked for a period of leave-without-pay to make a two-month expedition, exploring the coastline from Ketchikan to Skagway. She ordered twenty-four sea charts and forty-nine topographical maps to prepare for the journey. Her inflatable kayak, which she had been taking to sea since 1967, purchased in the three-year-gap between Molokaʻi expeditions, would suffice. It was light enough to be rolled, carried, and hauled. She compared looking at maps to the way musicians look at musical scores. Her imagination was taking flight to Alaska, and she was stuck at her desk, feeling 'fat and soft and white and mean'.[19]

Her request for leave was refused. She went home and saw her five-year plan stuck up on the wall with her list of twenty-five things she most wanted to do. 'Paddle Alaska' was number one. She looked at herself in the mirror and said, 'Getting older, aren't you lady? Better do the physical things now. You can work at a desk later.'[20] So Audrey, with her children grown up and enough money saved to live for a year, quit her job. 'I was truly free.'

In Hawaii, she often went barefoot in the kayak. Not here. It was not an easy start in her lightweight boat: 'The wind blew me backwards as I put on my gloves.'[21] To anyone else, this voyage would have seemed absurd, dangerous, if not downright crazy. Indeed, a local kayaking guide, Ken Leghorn, saw Audrey near Chichagof Island, towards the end of her voyage. Audrey was wet through, being blow around on top of the water, and singing. Leghorn later said, 'My first reaction was, "This is a crazy person." I thought it must be somebody who was totally unprepared to be out there. Then I found out it was somebody who has more long-distance sea kayaking experience than I'll ever have.'[22] Using an inflatable kayak was a novel approach to this sort of travel. Randel Washburne wrote in *The Coastal Kayaker* in 1983 that 'most inflatables belong in swimming pools'. Audrey had changed his mind by 1989: 'Her ingenious gear system allows self-sufficient travel for weeks at a time, and she regularly manages 20-mile travelling days.'[23]

The reason Audrey was able to spend her sixties and seventies making solo expeditions to Alaska and British Columbia in an inflatable kayak – a vessel that caused experienced fishermen to say, 'You're paddling 800 miles in that? You must be a real nut' – was because she had gradually trained herself to the challenge. From the terrifying moment when she leaped from the fifty-foot wall in Moloka'i to launching out in Alaska, she had cultivated herself into being Audrey Sutherland, pioneer of women's solo exploration.

In the late 1980s, Audrey became friends with Neil Frazer, a geophysicist and environmental scientist. He sent her the manuscript of his book *Boat Camping Haida Gwaii*, a guide for small-boat explorers of a remote archipelago in British Columbia. This initiated a friendship, centred on maps. Neil and Audrey would meet up and pore over the large-scale maps of the British Columbia and Alaskan coastline that she kept permanently under glass on her long dining room table. They exchanged information about cabins and camp sites they had found. (In British Columbia, industrial logging has made it difficult to find good campsites.) The maps had Audrey's routes marked on and they spent hours swapping stories and discussing topographical details. They were the only two people in Hawaii with this interest in common.

Neil explained to me that Audrey's years of kayaking had given her a sort of embedded wisdom, a set of instincts, that made her expeditions possible. She always told students they needed to be able to tie a bowline backwards and underwater (something she didn't want to have to test in Alaska). But it went much deeper than that. Neil explained that each voyage teaches you a little more: 'You have experiences that teach you what to do and not to do.' As you explore, you begin to 'expand your consciousness' into nature and react to the conditions instinctively. It's not the sort of thing you make notes about: it becomes second nature. 'You have learnt so much that you guide yourself through it instinctively... because of her experience, that's the kind of wisdom she had. Other people would have died attempting what she did.' Audrey had literally paddled herself into being capable of this extraordinary voyage at which other experienced water people blanched. Even Neil Frazer said of her swimming expedition to Moloka'i, 'I would never have done *that*!'[24]

This is an example of self-cultivation taking someone far beyond their initial capability. The more Audrey sampled different forms of expedition, the more capable she became of becoming a solo explorer of the Alaskan coast in an inflatable kayak, something it is fair to assume no one else had ever done. By cultivating your existing interests, you can gradually develop yourself into something quite new. Audrey was always singular, always outdoors, always solitary. But her Moloka'i and Alaska expeditions were unpredictable.

For philosopher Agnes Callard, self-cultivating is about improving yourself based on existing preferences. You will self-cultivate a taste for vigorous exercise, such as by going to a gym class, if exercise is a pre-existing interest. Callard distinguishes this from wanting to be a different sort of person, a sort you might not know much about (the Vampire Problem). But we don't have to see this as an all-or-nothing transformation. As Callard says, 'It often happens that our point of view... changes little by little... we transition slowly.'[25] There will be a transformative moment but change is an ongoing process.

Francis Ngannou went through such a transformation through a terrible struggle to emigrate to Europe. He grew up in Cameroon, working in a sand mine from the age of ten. He walked two hours each way to go to school. At the age of twenty-two, he started training as a boxer. He saved money and left Cameroon aged twenty-six. Smugglers took him on a life-threatening journey to Algeria. He reached Morocco where he was injured badly, went to hospital, and was arrested for attempting to cross the border to Europe. After a year and three more failed attempts, he went to Tangiers to cross by water. This failed so many times he gained enough experience to captain a raft himself. It was his seventh attempt, a year after he left Cameroon, that worked. After two months' interrogation in Spain, he made it to France, where he found a gym and a trainer. He started training for mixed martial arts aged twenty-seven and is now heavyweight world champion.[26] Like many people in this book, once he had his focus, he was determined to change his life, in his case making life-risking decisions. It was the ongoing process of transformation – through terrible trials – that combined persistence and development into a transformation.

These major transitions can start with sampling. For example, say you enjoy reading mystery novels and you eventually decide to watch a film adaptation of one. This is self-cultivation – you are pursuing an existing interest but slightly expanding it. But it may spark an aspiration to be a serious movie buff. You will now have to choose to watch many movies, learn about the genres and history, see the classics, and so on. It takes a long time to become a serious movie buff. The important difference for Callard is that with aspiration you come to see the world in a new way.[27] We can see, though, that sampling the world and expanding our interests might prompt us to start on a much bigger sort of transformation.

That's exactly how Neil Frazer described Audrey. She had a transformative moment when she flew over Alaska. But that was part of a long and ongoing process of transition that dated back to the 1960s. She wasn't what Callard calls aspirational – she never set out to become this sort of explorer. Instead, she constantly self-cultivated, expanding her interests to a point where they had become something new and extraordinary. As her consciousness expanded, journey by journey, accident by accident, and her instincts were honed, she came to see the world in a new way. After the second Moloka'i trip, with the inflatable kayak, she decided that the 'tender power' of Moloka'i was more compelling than the bruises and cuts which were healing while she sat at her desk job: 'I had to go back again. To be that terrified of anything, that incompetent, survive by that small a margin – I'd better analyse, practice, return and do it right.'[28]

Like the fractal patterns we saw in Chapter 4, which get more complicated as they repeat, Audrey was developing into a more accomplished explorer, learning new limits, acquiring new habits and instincts. Her transition took place over many years, in all her preparation and practice as well as on the journeys. As she wrote, 'I now know what to do, having learned most of it the hard way.'[29] But the key turning point was her divorce. Audrey married John Sutherland after the Second World War. John was an adventurous person, too. He had learned to surf on a visit to Waikiki, Hawaii, in 1937–8 and before the war became a surfer in California, where the couple lived. He was then a coastguard, before becoming an officer in 1942. He also served in Korea from 1950 to 1954. The family moved from California to the Hawaiian island of O'ahu in 1952. John worked variously as a fisherman and a military marine engineer. In 1957, after a tempestuous marriage, he moved back to California. Audrey decided to stay in Hawaii with the children. John rarely paid maintenance and didn't see the children. Eventually, he acquired his Master's Unlimited Captain licence, allowing him to captain any vessel.[30] The year 1957 wasn't just when John left – it was the year Audrey looked down at Moloka'i and decided she had to go there.

Once the transition was reached, she then began developing into the woman who paddled thousands of miles in cold Alaskan waters, taking all the inefficient preparation of her earlier life and cultivating it into something entirely unexpected. As well as a swimmer and explorer, Audrey was an educator and had worked as an elementary school supply teacher when she first arrived in Hawaii. As a single mother Audrey became a swimming instructor. She progressed to vocational counselling after she completed her part-time master's degree. This counselling work made her realize that exploring Hawaii wasn't enough. 'Helping people plan what to do with their lives often led to wondering whether I knew what to do with my own,' she told the journalist Linda Daniel in 1988. The inconsistency between her life as an office worker while forever 'roaming off' in her imagination was part of what drove her to quit and set off for Alaska.[31]

As she became well known within the kayaking and exploration community, she started giving talks about her travels, instructing people in the use of inflatable kayaks. It was at one of these talks that Neil Frazer met Audrey in the late 1980s, 'in the days before sea-kayaking became popular'. These talks were not just informational: 'she was kind of an evangelist.' At the end of these lectures, she used to say, 'Close your eyes. Sit very quietly for a minute. Imagine that you were just given five million dollars. Now think what you would do if you had that five million dollars.' After a pause, she would say, 'I want you to open your eyes and think what is stopping you from doing those same things without the five million.'[32] This often got a laugh. But Audrey thought people should follow their dreams, not be held back by fear. At the end of one talk, when she asked what was holding people back, someone stood up and said he had a wife, children in college, and ageing parents. This or something like it will be many people's response. It is difficult to follow our dreams when we have bills to pay.

To Audrey Sutherland, the single mother who raised her children with little financial support from her absent husband, who often got home from work so late her children had to cook dinner, whose house was so remote that for several years it had no television signal, whose son remembers cycling two miles into town to get a loaf of bread, who had waited to go adventuring until her children were old enough and until she had the money to quit her job, and who had studied eight years part-time for a master's degree, this was not a persuasive objection.[33] She replied: 'Then you need to ask yourself: What part of my goal can I achieve now? What can I do now to achieve my goal later?'[34]

AUDREY SUTHERLAND: LIVE IMMEDIATELY

That's the same advice Chris Gardner gives people, and is the attitude he used to become a successful stockbroker:

> I was talking with a young man recently, and I told him you've got to ask yourself two questions. While you're brushing your teeth, ask yourself: If tomorrow morning you could be doing anything in the world, what would it be? Second, what did you do today to make that tomorrow possible?[35]

Audrey took this attitude right to the end of her life, as shown in a late profile written by Lorenn Walker, *Aging with Strength*.

At age eighty-one, Audrey's goals included studying biology and zoology, which she accomplished. She also wanted to finish her book about paddling Alaska. Ten years later, in 2012, her Alaska book *Paddling North* was published by the Patagonia Company... As to future goals, Audrey laughs saying, 'I'm 91 years old, I don't have a lot of plans, but I do wanna go back to Alaska.'[36]

Audrey was able to achieve what she did in her sixties, seventies and beyond because she was always learning *now* something that would enable her to achieve her goal *later*. As Audrey once told an interviewer, 'It isn't a question of can you or can't you, but of deciding what you really want to do, and then figuring how... and once you succeed, you know the meaning of joy.'[37] In Chapter 4, we saw the chaos theory of careers which takes account of the role of chance and the way small things can have big effects on the course of our life. Audrey's advice to work out what you can do now to achieve your goal later is exactly what you would expect someone to advise if they understood this theory. Here is the career development strategy developed by psychologist Robert Pryor that takes account of the chaos theory of careers:

1. Work out what really matters now and how work fits into that.

2. Keep the mind open to opportunities.

3. Generate and try several possibilities.

4. Expect that some of them will fail.

5. Make failure survivable.

6. Seek and examine feedback to learn what works and what does not.

7. Utilize what works and examine what has emerged.

8. Combine and add as seems likely to improve career prospects.

9. Iterate the process starting back at 1.[38]

This is exactly how Audrey worked. She was a career counsellor, and it's as if she either knew of this theory or had intuited it for herself. In this way, she worked through all the obstacles between her and Alaska.

Perhaps the most persistent problem she faced was fear. Her first solo trip was to a field eight miles away from her house, aged fourteen, after an argument with her mother. She slept in the field, terrified that the glowing eyes surrounding her were lions. She woke up and found herself in the middle of tame cattle. 'It often turns out that what we're afraid of are very ordinary things.'[39] She faced similar fears fifty years later as she headed to Alaska. To capsize in those cold waters could be fatal, if not properly managed. She had started managing her fear young, but was still doing so in the last third of her life. Before she left for Alaska, she took her kayak to the ocean by her house and purposely capsized it five times each side. When she did capsize in Alaska, she brought herself up by reflex. She felt fear, but fear didn't make her panic because she was prepared.[40] Through this practice of fear management, the teenager who slept among the cows would become the older woman photographing bears standing twenty feet away. 'There is only one fear,' she said, 'and that's the fear of the unknown.' She believed that the animals she met – including a wolf the size of a Great Dane – saw her as less of a threat because she was a woman. Writing in *Sea Kayaker* magazine, she joked about this, noting that although shark attacks were incredibly rare, 'it is worth noting that 90 per cent of shark attacks worldwide are on men, even when men and women are swimming in the water in the usual 60/40 ratio; this may help you in your choice of companion...'[41]

Practicality is the essence of Sutherland's explorations and self-development. The English professor Jim Kraus, a friend of the family who rented Audrey's annexe, remembered talking to her about other writers. Her judgement on Thoreau was immediate and uncompromising: 'namby pamby'.[42] (She said the same thing about the poet W. S. Merwin's work.) Audrey was committed to practicalities and facts, to being challenged. There is something romantic and literary about Thoreau's engagement with nature that is a complete contrast to Audrey's observant, immersive, scientific approach. Audrey knew what plants she could eat, she knew the natural history of the areas she explored, she read guide books and ecology books. She used to recommend Euell Gibbons's *Beachcomber's Handbook*. Her closest precursor in writing style was the anthropologist Loren Eiseley, whom her son Jock remembers as one of her favourite authors.[43] Sutherland and Eiseley share a lapidary style, a straightforward tone and a naturalist's attitude. Nature is not an escape or a holiday. It was a challenge, to be respected and engaged with realistically.

Another of her models was Scottish-born American environmentalist John Muir.[44] Like Muir, Audrey is interested in the topographical, geological, and botanical details of the places she explores. Like Muir, and Eiseley, Audrey integrates herself and her anecdotes into the narrative, but she retains her purpose, which is to show you how she conducted her exploration, not a baring of her soul, or a philosophical reaction against society. She was concerned about consideration and environmentalism but was not an activist writer. Ultimately, her books are accounts of her journeys, based closely on her diaries, aimed at showing other people how they too might go on such journeys, albeit not perhaps exactly of the sort Audrey did. Jim Kraus remembered Audrey writing *Paddling North* based on the journals she kept while she travelled, and worrying that, as she compiled her years of adventuring into a narrative spanning only two years, she would slip from the factual to the fictional.[45] This is a fairly normal thing for memoir writers to do, to give an accurate impression rather than to recount something exactly as it happened. But the risk of not being accurate troubled Audrey. As in her life, she was a teacher in her writing, and wanted to give a faithful and useful account of herself.

'All my life,' wrote Muir at the start of his memoir *The Story of My Boyhood and Youth*, 'I've been growing fonder and fonder of wild places and wild creatures.'[46] The same was true of Audrey – and it was the lifetime's worth of experience of the wild places that enabled her to become who she did. Neil Frazer described the way Audrey's experiences accumulated, developing her expanded consciousness, so that she knew what to do by instinct. He described that as a sort of wisdom. Her son Jock talked about her faith in the ways events would turn out, her sense of some guiding spirit that kept her safe when the tide was against her. 'She wasn't mystical. But things could happen out of nowhere to help you out.' Michael Molloy, Hawaii University professor of philosophy, described *Paddling My Own Canoe* as presenting a 'spirituality akin to Zen'.[47] In more day-to-day terms, Audrey is regularly quoted in inspiration books. Richard McMahon called *Paddling My Own Canoe* 'much more than an adventure tale, the book is a life statement'.[48] She is often understood as a spiritual, philosophical, Zen-like, singular individual.

Her approach to personal development, though, is closer to Stoicism. All of the mystical identities ascribed to Audrey forget that she was not removed from the action of the world, she had not tamed her instincts, she was not on a higher plane. She was very much of the world, a buccaneering figure, whose instincts were honed to help her manage big waves and stray bears. She was immersed in the harsh and dangerous side of nature, as well as in its contemplative and calm aspects. Fire, as Seneca said, is the test of gold.

Audrey seems to have believed in the Stoic ideal that you cannot control the world but you can control yourself. When her children felt depressed, she told them to list the things they knew how to do well, a typically Stoic injunction to focus rationally on what you can control.[49] By relying on her instincts in bear encounters, she accepted what was happening and showed herself unthreatening and unafraid to the animal. She talks frequently throughout her books about the different people in her mind, the negative and the positive voices. In focusing on choosing to listen to the positive, practical voice, Audrey was being Stoic. She was focused on the central Stoic virtue of simplicity. Her life was pared down. She did carpentry on her house, which was a converted army barrack. Her camping gear was scoured from second-hand shops. In an interview with Paul Theroux, she said she lived on about $3 a day during her trips to Alaska.[50] British adventurer Alastair Humphreys cites this quote from Audrey as one of his favourites: 'I didn't need to get away. I needed to get TO. To simplicity.'[51] The Roman Stoic emperor Marcus Aurelius could have said that. Above all, she got, through her expanded consciousness, to be in tune with nature.

Audrey also used Stoic techniques. She broke down her fears into components to help her overcome them, such as practising capsizing. As Marcus Aurelius said, 'Your responsibilities can be broken down into individual parts... concentrate on those, and finish the job methodically.'[52] This is how her adventuring in Alaska started:

> I was working at the army as a career counselor and my territory was Hawai'i, Samoa, the Philippines, and Alaska, and I talked to every 10th grader in all of those places. So I was very familiar with Alaska and I saw it had a lot of potential for paddling. I had found a place that didn't have a lot of people and I went there and learned the basic skills to survive in that place.[53]

Perhaps her most famous quotation is one that says the only real security is the 'skill and humour and courage within, the ability to build your own fire and find your own peace'. Or as another ancient Roman Stoic, Seneca, put it, 'The greatest blessings of mankind are within us and within our reach.' The Stoics advise that we anticipate our troubles – think through all the bad things that might befall you – and, by doing so, prepare yourself against fate. This keeps you calm in the face of adversity. 'I go through all the what ifs each day before launching,' Audrey said, 'keep track of the wind and the tide.'[54]

When she looked in the mirror and said, 'Getting older, aren't you lady? Better do the physical things now. You can work at a desk later,'[55] Audrey was being Stoic. Fate is at your elbow, said Marcus Aurelius. Death overshadows you. 'While you're alive and able – be good.'[56] She remained fit all her life, but it was her mental attitude that enabled this moment of change. 'Sometimes it is the body which is the first to surrender to old age,' warned Michel de Montaigne, 'sometimes the soul.'[57] Audrey did not surrender in body or soul. She inspired herself to go to Alaska with Stoic ideas. Think, too, of the advice Audrey gave to the man with the wife, children and parents, about how to pursue his goals, to whom she said, 'Ask yourself: What part of my goal can I achieve now?' How close that is to what Seneca says in *On the Shortness of Life*: 'What are you looking at? To what goal are you straining? The whole future lies in uncertainty: live immediately.'[58] It is by breaking a problem down into its parts, and working on them as we can, that we begin to live immediately.

That is one way to become a late bloomer. It is how Audrey Sutherland cultivated herself, stoically transitioning into the explorer she became. By going simple, going solo, going now. Living immediately.

10
The more you do, the more you succeed

Like Samuel Johnson, Audrey Sutherland is a study in the benefit of sticking power. Neither of them believed that they had to slow down just because they were ageing. They got great benefit from carrying on. The abilities they cultivated throughout their lives carried on being refined as they worked into old age. This chapter is about the way that our mental powers decline as we age, and the fact that the more work we produce, the more likely we are to be successful. Rather than worrying that we face an inevitable decline, we should aim to keep working for as long as we can. There is productive benefit in this persistence.

Perhaps the biggest obstacle to identifying late-blooming talent is that we expect less from people as they age. We joke that by middle age our backs ache, our memories are worse, and we don't understand how to use technology our children can pick up intuitively. You can't teach an old dog new tricks. In 2019, Arthur C. Brooks wrote an *Atlantic* column about this called 'Your Professional Decline is Coming (Much) Sooner Than You Think'. In 2022, he wrote a book about this inevitable decline.[1] Brooks takes an optimistic view that we can change our careers, but he is too determinist about cognitive decline. It is not inevitable that you will be less creative, capable, or competent at seventy than you were at seventeen.

There are two sorts of intelligence: fluid and crystallized. Fluid intelligence is your ability to take in new information and understand it and manipulate it. It is your think-on-your-feet intelligence. Crystallized intelligence is your stock of knowledge, such as your vocabulary. It is your acquired and learned intelligence. Scientific work has shown that, while fluid intelligence declines relatively young, crystallized intelligence continues to strengthen until much later in our lives. This is why people often complain as they age about their memory or their thinking speed getting worse. Unlike verbal skills and general knowledge, processing speed, reasoning, spatial ability and some aspects of memory decline as we age. This chapter is about the fact that these average changes conceal lots of individual differences.

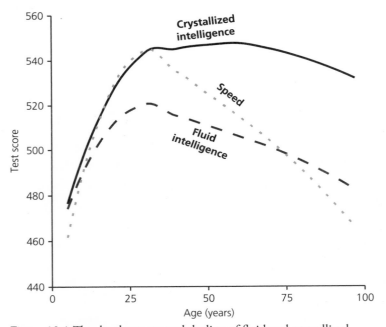

Figure 10.1 The development and decline of fluid and crystallized intelligence
Source: Stuart Ritchie, *Intelligence: All That Matters* (John Murray Learning, 2015)

Looking at the graph in Figure 10.1, you might be tempted to conclude that you can't teach an old dog new tricks after all. Brooks's advice is to change into a career that requires less fluid intelligence and more crystallized intelligence. But the distinction between fluid and crystallized intelligence (the difference is between dealing with novel problems versus being expert in something) is blunt. Can we really put intelligence onto a simple graph with three lines like that? There is more to intelligence than this simple division – and more variation among individuals than this chart can tell us.

The neurologist George Bartzokis researched the changing structure of the brain, focusing specifically on myelin, the material that sheathes our nerves. As we age, we acquire more myelin in our frontal and temporal lobes, peaking around age fifty. These lobes are where functions like memory, decision-making, processing language and emotion occur. The extension of these lobes means that, although we have less processing speed, and less ability to hold information in our memory, we are better able to think with what we do have. 'In midlife,' Bartzokis told *Time* magazine, 'you're beginning to maximize the ability to use the entirety of the information in your brain on an everyday, ongoing, second-to-second basis. Biologically, that's what wisdom is.'[2] This use of information is vital. Moments of insight – when we add the final piece to a puzzle or suddenly see connections between information and ideas – come about in various ways as we connect disparate bits of information in our minds.

Think of this as the linking up of different clusters of knowledge. The networks of connections between all the information in our minds are not uniform: there are clusters and hubs of information which are closely connected to each other but not well connected to other clusters. Once you link up one cluster of knowledge with another, moments of insight occur – but it often requires a long series of connections through our mental networks to make such links. The internet is similar. There are clusters of websites that are connected to each other: clusters of economics blogs, fashion sites, and market commentary sites all have strong sets of connections within their area, but they are not as well connected between clusters. Each cluster has hub sites – websites that are much, much more connected to other sites than the average. Once those hubs connect to each other, the clusters become more closely aligned and it is easier for the knowledge of fashion markets to be accessed by economics bloggers.

Your brain is analogous. The more distantly related the different pieces of information are, the less connected they will be in your brain. Everything you know about your work as an accountant sits in one cluster and everything you know about cartoons or kayaking sits in another cluster. Linking the two clusters up isn't easy or intuitive, just as linking economics blogs and kitchenware websites isn't so simple. Once you linked up different networks of knowledge, then, as the academic Melissa Schilling (who came up with the idea of knowledge networks) says, 'Relationships that had never been previously considered may suddenly seem obvious.'

These sorts of connections are at the heart of creative insight and rely on crystallized intelligence as much as fluid intelligence. The bigger your reservoir of knowledge, the more benefit you get from linking up different clusters of information. Linking two relatively small clusters of information is less likely to lead to creative insights than linking two large clusters of information.[3] Once you find some link between your work cluster and your hobby cluster, the more you know in each subject the more links you are able to make. Being a deep expert in one area can limit your insights and creativity, leading to incremental understanding. Making connections between different areas of knowledge is another way of making breakthroughs.

The more you prompt yourself to explore your different areas of expertise the more likely you are to chance upon some new discovery. It was by constant drawing with minor variations that artists like

Leonardo da Vinci and Michelangelo made their insights: in this way Michelangelo brought his insights from drawing nudes into designing architecture. Musician Brian Eno and artist Peter Schmidt devised a set of cards called Oblique Strategies that encourage such connections. When you reach a creative block you draw a card which will have instructions like 'Do something boring' or 'Emphasize repetitions' or 'Reverse' or 'Use fewer notes' or 'Use an old idea' or 'Make a sudden, destructive unpredictable action; incorporate'. These cards stimulate unexpected connections and ideas. You do not need to have the mental processing speed of a teenager to benefit from them.

Making previously unseen connections between your knowledge clusters can be worth much more than having high processing speed or exceptional memory. What matters is how you use your intelligence, not your level of raw horsepower. Brooks's advice might be useful for many people – and might trigger a period of late blooming – but we should be wary of the idea of an inevitable decline in our mental ability.

On 1 June 1932, almost every schoolchild born in 1921 and attending school in Scotland took the same intelligence test. This was the Moray House Test No. 12, similar to a school-entrance exam that measures IQ. Split roughly equally between boys and girls, 87,408 children took the test. The same thing was done in 1947, with another 70,805 children born in 1936. Ian Deary, and a group of intelligence researchers, contacted hundreds of these people many years later and gave them the same test they had taken at about age eleven. This allowed Deary and his colleagues to see what happens to intelligence over seventy years. The results are shown in Figure 10.2.

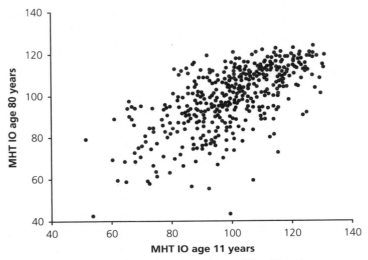

Figure 10.2 IQ scores from the Moray House Test No. 12
Source: Ian Deary et al., 'The Impact of Childhood Intelligence on Later Life: Following Up the Scottish Mental Surveys of 1932 and 1947', *Journal of Personality and Social Psychology* 86:1 (2004), pp. 130–47, DOI:10.1037/0022-3514.86.1.130

Deary and his colleagues were not looking at whether people's scores were higher in childhood or older age. Instead, they were interested in whether people retained their relative position in the group across many decades. That is, were the high scorers in childhood also high scorers in older age, and were the modest scorers still towards the middle or lower end when they were older?

To do this, they first took the raw scores at each age and gave them a standard average of 100. They then looked at the way people scored in childhood and again in old age. Those who are close to the diagonal line in the diagram did not change their relative position. Those who are above that line did better in old age, and those who are below that line did better in childhood. The important overall finding is that there is a lot of variation.

Look at the horizontal axis. This is the IQ as measured at age eleven (standardized to be a mean of 100 at that age). From 100, which is the average IQ, look up the graph and you will see that people who scored an IQ of 100 at age eleven were scoring between 40 and 120 when they were aged eighty. Although there is a general trend for people's IQ to be approximately the same at the age of eighty as it was at the age of eleven, this is by no means a sure thing. The average conceals a lot of variation.

You can read these results in different ways. Perhaps some people had a bad day when they took one of the tests. Perhaps the tests are not perfectly reliable. Perhaps the results would change with a bigger sample. But we know that these tests are a reasonably accurate way of measuring your ability to solve mental problems and that this correlates reasonably well with success. It is easy to overstate the importance of intelligence to career and life success, but it is well established that levels of education and income are correlated with intelligence.[4]

What's really interesting is how to explain the variation between people's scores age eleven and eighty. Is this variation caused by genetics or environment? Deary says: 'About half the differences in people's intelligence test scores in older age are not accounted for by childhood intelligence.'[5] That means that half of the changes in the scores (when people's scores improve or get worse over time) can be explained by their childhood intelligence. The other half has to be explained by other factors. (Other studies have found that cognitive changes in your seventies are not related to early-life cognitive ability.)[6]

Deary and his team were especially interested in the 'risk' factors for falling below the line across the life course, and the 'protective' factors that might be associated with relative improvement. Think of the people who scored an average of 100 in childhood but then scored higher than that in old age (i.e. people above the diagonal line) – was it something they did that improved their intelligence, or was it something out of their control?

It may be that we can prevent cognitive decline as we age through the right activities – or even improve our intelligence. Deary and his co-authors have described this as a question of 'marginal gains not a magic bullet'. No one thing has a large association with people's differences in cognitive ageing. And this is still not a well-understood area. As one group of researchers recently said, 'The evidence is patchy and often classed as low to moderate quality.'[7]

Being in a more stimulating intellectual environment, or doing stimulating, complicated activities, seems to be correlated with preserving cognitive ability, but the causation isn't clear. Perhaps people who retain their cognitive function are more likely to have or choose intellectually stimulating jobs and hobbies. Exercise is associated with better mental processing speed and general cognitive ability. Good diet is thought to be beneficial but it has a small effect and the results are uncertain.[8] But nothing on its own seems to explain much of the differences. For example, smoking accounts for only 1 per cent of the variance of cognitive decline.[9]

There are many recommendations for maintaining brain function, such as brain training exercises and games, but the evidence here is mixed. Using an app that promises to prevent cognitive decline is not reliable. There is a study that suggests playing games like chess or completing crosswords can be beneficial, but the evidence is limited.[10] Some evidence shows that the more years of education you receive, the better cognitive function you develop when you are young. This can prevent or delay some forms of decline like dementia through the advantage of starting with better cognitive function.[11] It is difficult to work out the causation of these interventions. Perhaps there are underlying neurological reasons why people with delayed cognitive decline exercise more or smoke less.

The study of SuperAgers – people in their eighties with the cognitive function of someone twenty years younger – shows that they moderately indulge in alcohol, take regular exercise, stay mentally active, and maintain good social relationships. SuperAgers seem to lose brain matter at a slower rate than other people, which accounts for their lack of cognitive decline. Like the other studies, however, it is difficult to know how the causation works. While we can't be quite sure what will prevent cognitive decline in any given individual, mostly, this science reflects common sense: healthy body, healthy mind. A recent review of this research found that what makes the most difference is when several factors are combined: sleeping well and exercising and not smoking and having a healthy diet.[12] Most factors are important cumulatively – there are beneficial effects of not drinking over long time periods, for example.[13]

What if we could change our attitude and, in so doing, change our lives? When the economist Steven Levitt ran a large online experiment to have people make major life decisions – about their jobs and mortgages and love lives – based on a coin toss, the ones who came up heads for change tended to be happier. Change may be daunting but it is good. We need more of it. If we expect more of ourselves, who knows what we might be able to achieve...[14]

Studies also show different cognitive peaks at different ages for different abilities. Raw speed in processing information – how quickly you can understand new things – appears to peak around age eighteen or nineteen. The ability to recognize faces improves until our early 30s, as does visual short-term memory. But our ability to evaluate other people's emotional states peaks in our forties or fifties. Vocabulary can peak as late as our sixties or seventies. And contrary to popular belief, the potential for high-functioning brain activity peaks in our fifties but remains high until our nineties.[15]

A recent study that tested different aspects of short- and long-term memory in people of all ages from sixteen to eighty-nine should make us doubt the simple cut off point for the decline of fluid intelligence. The tests included a wide range of tasks such as asking for definitions of words and general knowledge questions, arithmetic problems and comparison questions (e.g. how are forks and spoons alike), tapping a set of cubes in the reverse order that the experimenter tapped them in, finding the missing parts of pictures, copying pictures of shape patterns with blocks, looking at faces for two seconds and seeing if you could then tell them apart from new faces, looking at family pictures and trying to recall them, and retelling a story you have just heard. This testing supports the fluid–crystallized knowledge distinction. The vocabulary, information, comprehension, arithmetic, and similarities tasks peaked at significantly later ages than nearly every other task. That is, when you had to know something to pass the test, you did better older. Figure 10.3 shows the way that different tasks peak at different ages, on average.

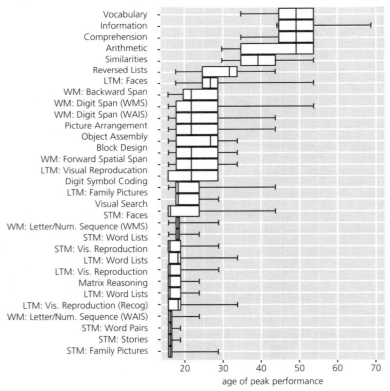

Figure 10.3 Age of peak performance for different tasks
Source: Joshua K. Hartshorne and Laura T. Germine, 'When Does Cognitive Functioning Peak? The Asynchronous Rise and Fall of Different Cognitive Abilities across the Life Span', *Psychological Science* 26:4 (2015), pp. 433–43, https://doi.org/10.1177/0956797614567339 [accessed 13 September 2023].

You can see that the fluid intelligence tasks of seeing a family picture and recalling the people and activities happening in the picture are at the bottom – the peak age for these is your teens and twenties – whereas, at the top, your vocabulary and general knowledge peak in your fifties and sixties, perhaps beyond. However, not all of the results came out on this simple fluid–early, crystallized–late dichotomy.

So the researchers ran large sample online tests of three tasks. They tested processing speed by giving you a symbol for each number between 1 and 3 and then showing you the numbers and having you match them to the symbol as fast as possible. They also tested visual and verbal working memory by showing a picture of an unfamiliar shape. Once the unfamiliar shape was taken away, another picture of a shape was shown and you had to say whether it was the same or not. Verbal working memory was tested by giving a list of numbers and asking you to recite it. There was also a vocabulary test. Finally, pictures of people's eyes were shown and you had to identify the emotion that person was feeling, based on seeing only that part of their face.

What this showed is that processing speed (matching numbers and symbols) peaks much earlier than working memory (unfamiliar shapes and reciting lists of numbers). These are both aspects of fluid intelligence, but they peak at different times. The idea that fluid intelligence is one thing and declines early isn't quite right. There are many aspects to intelligence and they peak at different ages throughout our lives. The authors of the study say: 'Not only is there no age at which humans are performing at peak at all cognitive tasks, there may not be an age at which humans are at peak on *most* cognitive tasks.'[16]

A recent study in *Nature Human Behaviour* shows that mental speed slows down not in our thirties, as previously thought, but in our sixties. The authors of this study show that sample sizes in previous work were often small. They used much larger data sets and looked at adults of all ages, rather than previous studies which compared young adults with older adults.[17] This study's most interesting finding was that when we make complex decisions, our caution about making decisions starts to increase in our early twenties. Figure 10.4 shows the way we become increasingly cautious as we age.

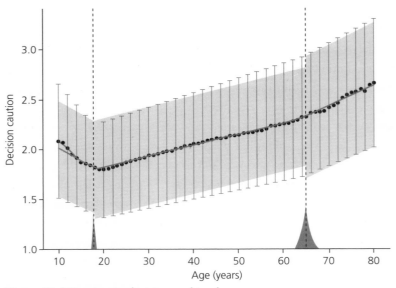

Figure 10.4 Caution in decision-making by age
Source: Mischa von Krause, Stefan T. Radev and Andreas Voss, 'Mental Speed is High until Age 60 as Revealed by Analysis of over a Million Participants', *Nature Human Behaviour* 6 (May 2022), pp. 700–8.

This study uses different sorts of tasks to test cognition from the other research surveyed here. It's not yet clear whether this will change intelligence researchers' view of the way mental speed changes as we age: the bulk of the evidence disagrees with this finding. What is true is that it is worth investigating further when and how we become slower at making decisions, whether it is mental speed or caution that slows us down, and whether our rising caution can be changed.

Of course, caution has many advantages – many people make reckless decisions when they are young. But caution can be limiting. One theory as to why people produce less academic and scientific research as they age is simply that they are more likely to dismiss new ideas: they know too much to have the confidence to just jump into something new. Many late bloomers reach a point of desperation when they finally do something they have wanted to do for a long time but felt unable to. Others feel freed by changing life circumstances. Being a little bit reckless can be a good thing.

There is also the question of what counts as intelligence. IQ is important. It is a strong predictor of career success. But it is not the only thing that matters. There is no IQ test for sociability, for example, but humans evolved larger brains with more cognitive capacity to deal with complex social relationships.[18] It is still true that people who are good at managing complex social relationships get a premium in the labour market: it is an essential marker of the best salespeople and leaders that they are able to carefully and insightfully manage the complexity of many social connections. This doesn't mean those people aren't smart – but IQ alone isn't enough. There are mental abilities involved in sociability that are also important but much less measurable. As people age, they increasingly value the emotions they experience in social relationships, and the stronger the network they belong to, the less cognitive decline they demonstrate. Volunteering, for example, is more cognitively exerting than solo activity. As people age they become more positive about their memories, perhaps more selective, partly in response to their awareness that their time left in life is getting shorter. From experience comes the ability to take a better perspective, realize that time is short, and focus on the more meaningful aspects of life.[19] Many older people, of course, experience negative emotions, especially those who were emotionally unstable earlier in life. But there can be advantages to our changing cognitive functions. Studies of forager-horticulturalist people suggest that as people age and become less able to do physical work, they specialize instead in the oral culture of telling stories. This is a way of preserving knowledge through the generations, especially between grandparents and grandchildren. This demonstrates the growing role of crystallized intelligence as we age and the way that adapting our abilities to our circumstances can matter as much as how smart we are.[20] The idea that older people are better able to use their experience to adapt to the world is also seen in a study that suggests people are better at conflict resolution when they are older.[21]

Intelligence is only one part of success. Mental speed has a central role in your ability to learn and develop. But cognitive capacity and practice are not enough. Several personality factors are necessary too, such as motivation, perseverance, effort, curiosity and openness. Having a strong working memory helps you sight-read music, for example. But without those other factors, you won't end up actually being good at sight-reading music. You do not have a cognitive destiny. The interaction of circumstances and personality factors makes a difference. As psychologist Wendy Johnson says, 'Every person has some distribution of possible expressions of intelligence and ability in every context.' [22] We all know the idea that some people do and don't live up to their potential. Cognitive decline is only one piece of that puzzle.

My point here is that graphs of average decline should not be taken in isolation and may not apply to you. There are other reasons to place less importance on pure intelligence. It is not always the case that high-ability people always grow up to achieve eminence – sometimes they lack the requisite personality factors. And unusual development histories can be important to create high-accomplishment people. Perhaps being weird is more significant than being smart when it comes to talent.[23]

Rather than accepting the blanket statement that as we age we go through cognitive decline, we should see themselves as adaptable. Changing focus, environment, collaborators, or what we work on can often make a significant difference, irrespective of our mental powers. Achievement isn't reliant just on our mental ability staying high but on whether we choose to keep using and adapting the capacity we have.

According to the 'constant probability of success' theory, the more attempts we make at something – whether it is writing scientific papers or composing music – the more chances we have of succeeding, irrespective of how old we are, or where we are in our career. People who keep trying have more successes (as well as more failures) than people who stop. This has been detailed and described for decades by psychologists like Dean Keith Simonton. British economist Ronald Coase is a good example. Economists often do their most important work fairly young, but Coase's two critical papers – 'The Nature of the Firm' and 'The Problem of Social Cost' – were published when he was twenty-seven and fifty years old respectively. They were both revolutionary and contributed to Coase's Nobel Memorial Prize in Economic Sciences in 1991. They underpin the Coase theorem, an important part of modern microeconomic theory about the nature of property rights. The essential factor in his success was that he didn't stop working just because he had already been successful. As Keith Sawyer says, 'The best predictor of exceptional creativity is *productivity*. It's lots of hard work.'[24]

The 'constant probability of success' theory says that the more attempts you make to hit a target, the more bullseyes you actually will make. Psychology has another well-known rule about how talent develops, popularized by Malcolm Gladwell as the 'ten thousand hour rule'. This is the idea that it takes a decade of deliberate practice to achieve mastery in a given discipline. This decade is enough time to acquire the thousands of chunks of knowledge needed to excel. The chunks might be chess patterns, musical scores, business ideas, writing techniques and so on.

The ten-year rule is too specific. Dean Keith Simonton studied 120 composers, covering a huge number of pieces in the classical repertoire. It took them anything from two to forty-two years from the start of practice to the creation of a masterpiece. The psychologist whose work Gladwell was drawing on, Anders Ericsson, has said that the pianists who win international piano competitions are likely to have spent 20,000 to 25,000 hours in practice whereas one international champion at memorizing strings of numbers took only two hundred hours of practice.[25] When the variation is that big, this seems less like a specific rule and more like a reinforcement of the basic idea that the more you do, the more chance you have of succeeding. It takes a lot of practice, deliberate and otherwise, to become successful.

What matters in this rule is the accumulated expertise, not the starting point. Mozart, for example, was largely a prodigy because he started so young. He completed his decade's practice before most people even begin theirs. He started composing aged six; twelve years later he composed his first breakthrough piece, the Piano Concerto No. 9 in E-flat major, K. 271. His earlier compositions are not as regularly recorded.[26] Indeed, the pianist Víkingur Ólafsson described Mozart as a late bloomer, during a 2022 concert.[27] Another example of this phenomenon is English philosopher John Stuart Mill, who learned ancient languages from the age of three. No wonder he was precocious.

The fact that someone starts later doesn't preclude them from succeeding later. Mozart started as a child, but others can discover their talent later on. Even though Mozart was born with rare gifts, he still had to graft to realize his talents. It doesn't matter *when* you start as much as it matters that you *do* start – and then keep going. As the nun and art teacher Corita Kent said, 'The only rule is work. If you work it will lead to something. It's the people who do all of the work all the time who eventually catch on to things.'

There's also reason to believe that deliberate practice is only useful in some disciplines. A 2014 meta-study found that 'deliberate practice explained 26 per cent of the variance in performance for games, 21 per cent for music, 18 per cent for sports, 4 per cent for education, and less than 1 per cent for professions'.[28] In high-certainty activities, like chess, deliberate practice to accumulate expertise works well. In environments and jobs where you have to deal with uncertainty, deliberate practice can be less useful. There is even a Yale study that shows that people with expertise are often surprised when faced with comprehensive explanations that show the limitations in their understanding. 'While expertise can sometimes lead to accurate self-knowledge, it can also create illusions of competence.'[29] It might seem pedantic to distinguish between deliberate practice and lifelong learning, but that's the distinction between learning to do something exact and learning to adapt to new things. For late bloomers, the latter option will often be the more important. As Dean Keith Simonton said, Nobel laureates in science and literature don't practise in the same way that pianists and golfers do.[30]

We all want rules to follow, formulas for success. But these guidelines seem too specific to be universally applicable. Once we start looking closely, they are less objective than they seem. The ten-year rule, deliberate practice, and the constant probability of success theory are all getting at the same general point: one of the key ingredients to success is to sit down and do the work. It doesn't matter when you start, what matters is what you do. The more time you put in, the more chances you have of doing something that works. That might be the result of practice, or luck, or determination, or talent, or some combination of all of them. Trying to establish a firm rule from this is a fool's errand. There is so much variation. A recent sociological study found that, as authors get older, their work changes less. The topics of their books become more similar with age; the rate of change slows down significantly throughout an author's thirties.[31] But the researchers also found huge variation within those results. Plenty of authors keep changing, and changing durably, into old age.[32]

This is the case with many of the findings discussed in this book: whatever the headline rule, there is a tremendous amount of variation. We should think of these 'rules' as trends or tendencies. People are unique, they work on individual projects, with specific aims, and in particular environments, each with their own circumstances. For chess, a highly specific activity, we can say it takes an average of 12,000 hours of practice to become a grandmaster, so long as you start young.[33] But for most people, and most sorts of activity, that level of specificity is unhelpful. People are too complicated.

According to a recent study of scientific careers, scientists tend to do their most significant work young because that is when they are most productive. Once scientists have prestige and tenure, they produce less. The ones who keep going have a better chance of doing impactful work. Nobel prizes are awarded for work done at all ages.[34] John B. Fenn, for example, won the Nobel Prize in Chemistry in 2002 for a paper published in 1991, after he had been forcibly retired from Yale. This is an example of what the authors of the study call the 'random impact rule'. Like the 'constant probability of success' rule it says that your best work can come anywhere in your career – early, middle, or late.

The people who keep trying to hit the target are more likely to do so. The big difference between the old and the young is that fewer people keep trying as they age. We saw earlier that perseverance alone is not enough: luck is also essential. According to this study, another group of attributes is necessary. As well as perseverance and luck, you need something called the Q factor.

The Q factor is defined as the ability of a scientist to take advantage of available knowledge in a way that improves or decreases the potential impact of their research paper. This means that as well as being able to do the maths, scientists need to be able to bring other relevant skills to bear on the problem. Having an idea isn't enough. Being right isn't enough. To succeed, you need to be good at getting your idea noticed. Q is unique to each scientist: it's about getting the right fit between the scientist and the project. Q can cover communication skills, education, talent, likeability, motivation, openness to ideas, collaboration skills and more. The *New York Times* described Q as 'an ability to make the most of the work at hand: to find some relevance in a humdrum experiment, and to make an elegant idea glow'.[35] What these researchers call the Q factor we might otherwise call the X factor – the hard-to-define combination of personal and soft skills that is crucial to success and changes for every project and person.

There is a great deal of difference between a scientist who writes in a readable style, knows how to give a talk you will remember, and can express their findings in quotable phrases and pithy headlines and one who cannot do those things. Think of the difference, too, that can be made by someone who can network effectively in a funding system, motivate a team of researchers, and allow the best ideas to come from anywhere in a project team. Finally, think of the difference between two brilliantly clever people one of whom is motivated by their work, one of whom is not. The Q factor makes predicting hidden talent quite complicated. Q is specific to a person *and* their specialism. Often, people are able to transfer from one sort of job more easily than we think. But not everyone will be able to transfer their Q factor. You can be brilliant at navigating the world of literary journalism and find yourself at a loss to replicate that success when you change to teaching in a comprehensive school. Samuel Johnson might not have found his erratic habits so conducive to life as a clerk or an academic.

Importantly, the Q factor, lifelong persistence and luck are all independent of one another. Highly productive scientists who lack Q will not be as successful as people with both. And, of course, anyone can be unlucky. For the right person on the right projects, persistence pays off, with some luck.[36] And we saw before that, by moving people to new places, we can change their luck quite significantly.

It is possible that taking account of the average age of success in different fields would explain these results. For example, Nobel prizes are awarded younger in quantum mechanics than in medicine. The researchers would say that's because scientists are often more productive earlier in life and so they try harder. As they age, this effort recedes. But it may be the case that what looks like an equal chance of success across your career is just an average of different ages of success across different disciplines. We will see in the next section that the average age of a Nobel prize winner changes more based on the period of time than the field of work. It may be the case that, while there are differences in the average age of Nobel winners, it is still possible to succeed at all ages. You don't have to win a prize to have an impact.[37]

The 'equal-odds rule' might help us explain this. This is the idea that each work a scientist or artist produces has the same statistical chance of being great as any other work. This does not mean every year of work has the same degree of quality. Other things get in the way. You can get your successes and failures in clumps, as many people do. But what the rule does say is that you will do your most significant work in the period when you do your most work.[38] Smash hits don't come out of nowhere. According to the equal-odds rule, it is no surprise that *Hamlet* – Shakespeare's most important play – was produced in the middle of the busiest and most successful stretch of his career. In a three or four-year window, he wrote *Henry V, Julius Caesar, As You Like It, Hamlet* and *Twelfth Night*. The equal-odds rule helps explain why the chaos theory of careers we saw in Chapter 4 is so important. Chaos and failure are not problems to avoid, but important and unavoidable parts of any career. Episodes of chaos and failure are part of taking many chances at success.

But we must remember that this is a statistical average, and we have seen earlier that there is significant individual variation in averages.

We have seen the huge number of factors that go into making perseverance effective. This is not going to be accurately represented in a single rule or principle. All of the factors we have studied – networks and influence, attitude and cognitive ability, deliberately slow learning, and changing circumstances – have to be looked at alongside average age of success in a field, Q factor, luck, persistence, the amount of practice someone has done, their level of mental ability and their life experiences. What would cause one person to give up won't make much difference to another. One woman's moment of inspiration is mere background to another. What is vitally important to one life often takes place, as W. H. Auden said, 'while someone else is eating, or opening a window, or just walking dully along'.

•••

Science and maths are fields where youth is thought to be better at making breakthroughs than age. Einstein famously said, 'A person who has not made his great contribution to science before the age of thirty will never do so.' The mathematician G. H. Hardy's famous quotation that maths is 'a young man's game' gets repeated all the time. These views are not as mainstream as they once were, but are not uncommon. Many sciences are supposed to require the agility of a younger mind. But youth has less inherent advantage than it seems. Many other conditions are relevant. Depending on the time you live, your culture, the problems you work on, and, perhaps most importantly, your own attitude, you can flourish at many ages and stages of life.

Everyone knows Einstein was a young prodigy. We forget that Copernicus didn't complete his theory of planetary motion until he was sixty. William Herschel was an organist; astronomy was his hobby. He never went to university. He discovered Uranus and was given a pension by George III. This meant he could quit music and do astronomy full time. He was forty-three. It is not only the precocious young who make great scientific discoveries.

The period a scientist lives in can affect when they do their best work more so than the field they work in. Before 1905, 69 per cent of chemists, 63 per cent of medical scientists and 60 per cent of physicists did their Nobel prize-winning work before age forty. Something like 20 per cent of their prize-winning work was done before age thirty. By the end of the twentieth century, almost no prize-winning work was done before the age of thirty. And in physics, great achievements before the age of forty happen about one-third as often as they did a century earlier. The average age for doing prize-winning work increased by seven years for medicine laureates, ten years in chemistry, and thirteen years in physics. Most strikingly, at the start of the twentieth century, 66 per cent of prize-winning work in chemistry was done by age forty. By the end of the century, that number was close to zero.[39]

Earlier in the century, more work was theoretical and so large imaginative breakthroughs could be made early in people's careers. Later in the century, the work was more empirical, involving more data collection and analysis, which inevitably attracts a different temperament and intellectual style.[40] Scientists also graduated at older ages, having spent more time in graduate school as the accumulated burden of knowledge required more and more study before they could start being innovative. This is not yet properly understood.

One reason why success happened later on in scientists' careers throughout the twentieth century may be the 'burden of knowledge'. As more breakthroughs were made, there was more to learn before an individual could become innovative. Studies have found that the age when a mathematician gets their first solo-authored article in a top journal went from thirty to thirty-five between 1950 and 2013. The same thing happened to economists between 1970 and 2014. Studies have also shown that as well as Nobel prize winners getting older, they are spending an additional four years in education. One way scientists are getting round this 'burden of knowledge' problem is by working in teams much more often than they did in the past. However, this also makes them more specialized.[41]

The authors of a study at Kellogg School of Management say that the professionalization of science during the Enlightenment may have reshaped careers. The fact that you need a PhD and you have to submit to peer review and jump through certain institutional hoops to get tenure all affect at what age innovations happen. Institutions can speed up careers, of course. Copernicus managed a cathedral before he was a scientist; if he had been able to join a modern PhD programme aged twenty-one, he might have had his breakthrough sooner. Who knows? But the more requirements that are piled up at the start of a career, the longer it takes for someone to be ready to make a creative contribution.

If there are many more difficult foundational concepts required to become a qualified physicist now than in the past, we might expect slower careers. However, this will also depend on the individual. David Galenson has applied his ideas to scientists as well as artists. He distinguishes between experimental and conceptual thinkers. Experimental thinkers work incrementally towards success, often slowly because there is more to learn, or because they learn slowly. Conceptual thinkers require less initial learning to form a more complete initial vision. To implement a radical new theory, you do not always need to understand every detail.

Galenson studied Nobel prize-winning economists to test this theory and found that economists with the most conceptual ideas did their important work twenty years earlier than the most experimental thinkers.[42] This is why Nobel prize winners in physics and maths often do their work younger than winners in history and medicine. Maths is conceptual; medicine is experimental. However, these differences are not definitive. There are experimental and conceptual thinkers within each field, and their most important work is done at relatively younger or later ages. You can be an experimental thinker in physics and bloom later than your conceptual colleagues.

And the time when you are working makes a difference. The early twentieth century was a time of breakthroughs by young physicists because quantum theory rendered much previous knowledge redundant. Werner Heisenberg, famous for his uncertainty principle, which he concocted at age twenty-five, was so conceptual in his research and his knowledge of classical electromagnetism was so poor that he nearly failed his PhD. There is no rule that you have to be young to make a scientific breakthrough. Indeed, in ageing societies such as we have in many Western countries it might be more likely to expect breakthroughs to come from older scientists.

There are reasons to think that the culture you work in makes a significant difference to your chances of success. Between 1964 and 2014, two thirds of all Nobel prize-winning scientific research was done in the United States, which had 5 per cent of the world's population.[43] But to really understand what creates scientific success, we should look not just for rules and averages but for individuals. As the authors of the Kellogg study said, 'Age and scientific genius are empirically characterized by great variation across individuals and over time.'[44]

The idea that great mathematicians have to be young is equally difficult to sustain. English mathematician G. H. Hardy made his famous claim in *A Mathematician's Apology*, a rhetorical essay full of unsubstantiated claims. As well as saying mathematics was a 'young man's game', he said, 'I do not know of an instance of a major mathematical advance initiated by a man past fifty. If a man of mature age loses interest in and abandons mathematics, the loss is not likely to be very serious either for mathematics or for himself.'

Ironically, Hardy admitted to being a late bloomer himself. Of his collaborations with the mathematicians John Edensor Littlewood and Srinivasa Ramanujan he wrote, 'It is to them that I owe an unusually late maturity: I was at my best a little past forty.' Another irony of this book is that Hardy uses Euclid's theorem of an infinity of prime numbers as a way of demonstrating how maths works.[45] This theorem gave rise to the twin prime conjecture, a problem that has remained unsolved for over a hundred years. The most recent major advance towards solving this problem was made by Yitang Zhang, aged fifty-five.

Despite examples of mathematicians doing important work after fifty – including Littlewood, Hardy's one-time collaborator – the idea of youth is still privileged in mathematics.[46] The Fields Medal, the most prestigious maths prize, has to be awarded to a mathematician aged forty or under. When the Fields Medal was established, the aim was to find underrated mathematicians, people who showed promise, not who were already widely recognized. In theory, the age limit was set to help the prize committee discover unappreciated talent. But this is not quite the case.

The first Fields Medal committee relied on a memo, written by the Canadian mathematician John Charles Fields, called 'International Medals for Outstanding Discoveries in Mathematics'. The memo said the medals were to be awarded 'in recognition of work already done' and 'an encouragement for further achievement'. The first awards were in 1936 and the second not until 1950, delayed by the Second World War.

The 1950 committee discussed criteria for nominating people. The chair, Harald Bohr, wanted a young mathematician called Laurent Schwartz to get the medal. The other leading nominee was André Weil. Bohr suggested a cut off of age forty-two, seemingly because André Weil had turned forty-three the previous year. Bohr argued, for reasons of international politics and 'the encouragement of further achievement', that age was an important factor in choosing the winner. But really he was concerned to have his candidate succeed and used the arguments necessary to ensure the outcome. It was committee politicking that ensured the Fields Medal was a prize for younger mathematicians. In 1966, forty was chosen as a convenient round number for the age limit.[47]

This has fed an impression that the best maths is done by young people. But there is no connection between age and declining productivity in maths. In 1978, sociologist Nancy Stern published a paper about mathematics, age and productivity. She looked at the number of papers mathematicians wrote at different ages, and she concluded that: 'There is no apparent overall relationship between age and mathematical productivity.' Table 10.1, which summarizes her results, shows you can be productive as a mathematician at any age.[48]

Table 10.1 Age and mathematical productivity, 1970–4 (mean number of papers published in 1970–4 by mathematicians of different ages)

Ages	Mean number single-authored papers	Mean number co-authored papers	Mean number total	N (sample size)
Under 35	3.27	1.73	5.12	101
35–39	3.97	3.36	7.33	96
40–44	3.24	2.94	6.24	67
45–49	2.37	1.13	3.49	63
50–59	2.16	3.03	5.22	73
60+	3.43	2.69	6.11	35
TOTAL	3.11	2.49	5.64	435

Source: Nancy Stern, 'Age and Achievement in Mathematics: A Case-Study in the Sociology of Science', Social Studies of Science 8:1 (February 1978), pp. 127–40.

A few years before Stern's paper, Stephen Cole investigated age and scientific performance. He found that there was a 'slight increase in productivity through the thirties' and then a 'slight decrease in productivity over the age of 50'. Both, he said, were 'explained by the operation of the scientific reward system'. The ones who keep publishing form a 'residue' of the best members of their cohort; the others were disincentivized from carrying on.[49]

Cole says that most important discoveries are made by young scientists 'because most scientists are young' – we should not take from that observations that older scientists cannot make important discoveries. Although productivity in the fields Cole studied peaked in middle age, he found that 'in most of the fields studied the scientists over the age of 60 were not much less productive than those under 35'.

That measures pure quantity. Cole also looked at the number of citations the scientists achieved for their work – that is, the number of other scientists who quoted their work – to see what the relationship between age and quality of work was like. He found, 'Scientists over the age of 45 are slightly less likely to publish high-quality research than those under 45.'[50] That's it! Slightly less likely. Like Stern, Cole found that productivity for mathematicians does not significantly change with age. Cole also found that the mathematicians who published more papers and better papers were no more likely to be creative when they were young. And less than 10 per cent of the sample changed their productivity over their career. Good mathematicians published a lot of interesting work irrespective of their age.

Cole was also careful to look at quality of work, to make sure that this productivity didn't mask the possibility that only the best work was done young. He found that of the most cited papers, '22% published their most cited paper in the first five-year period [after getting a PD], 21% in the second, 21% in the third, 23% in the fourth, and 13% in the last'. The last number was lower because the papers were too recent to have garnered as many citations as previous work.[51]

We can see that age is not a very important factor in productivity. But we do know that, on average, age brings cognitive decline. The way mathematicians and scientists remain productive is important. Reviewing a book that challenged the idea that maths is a 'young man's game' the mathematician Anthony G. O'Farrell summarized thus:

> A reasonable summary would be productivity can be maintained, but only if appropriate steps are taken to compensate for declining energy, memory and computational ability, and that the most reliable recipe is [to] combine your accumulated technique and cunning with the energy of a younger collaborator.[52]

That sounds a little downbeat – but it's far more optimistic than Hardy. And when we consider that the latest research suggests we don't lose mental speed – or don't have to – until much later than previously thought, it becomes more optimistic still. We saw earlier that the neurologist George Bartzokis showed that, as we age, we acquire more myelin in our frontal and temporal lobes, peaking around age fifty. The extension of these lobes means that, although we have less processing speed, and less ability to hold information in our memory, we are better able to think with what we do have. So O'Farrell's suggestion for older mathematicians to couple their accumulated wisdom with younger collaborators' energy and insight is good practical advice.

•••

Yitang Zhang is a remarkable example of how a late bloomer with almost no academic track record surprised the world with an exceptional and unexpected discovery in mathematics.

When Yitang Zhang submitted his paper purporting to have made significant progress towards solving the twin prime conjecture – an old and difficult problem in number theory – nobody knew who he was. Zhang sent his paper to the prestigious *Annals of Mathematics*. The editor had to send it for review by someone who was qualified to look at this complicated problem. 'In this case,' the editor of the *Annals* told the *New Yorker*, 'the person wrote back pretty quickly to say, "If this is correct, it's really fantastic. But you should be careful. This guy posted a paper once, and it was wrong. He never published it, but he didn't take it down, either."'[53]

This guy posted a paper once. That's not what they usually say about people who are about to solve one of the biggest problems in number theory. When Zhang's paper was published – within a few months, much more quickly than the usual year – many mathematicians' first thought was, 'I've never heard of this guy.'

One of Zhang's big advantages was that he doesn't believe age is a barrier to success. When an interviewer pointed out that Fields Medals are given to mathematicians aged forty or under, and that Zhang was fifty-five when he worked on the twin prime conjecture, and was sixty now, Zhang replied, 'I don't care so much about the age problem. I don't think there is a big difference. I can still do whatever I like to do.'[54] We have seen several times that stopping is the biggest barrier to success. There are various explanations why people stop working so hard – they have families, they get tenure, they have changing interests, they have made their money, their accumulated expertise stops them from experimenting, maybe even laziness – but anyone ambitious enough to want to change their lives or work on big problems can advantage themselves simply by not quitting.

Zhang was born in Shanghai in 1955 and grew up in Beijing after the age of thirteen. His father was a college teacher and engineer. His mother was a secretary. He first learned about famous mathematical problems like Fermat's Last Theorem aged ten. In different interviews, he has said that he did hear about the twin prime conjecture as a child, and that he did not.[55] He had a book called *One Hundred Thousand Whys*, a popular children's book in China that introduces children to the basic questions of chemistry, physics, maths, geology, astronomy and meteorology. The book 'aims to explain to Chinese children the scientific principles behind natural phenomena and commonplace actions which they can observe in their everyday lives'.[56]

Zhang lived through the Cultural Revolution and was sent to a farm with his mother. Due to political problems faced by his father, Zhang was not allowed to go to school and spent some years working on a farm. It was during this time that he formed the habit of solving problems in his head, because he had no one who would help him. After 1978, he was allowed to go to Peking University, aged twenty-three, after cramming for several months to make up for lost schooling so he could pass his entrance exams, where he studied maths. He was the best student in the department. Zhang was interested in number theory at this time, but his professor wanted him to study algebraic geometry. He was blocked from going to study at the University of San Diego. 'They didn't have much respect for personal freedom, personal choice,' Zhang said.[57] Instead, he went to Purdue where he was assigned the Jacobian problem, another algebraic subject. He was aged twenty-nine and was about to start his PhD.

The Jacobian problem, which he studied with T. T. Moh, was the basis of Zhang's PhD. Once he finished, aged thirty-six, he told Moh he wanted to go back to number theory. At this point, their relationship broke down. Zhang and Moh have different accounts of what happened. One point of agreement is that Zhang wanted to work on difficult problems. His enthusiasm for the Jacobian problem struck Moh: 'I felt it was odd to select such a difficult task.' Moh also noted what many later observers would see: 'Yitang spent all of his free time thinking of mathematics.'[58] But Moh believes Zhang was *not* forced to study algebraic geometry in Beijing. 'It was possible that what happened was Yitang pretended to be interested in algebraic geometry and fooled Prof Ding to recommend him... Yitang published no paper in Algebraic Geometry. Yitang wasted 7 years of his own life and my time and an opportunity of a young Chinese Algebraic Geometor.'[59] Moh also believed that Zhang was more interested in being famous than in research for its own sake and states that Zhang believed he should get a Fields Medal for his PhD thesis, which was impossible as it was based on an incorrect theory of Moh's. A more insightful way of thinking about this side of Zhang's personality is to note that he believed as a child that he would one day solve a major problem in maths; aged nine, he came up with a proof for the Pythagorean theorem.[60]

This is clearly part of why Moh did not help find Zhang a job when he graduated, a decision Zhang believes held back his career:

> Sometimes I regretted not fixing him a job. But really, who could tell whether it was a good decision or not?… Maybe it was his destiny to endure and turn out to be great in number theory, while he showed clearly he could not do anything meaningful in algebraic geometry.[61]

Zhang claims Moh refused to write him a letter of recommendation, without which it was impossible for Zhang to get an academic position. Moh says that when Zhang graduated there was a new system coming into place, the 'tenure track', which meant students had to look for jobs on their own:

> I told him the normal way of seeking jobs. When I looked into his eyes, I found a disturbing soul, a burning bush, an explorer who wanted to reach the north pole, a mountaineer who determined to scale Mt. Everest, and a traveller who would brave thunders and lightnings to reach his destination. Yitang never came back to me requesting recommendation letters. Apparently, he did not seek a job.[62]

Both stories are credible. Zhang is a hugely independent person, able to retreat into his own thoughts in almost any environment, according to colleagues. However, Moh's essay has a rattling, hostile tone; a dislike of Zhang comes across on every page. One thing seems clear. Zhang was not well suited to academic structures. As Moh said, 'I was sure of one thing – he could not survive the life of "tenure-track," "tenure," and "promotions." It was not his type. I regarded him as a free spirit, and I should let him fly.'[63] Certainly, Zhang lacked the social skills needed to network, get contacts, and become part of the mathematics community. 'My personality didn't allow me to be very public, to be known by everyone, because maybe I'm too quiet.'[64]

And so Zhang went his own way. Unlike his fellow students who went to work in computing and technology firms, he had no serious job. In the years after his PhD, he worked for various branches of the takeaway restaurant Subway and did accounting work. 'I kept thinking about math during that time, every week.' This is not to say he was happy at the time: 'Sometimes I think about it. I just think of it in a very peaceful way. It is past, so I don't worry about that. Disappointment – that was the past.'[65] Sometimes during this period he lived in his car.

It was in 1999, when he was forty-four, that Zhang got his first academic job, as a part-time calculus teacher at the University of New Hampshire. It wasn't until 2009, when he was fifty-four, that he started working on the twin prime conjecture, although he had spent his time at New Hampshire thinking about number theory. When asked why he, and not somebody else, had solved this problem, he said, 'I think the important reason is that I persisted for several years. I didn't give up… The most important motivation is to really love mathematics.'[66] Zhang had independently realized the constant probability of success rule: 'There are a lot of chances in your career, but the important thing is to keep thinking.'[67] Zhang structured his life around his persistent interest, ensuring that he could always keep thinking. This is how the *New Yorker* described his life:

A few years ago, Zhang sold his car, because he didn't really use it. He rents an apartment about four miles from campus and rides to and from his office with students on a school shuttle. He says that he sits on the bus and thinks. Seven days a week, he arrives at his office around eight or nine and stays until six or seven. The longest he has taken off from thinking is two weeks. Sometimes he wakes in the morning thinking of a math problem he had been considering when he fell asleep. Outside his office is a long corridor that he likes to walk up and down. Otherwise, he walks outside.[68]

Apart from the fact that the longest he has taken off from thinking is two weeks, these seem like inconsequential details. Many academics live some version of this life. But each detail tells. Zhang's life is structured so that he can move between concentrated and diffuse modes of thinking. Diffuse thinking is when you are no longer focused in on a task and you do something like wash the dishes or take a walk. Often, good ideas occur to us during this mode of thought, when the post-concentration mind wanders. Hence the common observation 'I have all my best ideas in the shower!'.

Taking the bus can be a technique for having ideas. It's not just Zhang. The speechwriter and playwright Ronald Miller did much of his best work while sitting on a train. The librettist Michael Stewart, who wrote *Bye Bye Birdie* and *Hello, Dolly!*, could only write on the train, 'which meant that whenever the producer wanted rewrites he had to spend days, and sometimes nights, with his librettist going to and fro on the New York subway'.[69] The scientists Henri Poincaré and August Kekulé had great ideas on the bus. For Linus Pauling, it was a bout of the flu and reading detective stories that gave him a breakthrough.[70] Similarly, when Noël Coward was forced to spend a week in bed with flu, he wrote *Private Lives*. Cognitive ability isn't enough – using your smarts in a way that produces the best ideas is what matters.

Psychologists Robert and Elizabeth Bjork have found 'studying the same material in two different rooms rather than twice in the same room leads to increased recall of that material'.[71] There are several studies that show interleaving separate topics together can provide spaces between practice and enhance your learning. This might work because, 'having to resolve the interference among the different things under study forces learners to notice similarities and differences among them'.[72] The same branch of psychology has also found that generating your own answer to problems is far more effective than being given answers: 'Any time that you, as a learner, look up an answer or have somebody tell or show you something that you could, drawing on current cues and your past knowledge, generate instead, you rob yourself of a powerful learning opportunity.'[73] Robert and Elizabeth Bjork stress the point that students need 'prior learning' to make testing work and that the optimum level of difficulty therefore varies for each student.[74] Another finding from psychology is that testing yourself is a far more effective learning method than making notes and revising material. As Robert and Elizabeth Bjork say, 'learning requires an active process of interpretation'.[75] This suggests that Zhang's childhood, where he didn't have anyone who could give him the answers, was an advantage.

Zhang is now sixty-seven and has published a paper claiming to have made progress on another significant problem in pure number theory, the Riemann hypothesis. Other mathematicians are looking at his work, but it seems likely that he has made another breakthrough. His advantage has been not his intelligence – although that certainly matters – but his persistence, his obsessiveness and his attitude.

As we will see in the final section, this is how Frank Lloyd Wright became the greatest American architect of the twentieth century – and it's why there is more potential available in middle life than we realize.

Part Five
Right Time – Midlife Transitions

'This spell of time that has been given to us rushes by so swiftly and rapidly that with very few exceptions life ceases for the rest of us just when we start getting ready for it.'

Seneca, *On the Shortness of Life*

11
Frank Lloyd Wright: the re-examined life

Standing in the grounds of the small Unity Chapel, an isolated and run-down building in the Helena Valley in Wisconsin, looking north to the river, you can see three buildings set in the hills – modernistic but oddly suited to their environment. Like the lighthouse on Lake Michigan in the east, or the tall trees of the valley, the Romeo and Juliet Windmill is unmissable, clad in the cedar that surrounds it. Next, the Midway Barn is a low, flat version of the great Wisconsin barns that are dotted along the road running east to Madison (the state capital) and shares their distinctive red colour. Lastly, Taliesin, a house wrapped around the crown of a hill, submerged in dozens of oak and red cedar trees, recreates the grey and brown of the hills, stones and tree bark. Above the valley, turkey vultures and bald eagles turn in widening gyres.

All three buildings were designed by Frank Lloyd Wright (1867–1959), now recognized as one of the United States' greatest architects. His family settled in this valley in the nineteenth century and built the Unity Chapel. From the age of eleven, he visited his uncle's farms here, coming from Madison for the summer. As a young man, Wright went south to Chicago to become an architect, training with Louis Sullivan who taught him that form and function must work together. Twenty years later, he returned to the valley, as a scandalous, inventive, indefinable figure. Wright declared himself, 'by birth and nature a Wisconsin radical. Radical is a fine word meaning "roots." Being radical I must strike root somewhere. Wisconsin is my somewhere.'[1] From here, in middle age, Wright reinvented himself as one of the twentieth century's most original architects. Had he not been a late bloomer – or a second bloomer – Frank Lloyd Wright would never have built many of his most famous creations. Wright was able to be a second bloomer because he never believed he was less than exceptional. And because he had a midlife crisis.

As we will see, Wright's immense self-belief – which developed young – was part of what pulled him through his trough and into this second phase. But as well as being the source of his creativity, Wright's ego made him domineering and violent. More than any other late bloomer in this book, the dark side of Wright's personality is a driver of his success. He gathered devoted admirers around him, people he could impose himself on, emotionally, psychologically and physically. Katharine Graham had to be free from her domineering husband to succeed: Wright is her opposite.

Wright was supposed to be a prodigy, a born architect. His mother decided while he was still in the womb, so the story goes, that he was going to design great buildings. She bought him a set of Froebel Blocks. From his childhood, Wright was arranging and organizing these shapes – an essential influence on his later work. It is much commented on that he learned from an early age to see through into the basic structures of geometry – what Anthony Alofsin calls 'a perception of geometric forms'. From his Prairie houses and early temples all the way though to his late works, this geometric abstraction is seen again and again.[2] His mother laid other foundations: she read John Ruskin's art and architecture criticism to him when he was a child and engravings of the great Gothic cathedrals hung over the boy's bed. His father immersed Wright in literature and music. Wright often compared buildings to compositions. (At Taliesin, he played Bach and Beethoven at full volume on speakers propped up to send the music across the valley where apprentices worked the fields and repaired the buildings.[3]) Aged fourteen, he read Victor Hugo's *The Hunchback of Notre Dame* and took from it the tragic lesson that, after Gutenberg, books had displaced architecture as the predominant form of cultural expression. Wright decided he would reverse that displacement and restore architecture to its rightful place as the mother of the arts. This idea was still animating him in his eighties as he designed the Guggenheim Museum in New York.

Wright's career started in the 1880s and was widely thought to be over in the 1930s. He was, by then, although rejected by the modernist academic and architectural establishment, perhaps the best-known architect in the United States – although at least two of his late commissions, for the Annunciation Greek Orthodox Church in Wauwatosa, Wisconsin, and the Guggenheim Museum, were made by people who had initially thought he was dead. Before 1909, he had designed houses and religious buildings in the suburbs of Chicago. His innovative Prairie houses were widely acclaimed. He and his wife Catherine were conventional middle-class people, accepted into their respectable community.

In 1909, aged forty-two, successful as an architect of Prairie-style homes, built horizonally with open interiors, Wright abandoned his family, put his business in the charge of an associate, and went to Europe with Mamah Borthwick, a married client. His practice had slumped in 1907 and he had first asked Catherine for a divorce in 1908. They had grown apart and Wright believed, as the Arts and Crafts generation had done before him, in the integration of work and home. Leaving was a bold statement. He was no longer bourgeois but eccentric, a respectable but innovative architect: he was a scandal. His own son hit him and knocked him down.

When he returned from Europe, he went back to Wisconsin, to the Helena Valley, and built Taliesin. This was a turning point: it is a building of ideas and experiments that extended his early ideas and established a new direction. From this valley, Wright reinvigorated his stalled career. This was the start of a long difficult period of his life, personally and professionally. Between 1911 and 1925, Taliesin burned down twice, his lover Mamah Borthwick was killed in strange, gruesome and tragic circumstances, and his subsequent marriage failed with violence alleged on both sides. Wright was a fringe figure in the architectural establishment, regarded as old-fashioned, ignored, or derided by the modernist establishment and proponents of the ideas of Mies van der Rohe and the International Style. As Tom Wolfe said, by 1932 Wright was considered to be 'half-modern' in comparison to the European modernists. 'Which was to say, he was finished and could be forgotten.'[4] He was also frequently short of money.

In this period, Wright received few commissions in the States and the ones he did receive often failed. But it was not an idle time: in 1923, he completed the Imperial Hotel in Japan, an astonishing feat, on a bigger scale than he had worked before, physically and imaginatively. The hotel proved itself by surviving an earthquake the year after it was built. A decade later he wrote proudly: 'They will never again build buildings in earthquake zones as they did before the Imperial was built in Tokyo.'[5] At home, his success was muted. His attempt to create affordable homes was a financial failure. Wright didn't lack ambition in this middle period, but he did have to pivot to writing and lecturing to make money, and to running an apprenticeship programme. During the Great Depression, his career as an architect seemed to be finally over. One historian says, 'Wright had vanished from the public imagination.'[6]

But then there came a second act, with commissions for three iconic buildings in the early 1930s – Fallingwater, Johnson Wax and the Herbert and Katherine Jacobs First House (Jacobs I). This second career, from 1935 to 1959, was Wright's most innovative period, with the creation of the Usonian, heliocentric and textile block homes, new and original designs based on the landscape of the American West, and monumental buildings like the Guggenheim Museum and the Johnson Wax Company. It was as though he were living his life again: he reimagined and reconstituted his career the way he constantly reimagined the patterns he had learned as a child.

So Frank Lloyd Wright was both an early and a late bloomer. He did more than half his life's work in the last quarter of his life, after the age of sixty-eight. His final decade was his most productive. It was

Wright's strong belief in his own abilities and in the importance of his work that led him to create his most experimental buildings in old age. At sixty, his career was in decline; aged eighty, he was ascendant. As the equal-odds rule would predict, Wright worked prodigiously. The year before he died, aged ninety-one, he produced a hundred drawings for a proposed cultural centre in Baghdad.[7]

This double-peak career shape can be seen in a graph of the number of buildings completed to one of his designs in every year of his career (Figure 11.1). This is not entirely representative because it takes longer to construct than to design a building – and many external factors affect when or whether a design is completed. However, the two peaks in Wright's career are clearly visible. After a slump around the start of the First World War, Wright's practice remained almost dormant until the commission for Fallingwater in 1935. Many architects – like Wright's mentor, Louis Sullivan, or his draughtsman Russell Barr Williamson – never recovered from a slump like the one Wright went through after the 1911–19 decline in work.

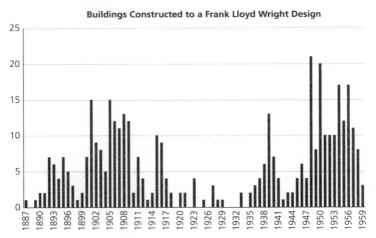

Buildings Constructed to a Frank Lloyd Wright Design

Figure 11.1 Number of buildings constructed to a Frank Lloyd Wright design, 1887–1959
Source: Data for graph taken from William Allin Storrer, *The Architecture of Frank Lloyd Wright: A Complete Catalog*, 3rd edn (University of Chicago Press, 2002).

There is a qualitative aspect to Wright's career that isn't picked up in Figure 11.1: Wright was able to produce his second peak because of his ability to remain innovative, to rework his ideas in new contexts, to constantly re-examine life. Between 1911 and 1917, Wright made over a hundred designs for the System-Built Homes programme, an attempt to make affordable housing according to his architectural principles. The System-Built Homes represent some 10 per cent of his total output; most of them were never built. A combination of the outbreak of the First World War, Wright working in Japan, and the difficulty of making the idea financially viable put a halt to the project. Nicholas Hayes, author of a book about an overlooked System-Built home, the Elizabeth Murphy House, found a note in the archives showing that, one year after the programme was cancelled, Wright was still thinking about using design elements in later projects. And he returned to the idea of affordable architect-designed homes with Jacobs I in 1936, part of a set of buildings known as Usonians. Despite the failures, this middle period was ambitious.[8] The Bogk House, from 1916, shows the influence of the Imperial Hotel (the preliminary plans for which were begun in 1913), and is testament to Wright's idiosyncratic style. It stands out on its street in a Milwaukee suburb as a singular, monolithic, alien house, unmistakably Wright, so utterly different from the Prairie houses he had been building a few years earlier. His ability to work with the aesthetic of monumental buildings on a smaller scale was seen again when he drew on the great Gothic cathedrals for inspiration in the Johnson Wax Headquarters, in Racine, Wisconsin (constructed 1936–9).

In his final decade, Wright built monumental, innovative spaces like the Beth Shalom Temple and the Guggenheim Museum, one of the most astonishingly futuristic buildings of the post-war period, which looks like it was dropped onto Manhattan from outer space rather than formed from the geometric imagination of a septuagenarian. He came to these spectacular new forms not through repetition but rearrangement. He was continuously varying his ideas. The ideas behind the Johnson Wax Headquarters are first seen in a design of 1931.[9] The idea of a continuous spiral ramp occurs first in a design from the 1920s; by the time he was commissioned to work on the Guggenheim, a new sort of concrete was available that made the idea feasible, and he had a patron who shared his visionary ideals. When Wright designed his first spiral ramp for a Planetarium he was 'pushing the technology of his times to its very limits'.[10] That is not to say that the Guggenheim design was a rehash, a salvaged design that he rejigged for a new client. Instead, it shows the extent to which Wright was able to see vast possibilities in even the simplest shapes and to work with new materials. The tree-shaped pillars of the Johnson Wax Headquarters were only possible because Wright was working with the latest forms of reinforced concrete. Wright's second phase was the result of re-examining the ideas of the first phase in new and surprising ways. As he said in 1931, some years before the revival of his career: 'This creative faculty in man is that quality or faculty of getting himself born into whatever he does, and born again and again with fresh patterns as new problems arise.'[11] After 1934, with Fallingwater, the Johnson Wax Headquarters and Jacobs I, Wright's career is born again and again with fresh patterns as new problems arise.

To understand how he did this, we can look at the drawing practices of Michelangelo.

•••

In the history of architecture, few design drawings survive before Michelangelo. There are several reasons for this. The printing press had made paper abundant, and artists like Leonardo were discovering the uses of drafting and sketching in creative ingenuity. And the Renaissance was a time of generalists. Many of the great architects of the era – Donato Bramante, Giorgio Vasari, Baldassare Peruzzi – had been painters and sculptors first. It was an era of late blooming. Brunelleschi was a goldsmith who became an architect in middle age and designed the dome of Florence cathedral, solving a problem that had puzzled architects for a thousand years – how to replicate the great domes of antiquity. Architecture shared the technique of drawing with painting and sculpture. All three arts had come to rely on drawing as a method of generating ideas. It is common to hear writers say that they do not write down their thoughts but that writing is *how* they think. Drawing played the same function for the painters, sculptors and architects of the Renaissance, foremost among them, Michelangelo.[12]

Michelangelo was in the middle of his career before he became interested in architecture, and was an old man when he was commissioned by the pope to build St Peter's Basilica. Instead of retiring, the septuagenarian artist became the Renaissance's greatest architect. Like other artists, Michelangelo became an architect by drawing.

Unlike Brunelleschi, Michelangelo didn't learn architecture by travelling to Rome and examining ancient buildings. He *was* inspired by classical styles, forms and rules, but through books. He studied a codex full of classical orders of architecture. Rather than take a systematic approach, he took what he needed. He learned the forms and shapes of this codex by drawing them, just as he had learned to do with nude figures in preparation for his paintings. This was not Michelangelo's invention. It was becoming common practice among artists. He learned as they did that drawing was a way of thinking, a means of uncovering new things in art.[13] As the art historian Cammy Brothers, whose excellent study *Michelangelo, Drawing, and the Invention of Architecture* is the basis of this section, writes: 'Leonardo da Vinci demonstrated the potential of drawing as a form of research and as a medium for the generation of new ideas.'[14]

Michelangelo's drawings are full of repetition. He draws the same figures over and over with slight variations in posture, pose, angle. It's how he encoded basic forms into his memory *and* how he discovered ways of being original. Through drawing, he achieved a deep understanding of shape. Hence his invocation to one of his students, 'Draw, Antonio, draw, Antonio, draw and do not waste time.'[15] It is in this repetition, this refiguring, that ideas are chanced upon. It meant Michelangelo came to each project with a head stocked with shapes that could be reinterpreted, reformed, to find something new. The skill he needed for architecture was one he learned from painting, and his interest in anatomy. As Vasari said, 'In flaying dead bodies to understand anatomical matters, he began to perfect the great sense of design he later acquired.'[16] (Michelangelo was beaten for his secret drawing habit as a child. Sometimes to be a late bloomer, you must start very young.)

From the codex, he learned a new series of forms that could be refigured and reworked in his various building projects. To start with, he saw architecture as a way of framing sculpture. As he worked on the Sistine Chapel, where the painting had to fit into spaces left by the architecture, he came to see architecture as interesting in its own right and as an important part of the overall effect. The architectural frame and the sculptural or painted figure were now unified in his imagination. What started as a means of acquiring drafting techniques for bases, capitals, pediments and cornices became a new way of seeing, akin to his ability to imagine the human figure within the marble block. From this basis of drawing scrolls and columns he went on to be the man who reinvented classical architecture.[17]

This is not all it takes to describe and explain Michelangelo's architecture. 'In a sense,' writes Brothers, 'his architecture still seems to come from nowhere.'[18] But we can see the central importance of repetition to his development. He wasn't abstract. He came to his architectural ideas as he did his artistic ideas: through drawing, repeatedly, with small variations, until he found the right answer. He took forms like human anatomy or architectural structures and applied a monkish *ruminatio* to them – chewing them over the way a monk meditates on a Bible passage. Creativity is the result of this sort of hectic, repetitive work. That is exactly how Frank Lloyd Wright was able to sustain such a long, inventive career. He was turning, arranging and refiguring the shapes of his childhood in his imagination seventy and eighty years later, like Michelangelo sketching arms and columns. This was how the Guggenheim was designed. Wright turned shapes for his whole life.

What drawing was to Michelangelo, imagination was to Wright. The old master had made continuous drafts on paper to find his forms; the new master thought it all out carefully in his head before picking up a pencil. Wright's memory meant he could do this work without actually drawing. Famously, when Edgar J. Kaufmann telephoned Wright and said he would be popping by to see progress on the designs for Fallingwater, Wright had nothing on paper. Unfazed, Wright walked out into the drafting studio and drew three complete, detailed drawings of plans for the house, straight down on the paper without hesitating. It took him two hours. When Kaufmann arrived, he was incredibly impressed. So thoroughly had Wright imagined the building in his mind in the preceding weeks that he was able to produce it as if from pure inspiration.

•••

We could describe the way Frank Lloyd Wright walked out of his life in 1909 in several ways. It looks a lot like a midlife crisis. He was bored and disaffected with his work, his marriage had gone stale due to divergent interests, and he was itching to change something, anything. We could talk, too, about Walt Whitman and Ralph Waldo Emerson, his heroes, the great prophets of American individualism, and see Wright as a bohemian trapped in a bourgeois life, like Charles Strickland in Somerset Maugham's novel *The Moon and Sixpence*. Or we might put the whole thing in more modern terms: he was reaching the nadir of the happiness curve (discussed in the next chapter); it was all a phase, a natural stage of life, which happens to most people. Rather than ride it out, he bolted. Possibly each of these factors played a part. Certainly he *felt* trapped and depressed. What use is further speculation? Perhaps his work would have developed just the same if he had stayed with his first wife, Catherine. Perhaps not. It seems unlikely that such a romantic individualist would be able to develop while he felt dishonest in his life. But if he was merely slipping down an inevitable biological happiness curve, it could all have amounted to the same thing. We can't know. Whatever the cause or consequence of that break in 1909, Wright was now 'loos'd of limits and imaginary lines'.[19]

Direct experience of European architecture reinforced Wright's idea that there should be no ornament distinct from function and this informed his later work and proselytizing. He was able to study the plans of European buildings, to see the connection between folk tradition and ordinary buildings (which informed Taliesin), and came away more firm in his mission to create an original American architecture rather than replicating old forms from other countries. Visiting Italy in 1909–10, he saw that classical architecture was organic with its environment and came to believe that to impose those styles on other times and places was discontinuous. To reproduce classical forms in modern America was not real. 'We are the only power nation, dead or alive,' he said, 'with no architecture of our own.'[20] Emerson and Whitman had always been important to Wright, and now he believed that training only the intellectual side of an architect rather than the spiritual side would lead to imitative rather than inventive building.[21] As Anthony Alofsin said, 'Wright returned from Europe a crusader.'[22]

The next two decades lead up to the major turning point of his late career. Isolated at home, alone in his profession, this crisis was a starting point. The period of Wright's troubles, approximately from 1909 to 1930, was when he finally realized his vision. After 1910, Wright is no longer the same architect. The model of form and function being one which he had learned as a young man from his mentor Louis Sullivan was 'expanded and reworked'.[23] Sullivan had given a sense of the whole in his ornament. Wright wanted wholeness to be a feature of the entire building. From now on, Wright made spaces, not buildings. As he did with shapes, so he did with ideas, turning them over in his mind to find new possibilities.

The hearth had been the centre of his Prairie homes before 1909, a focus of domestic space. The Larkin Building, of that period, in Buffalo, New York, had a huge, light, central atrium emphasizing functional space. He had separated the corners of the building from the walls with glass channels that contained brick spandrels. In this and other ways, he pulled the walls apart, making the building a space with a series of screens around it, rather than a box of walls. As Donald Hoffmann writes, by disrupting the usual box-pattern of the walls, 'interior space broke free in every direction'.[24] Similarly in the Unity Temple (1905–8), he made the worship space 'the soul of the design'.[25] Although he was designing like this, he did not yet have a theory of space. After Europe and Japan, the idea of space was increasingly central to his intentions.

The idea of continuous space reaches new heights in his late circular projects such as the Annunciation Greek Orthodox Church and the Guggenheim – their shape and structure emphasize not the walls but the constant flow of the interior. The glass rifts of the Larkin Building recur more strongly at Fallingwater, breaking the continuous wall to emphasize inner space. At the Guggenheim, the floor constantly slopes and the glass rift becomes the dome roof. In the Johnson Wax Headquarters, there is a clerestory of glass tubing between the wall and the ceiling bringing light down into the office. Similarly at the Annunciation Greek Orthodox Church, the roof rests on a clerestory of circular windows. The early-evening light comes down from these windows and reflects off the golden screen around the altar and a golden glow suffuses the whole interior of the church. The idea of an 'unlimited overhead' was first used in the Unity Temple in 1908. Fifty years later, Wright was still evolving and reconfiguring this concept.[26] In this way, he was 'born again and again with fresh patterns as new problems arise'.[27]

Most important to the concept of a build as a space is Taliesin, an extraordinary innovation: he wouldn't build anything like it again until Fallingwater in 1935. Even in the late 1950s, when the commissioners of the Annunciation Greek Orthodox Church visited Taliesin, they couldn't believe the buildings had been first built in 1911: 'I couldn't help but feel as though they were first built yesterday,' one of them said.[28] It is constantly difficult, when visiting Taliesin, to remember it was designed before the First World War, while Le Corbusier was a draughtsman and Mies van der Rohe was an apprentice. At Taliesin, in his mid-forties, during his crisis, he experimented with the concept of space in order to create a new American architecture. It was 'a manifesto of what he believed architecture should be', according to Neil Levine.[29]

Taliesin is built not on the hill but around it; the hilltop is in the middle of the three sides of the house, as a ledge rock later protruded into Fallingwater built above a waterfall. He came back from Europe ready to build Taliesin, reinventing the idea of a European estate in an informal, irregular, organic manner to integrate it into the Wisconsin landscape. The 'total freedom of movement and infinite expanse of space' within the Robie House, one of his early breakthroughs, was taken to new levels in Taliesin where 'almost all the rooms are connected to each other, and entered at their corners'.[30] In every room, the view expands and changes: the view flows with the surroundings, diminishing the distinction between inside and outside. At Taliesin you never feel boxed in: the space is always opening up or closing in around you. It is one continuous passageway of corridors, rooms, nooks and crannies, and snugs, like a river with inlets and rivulets diverting everywhere. The same thing is true of the Guggenheim, built nearly fifty years later.

Wright achieved this constant shifting and expanding of the view by building Taliesin on a diagonal axis, another element that now became central to his work.[31] Other ideas from Taliesin would become part of the reconfiguring shapes that defined his late period. The corner window in the living room has no join, a way of 'breaking the box' of modernism and of integrating the house with nature. At Jacobs I, part of the cluster of buildings that restarted his career in the 1930s, the door to the living room opens onto the garden at the corner. In the Elizabeth Murphy House, built a few years after Taliesin, part of the failed System-Built Homes project, there is a wall immediately to the left after you go in through the front door, which blocks the view of the living room, drawing you into the centre of the house where you have a more open view – the same as the original front door leading into the living room at Taliesin.

Taliesin was a personal retreat, a place for Wright to be independent and to live with Mamah – their unconventional partnership was the main inspiration for Taliesin, a marriage of the hill and the house.[32] But the first of many misfortunes came in 1914. A servant started a fire and killed seven people with an axe as they tried to escape, including Mamah and her children. The residential wing of the building was destroyed. More was to follow. In 1923, Wright married his second wife, Maude 'Miriam' Noel (his first wife, Kitty, granted him a divorce in 1922). This was a fractious and unhappy marriage. She was a morphine addict and mentally unstable. When they divorced, she accused Wright of violence. The divorce left Wright with burdensome debts. In 1925, he met Olgivanna Hinzenburg (née Lazović): they were together for the rest of his life. They moved to the rebuilt Taliesin. But that year Taliesin burned again, in a fire started by an electrical fault. A collection of Japanese art was destroyed, which Wright had collected since 1902.

The vanished art was worth up to half a million dollars, a loss Wright could not afford, not to mention the misery of losing irreplaceable art. He rebuilt Taliesin, again. But his creditors dogged him; at one point, the house was in their possession. So precarious was his situation – high debts and little work – that he created a consortium where investors could place capital with guarantees against his future work. His irresistible, incorrigible self-belief never wavered.

Shortly before the first Taliesin fire, Wright started working in Japan from 1913 to 1922. Like Taliesin and Europe, this transformed his view of architecture. Anthony Alofsin writes: 'The archetypal geometries of the circle, square, and triangle that he found in Japanese art corresponded with the spiritual qualities of infinity, integrity, and structural unity, respectively.'[33] The pure geometry he had learned as a young child was being refigured and turned over in his mind, finding new perspectives and new beliefs. Japan's influence remained profound in Wright's work for the rest of his life, especially the idea that pre-industrial Japan had lived, as Wright saw it, in constant harmony with nature.

In 1921, shortly before he finished the Imperial Hotel, he wrote to his daughter, 'Once upon a time I never could strike the bottom of my physical resources – but now I find that very grey hair and *fifty-three years* – indicate something that I will have to pay attention to…' He made another realization in Japan, that he had, until now, been working in the wrong way. Here is what he wrote to his friend and client Darwin Martin:

> My experience in the building of the great building in Japan has taught me how difficult of realization my ideal in Architecture is. I had to come to close grips with everything in the field as the whole affair including furniture was made by my own workmen 'on the job.' I realize how inadequate my superintendence has always been – how rash I was to aim so high and how much my clients had to give in patience and forbearance to get the thing which in the beginning they did not really want – perhaps.[34]

This is exactly what made Michelangelo succeed as the architect of St Peter's – not being just the designer but also the builder. Learning to supervise everything was the secret behind the construction of the great basilica. Michelangelo implemented a system to have food and water brought to stone masons high up on the scaffolding. He took up the chisel and showed them how to carve accurately. He inherited a mess of a site, which had been passed from one meddlesome architect to another and looked, in the words of Michelangelo scholar William Wallace, 'much more like a Roman ruin'.[35] Michelangelo made significant changes to the existing design, asking the workers to undo twenty years of labour. He was right but he had to prove himself, so he descended into the details to show his workers his expertise. Wright seems to have had a similar realization. The results were clear. The hotel had been severely criticized and was expected to suffer badly during an earthquake. The year after it was finished, Tokyo suffered its most severe earthquake of the twentieth century. The hotel survived, absorbing the shock and, despite some damage, operated proudly for many more decades. Shortly afterwards, Wright was included in *Who's Who in America* for the first time. When asked for his special accomplishments, he replied, 'The Imperial Hotel of Tokyo, Japan and 176 other Buildings of Note.'[36]

The Imperial Hotel relied on cantilevered steel-reinforced concrete, a material and a technique that were centrally important to Wright's later work, most famously at Fallingwater. Many lessons had been learned about how to reinforce buildings after the San Francisco earthquake of 1906, and Wright had already designed an unbuilt skyscraper that anticipated some of his thinking in the Imperial Hotel.[37] His ideas always matured through projects and flexed to current demands and available materials. One of the hotel's most controversial aspects was the use of floating foundations. Rather than drive deep pillars into the ground to connect the hotel with solid ground, the piles were only driven into the soft mud below the hotel. Wright believed, after some testing, that this would let the building float on the mud during an earthquake like a ship on top of waves. He made the building light, by giving it a copper roof, and lowered its centre of gravity with sloping walls.[38] The hotel was cantilevered with concrete slabs capable of bearing great weight. The cantilevers were extended to display the building's structure – the same technique that makes Fallingwater so compelling. Wright said, 'The cantilever which looked both dangerous and absurd to the critics absolutely trimmed and balanced the structure in the undulations, upheavals and twists.'[39] He had to ignore much carping before the hotel passed the earthquake test.

Importantly, with cantilevered steel-reinforced concrete, Wright made an organic building, one where the form arose from the function. The alternative to cantilevered steel-reinforced concrete was a rigid steel frame. Wright disliked this, partly because he thought they would suffer more in earthquakes but also because they imposed classical styles on Japanese buildings. His techniques allowed for modern architecture that was in tune with its surroundings. As Joseph Siry writes: 'The Imperial Hotel's technical integrity paralleled its aesthetic merit, intended as a tribute to Japan. Its survival validated Wright's conviction that its structural principles of cantilevered concrete, more than the steel frame, pointed the way for modern architecture, not just in Japan but worldwide.'[40]

By the start of the Great Depression, Wright's career had finally stalled, with hardly any commissions in the late 1920s and early 1930s. When he established his apprenticeship programme at Taliesin in the late 1920s, there was often no architectural work for the apprentices to do. Instead, they farmed the land, repaired the house, and worked on Wright's vision for Broadacre City, a crank idea to replace modern urban centres with more rural car-based alternatives. Without work, his reputation was in decline: he was an old man in Wisconsin, a romantic of a former time. To the architectural establishment, he was the eccentric past. But Wright knew that life does not give you prizes: you must fight for them. Whitman had taught him well:

Listen! I will be honest with you,
I do not offer the old smooth prizes, but offer rough new prizes,
These are the days that must happen to you:
You shall not heap up what is call'd riches,
You shall scatter with lavish hand all that you earn or achieve,
You but arrive at the city to which you were destin'd, you hardly settle
yourself to satisfaction before you are call'd by an irresistible call to depart,
You shall be treated to the ironical smiles and mockings of those who
remain behind you,
What beckonings of love you receive you shall only answer with
passionate kisses of parting,
You shall not allow the hold of those who spread their reach'd hands
toward you.[41]

Wright did not see himself as a washed-up case. He must have looked and sounded like the past, the shadow of Grosvenor Cleveland's America. But he was vital, energetic. He had long believed that an honest arrogance was preferable to a hypocritical modesty. From criticism, he took combative inspiration. He wrote to the architectural critic Louis Mumford, 'Any man will learn as much from his enemies as from his friends. They keep him in fighting trim.'[42] And Wright never stopped working with the latest materials, experimenting with ideas, or rethinking his concepts.

In the decade when he was short of work, Wright might have gone to seed the way his mentor, Louis Sullivan – and his father – had done. Wright visited Sullivan, who lived in hotels and drank too much, bought him an overcoat, and wrote consoling letters. But he did not follow his *lieber Meister* down that path. In a review of a biography of Sullivan, Wright explained that Sullivan's decline was not because 'his contemporaries did not recognise his talents' – on the contrary, they did recognize them and so 'built a wall of gossip' around Sullivan to keep their clients to themselves.[43] The same thing happened to Wright – drive round the suburbs of Wisconsin and you will see houses designed by Wright's former draughtsman Russell

Barr Williamson which are brazen copies of Wright's style, albeit with tell-tale ornamental pieces, like classical capitals, that Wright would have *scorned*. So Wright had learned to yield nothing, to dominate his own fate. He knew what Whitman knew, that 'from any fruition of success, no matter what, shall forth something to make a greater struggle necessary'.[44]

From this greater struggle came forth a whole second career. As Mumford predicted in 1930, perhaps the nadir of Wright's career and reputation, 'The day of your power is just beginning.'[45] Wright concurred: 'Between us I believe there is much to be accomplished. A crusade.'[46] The crusade began with Wright's new apprenticeship scheme at Taliesin, which would provide him with the commission that would make his mark incontestable. This was another long-meditated idea. He had written to his friend and client Darwin Martin in 1905, during the construction of Martin's house, 'I am getting discouraged but will make some desperate effort this coming year to build up a coterie of capable, honest workmen.'[47]

It wasn't easy. In 1931, Wright wrote, 'I've had so hard a time the past year getting pennies enough together to keep working.'[48] Financial troubles were perpetual. Bills were unpaid. A huge debt to Darwin – which had secured the mortgage on Taliesin – was ignored for years. Money was spent on luxuries while the apprentices scraped together food and firewood. Nor was the apprenticeship as successful as he wanted. Turnover among recruits was high, there were no commissions, he was unable to countenance anything other than a band of apostles, and his grand vision of Broadacre was ignored despite endless promotion.

The Taliesin fellowship was the route back to architecture. It was a fraught project with a high turnover rate of apprentices, many of whom felt they did a lot of grunt work without learning much architecture. Apprentices were supposed to revere the maestro. Once they became too sure of themselves, Wright disliked the competition. But the ones who stayed, who were able to be deeply loyal to Wright without losing their sense of self, were part of a singular enterprise. And they became Wright's network. The father of an apprentice supported the Broadacre City project. He then commissioned Fallingwater. Without him and his son, Wright wouldn't have had his renaissance. What seemed like a career change into an architectural apprenticeship without much architecture became the source of new commissions. When Wright lacked a network he created his own, putting himself at the centre of its sphere of influence.[49]

Wright frequently got in his own way – the grand vision he had of himself had a nasty side. He told racist jokes. He disapproved of homosexuality. He was openly sexist, with even the most talented female apprentices relegated to needlework. People who left the apprenticeship received vicious letters demeaning their personality and ability. As a young child, his daughter Iovanna saw Wright throw Olgivanna to the floor and hit his other daughter Svetlana's head against a cabinet. This could be the result of his own unhappy childhood, of his colossally aggrandized ego, his patriarchal attitude, or all three.

Wright always had an absurd sense of himself. His mission to restore architecture to its proper place among the arts was so important to him that when the University of Wisconsin wanted to make architecture less central to the syllabus of an earlier version of the Taliesin apprenticeship he proposed to them, Wright walked away from the partnership. Combined with his belief that all architectural education was wrong and misguided, this meant he distrusted educators so much that his youngest daughter didn't go to school until she was nine. She arrived not knowing the alphabet. Wright was a genius but also a crank. If he wasn't, he could never have had such original ideas.

Wright's Whitmanesque defiance of the world looked glamorous and inspired, but his failures and frustrations resulted in aggressive, demeaning, patriarchal behaviour. Without his 'honest arrogance' he might not have achieved what he did. But his tendency to fall out with the world was part of a bigger tendency to take what he wanted and damn the consequences to other people.

Wright was never forced to control his egregious tendencies. They are bundled up with his singular view of the world, but he did not need to be violent or so controlling. He *wanted* to be a prima donna, as he referred to himself. 'If we are to live our own lives we must be true, but true to what?' he asked in a 1939 lecture. His architectural answer was unity, an architecture with a 'sense of the whole'.[50] This sense of the whole is missing from his life – his vision for architecture didn't just come first, it was his only touchstone. He learned a lot from his midlife crisis, but he could have learned more.

Despite his flaws, the apprenticeship rolled on, with enough new apostles to keep it just about viable. And when the new commissions arrived, Wright was ready. Taliesin, Broadacre, and the Imperial Hotel had laid the basis for a new burst of invention. As Kathryn Smith writes, 'Although no-one could have predicted it at the time, Wright's structural experiments and spatial planning breakthroughs of the 1910s and 1920s were groundwork for his most productive period, which began in the mid-1930s and continued until his death in 1959.'[51] Smith dates 1925 as the real turning point in his twenty-year re-evaluation. That was when the chaos of financial and family problems was at its peak, but those problems made it necessary to earn money. Wright himself attributed the 'patient, persistent effort' of those years to the 'children of my mind' that he found unignorable. Like any poet, he had to do his work; he was compelled. But he also had to avoid bankruptcy as he struggled to keep possession of his house and moved from one volatile marriage to another.[52] The year 1925 was also when he designed the Gordon Strong Planetarium, the first time he proposed a single spiral as the shape of a building, the idea which recurred in 1943 with the Guggenheim. The year 1925 as a pivot in Wright's life shows us the role of luck, too. Austin's three sorts of luck from Chapter 4 – the luck that comes from being busy and energetic, the luck that comes to people who are receptive to it, and the luck we create through our own idiosyncrasies – are all visible here. Wright began a new period of experimentation in his career, he was open to the influence of his third wife, Olgivanna, and his arrogant personality enabled him to establish connections through the Taliesin apprenticeship scheme that restarted his career.

The fundamental lessons about shape he absorbed in his childhood are vital to this final phase, where Wright reimagines these shapes like kaleidoscopic patterns again and again. The most important shape to this part of his career is the spiral, the shape of the Guggenheim.

To Wright, geometry was eternal, fundamental. He compared it to Plato's 'eternal ideas' of the Forms – the idea that everything, every horse or house, pillar or plate, is based on an ideal Form that exists in eternity. Certainly, there were Forms in Wright's mind that enabled him to work in this way. This quality gave shapes a 'spell-power' to him. Wright's perpetual variations on geometry are an attempt to express this spell-power; he was searching for the enchantment of shape arrangements. Each shape represented a basic ideal from nature and corresponded to certain human moods: 'the circle, infinity; the triangle, structural unity; the spire, aspiration; the spiral, organic progress; the square, integrity'.[53]

In 1955, a few years before he died, he designed the Annunciation Greek Orthodox Church, Wauwatosa, Wisconsin, inspired by Francesco Borromini's church in Rome Sant'Andrea delle Fratte as well as by the Hagia Sophia, formerly the central church of Orthodoxy. This church is one of Wright's 'most geometrically pure and precise floor plans'. And yet, he reinvents Borromini: as Robert McCarter says, Wright's use of circles and ellipses gives the impression of a building lifting off the ground, 'like nothing so much as a flying saucer'.[54] The spiral means organic progress; the circle, infinity. In the Guggenheim and the Annunciation Greek Orthodox Church, those ideas were brought to their high point in Wright's work, right at the end of his life. Two icons of futurism from an octogenarian.

The Guggenheim is often compared to the shape of the shells Wright kept on his desk, or to an ocean wave (he gave a copy of Hokusai's *One Hundred Views of Mount Fuji*, including *The Big Wave*, to Hilla Rebay, the Guggenheim's first curator and director). But the closest correlate for this spiral are the birds of prey in the Helena Valley circulating above Taliesin, which Wright would have known in his childhood and which circle there still. His career is like a widening spiral, working round and round, and up and up, with Wright producing dozens of drawings in his final year. Circles and spirals recur throughout the late period – in the stairs at the Johnson Wax Headquarters, in the circular floors of the Johnson Research Tower, in the design for Monona Terrace, in the stairs at the Annunciation Greek Orthodox Church which are designed around the motif of the cross inside a circle, in the Guggenheim where the spiral ramp moves up to the circle of the glass dome. As he aged, rather than imitating his earlier style, Wright was inspired by the infinite circle and the organic spiral to keep reconsidering, reconfiguring his ideas into startling originality.

In the staircases at the Annunciation Greek Orthodox Church, circles and spirals are integrated (Figure 11.2). That church's motif is a cross inside a circle, a symbol of Orthodoxy. The stairs spiral around a vertical rail with bulbs pointing out to represent the pattern of a cross. The bulbs are not shaded, so another circle is introduced to the pattern. Standing at the bottom, looking up, you see the interplay of circles and spirals reaching upwards – they are designed to encourage parishioners to look up and think about God – and at the top, the spiral forms into a circle, the symbol of organic progress resolving into the symbol of the infinite. This is a reimagined technique. The lamps at Taliesin are designed as a vertical rail with perpendicular bulbs shaded in wooden boxes. In Jacobs I, a rail like this runs along the ceiling. At the Annunciation Greek Orthodox Church, Wright transformed this into a symbol of organic growth reaching the infinite, a symbol of God, but also of his own work, which, by drawing on ideas of eternal geometry, continued to change and grow throughout his life.

Figure 11.2 One of the three spiral staircases in Frank Lloyd Wright's
Annunciation Greek Orthodox Church, Wauwatosa, Wisconsin
Source: Henry Oliver

12
Reasons to have a midlife crisis

Twice, Frank Lloyd Wright came to a crisis point and turned it into a moment of transformation: in 1909, when he left his family, and again during the Great Depression. He is an example of a particular sort of late bloomer: an early success who reinvented himself for a second career. From his moments of crisis, he re-emerged as a more creative architect. He shows us that there can be benefits to having a midlife crisis.

When we look for potential late bloomers, we should not just think about unsuccessful people. As well as the people who might do something but haven't done it yet, we should look for people who have already done something interesting – and who could do so again. Plenty of people are stuck in the position of Charles Duhigg's peers at the business school reunion: successful but unhappy. The midlife crisis has been a stereotype of the middle-aged for decades. Many people in this position are not going to be late bloomers. The solution is not for every jaded middle manager and disgruntled consultant to walk out of their life and turn to painting, the way Charles Strickland abandons his respectable life as a stockbroker in Somerset Maugham's novel *The Moon and Sixpence*, which was based on the life of the Post-Impressionist Paul Gauguin. A change of attitude – finding the usefulness in the work you already do – is underrated for many people. Those who are bored or frustrated and who need something new or something bigger don't have to overhaul everything. But there are people for whom a new career, a new industry or a new life is the right answer.

Discontent affects many in middle age. According to the U-bend theory of happiness, adults start out happy, with the freedom, excitement and expectations of youth; then as they approach their mid-forties they slide, in Tom Lehrer's phrase, down the razor blade of life; and finally, as they age, their happiness improves and keeps on improving. In *The Happiness Curve*, Jonathan Rauch distinguishes this from a midlife crisis. Rather than acting as though they are in a crisis and doing something rash, many people at the bottom of the happiness curve get used to their dissatisfaction. It is not a crisis but a way of life. This is because, Rauch argues, the happiness curve is not about stressful jobs, abandoned dreams or grumpy teenagers. Instead, it is a natural phase.

As with all the studies we saw in Chapter 10 on intelligence, this is an average that not everyone follows in the same way. But it is a pattern that recurs for intrinsic reasons. Happiness, says Rauch, 'isn't rational, predictable, or reliably tethered to our objective circumstances'.[1] According to economists David G. Blanchflower and Andrew Oswald, ageing from twenty to forty-five brings as much as one-third of the unhappiness you would expect from being unemployed, which is one of the most upsetting things that can happen to you.[2] Nothing bad needs to happen for this effect to take place. And very often it doesn't result in any sort of midlife crisis. Most middle-aged people aren't having a midlife crisis, according to this theory, because nothing's actually going wrong in their life: people just naturally feel dissatisfied in middle age.

Let me make a strange argument: more people *should* have a midlife crisis. Declining happiness might be a natural phenomenon that you can't 'cure' but it can also be the inspiration to change. Many people respond to their happiness curve by obsessing about their problems, be they personal or professional. This is the wrong approach. We need to get outside of ourselves. As the philosopher Kieran Setiya says, to prevent (or cure) a midlife crisis you have 'to care about something other than yourself'.[3] For many people, the solution is a middle path between the demands of daily living and the recreation that absorbs you in something else. In 'The Country Husband', John Cheever's short story about a midlife crisis, the solution prescribed by the psychiatrist is to practise woodwork in the evenings, a typically mid-century recommendation. But for potential late bloomers, leaning into the crisis is sometimes the best answer. You don't have to believe in Freudian psychology to agree with the observation of many therapists that, in the words of Andrew Jamieson, most people's 'natural inclination is to preserve at all costs the familiar'.[4]

Marriage counsellor J. H. Wallis wrote in 1962 that middle age is a 'second puberty'. In adolescence, your body changes, you crave vocation, you experience a shift in your sexual drives, and your view of authority becomes less tolerant. In middle age, your memory declines, your young ambitions meet realistic limits, your own authority is less powerful, and your body changes. Maturity is not a given, Wallis says, 'despite greying temples' and a 'successful air'. He argued that we must see middle age as an opportunity for development, the same as adolescence. 'It is,' he said, 'as though we are giving the middle aged another chance.' The difference between adolescence and middle age is that teenagers are expected to discover themselves and explore the world. When middle-aged people 'feel the stirrings' of 'new potentialities', they are more likely to feel 'baffled' and 'rather sheepish'.[5] We should normalize this time of life as a period of change and opportunity. When Audrey Sutherland started going on her first explorations to Moloka'i, she said it was possible partly because her children were getting older, more self-reliant. Their transition to adulthood was under way. 'I need transition too,' she wrote, 'there was a strong feeling of "what next?".'[6]

Vita Sackville-West's novel *All Passion Spent* is a good example of children reacting badly to their parents doing new things. A recent widow, Lady Slane declines to be cared for by her children and instead goes to live alone in a cottage where she makes new friends. Her children find this thoroughly unsettling and object to their mother's independence. Lady Slane is unfazed and develops a new life for herself, cutting herself off from former obligations. Eventually, she serves as an inspiration to her great-granddaughter, who goes off to start a creative career, something Lady Slane had been unable to do. In Doris Lessing's book *The Summer before the Dark*, Kate Brown reacts to her children leaving home and her husband being absorbed in work. She slips loose of her self-restraint and goes on a there-and-back-again adventure involving romance, illness and disillusion that could easily have been the story of a twenty-year-old. Kate returns to her old life having gone through a process of understanding who she is – and to a life that isn't so different from how she had been living. Rather than going through a major spiritual transformation like in Hermann Hesse's *Siddhartha*, a novel about the slow process of becoming a Buddhist monk, Kate gains some perspective and a sense of inner freedom. She is not a mother or a wife or a representative of her class – she is herself. These novels demonstrate the ways that longing for something else can lead to myriad different lives, some involving more change than others. Acting on the crisis or the slump, rather than accepting it, can be transformative. These characters escape their own competency traps as wives and mothers. They put themselves into situations late in life where they would struggle to adapt and they are the better for it. This is often the way late bloomers begin.

People with existing career success can often reach a second peak late in life, after a stagnant period or a slump. Steve Jobs was twenty-four when he visited the Silicon Valley lab of Xerox PARC and saw personal computers with menus, mice and windows – the catalyst for the Apple Macintosh. But Jobs lacked the management skills required to be a great leader. He was fired from Apple in 1985 and lost a considerable amount of wealth. His last two projects at Apple flopped, and for several years after he left he had no successes, losing money at both NeXT and Pixar. When Pixar went public years later, Pixar CFO Lawrence Levy said it carried 'the full weight of his [Jobs's] return from the wilderness'.[7] In a book written before Jobs returned to Apple (kicking off the era that would produce the iPod, iPhone, and iPad and would redefine the nature of corporate collaboration and creativity), Warren Bennis and Patricia Ward Biederman wrote: 'His behaviour clearly undermined his authority.' He was a success, but he was not yet the Steve Jobs of legend. He was at risk of leaving his potential unfulfilled. So damaging was Jobs's behaviour that Bennis and Biederman asked, unaware of Jobs's impending second act, 'What was the real cost of Jobs' uncivil behaviour? How much did he slow down the Mac effort, instead of advancing it, by ratcheting up the stress levels?'[8] They saw some of his late-bloomer potential, saying that his time at Pixar 'mellowed' him and that he had 'learned to lead without bullying'. This, for Bennis and Biederman, 'gives the lie to F. Scott Fitzgerald's observation that there are no second acts in American life'.[9]

What Bennis and Biederman couldn't predict was that the skill for creative collaboration Jobs learned at Pixar, as well as his charismatic ability to inspire people to achieve far more than they believed possible, meant that he was able to transform Apple when he returned to the company in 1997, aged forty-two. He restructured the business, encouraged collaboration, doubled down on integrated hardware and software (against the conventional wisdom about Apple's products), focused on design, created the famous 'Think Different' advertising campaign, and narrowed the product line. He'd learned a lot in his ten years away from the company. He took Apple from being three months away from bankruptcy to being one of the most valuable companies in history. He also removed many middle managers and put the whole company under one profit and loss account, eliminating silos and encouraging the sort of collaboration that created the new generation of Apple products. Even though he co-founded Apple, his biggest contribution came in his second peak.

This extract from a 1996 interview with Terry Gross shows the importance to Jobs of the failures of his time at Pixar and the way that this helped him learn and improve for his later success:

> *TG:* Do you think that when you were ousted from Apple that people kind of wrote you off? I mean, here you are with these big successes now.
>
> *SJ:* Oh golly, I don't know. I'm sure that a lot of people did, and that was fine. It was a very painful time, as you might imagine.
>
> *TG:* What, to be forced out of the company you created?
>
> *SJ:* Oh, of course. That was a very painful time, but you just march forward, and you try to learn from it. One of the things I always tried to coach myself on was not being afraid to fail. When you have something that doesn't work out, a lot of times, people's reaction is to get very protective about never wanting to fall on their face again. I think that's a big mistake, because you never achieve what you want without falling on your face a few times in the process of getting there. I've tried to not be afraid to fail, and, matter of fact, I've failed quite a bit since leaving Apple.

Six years later, he sent an email to all Apple employees with only these words: 'We are what we repeatedly do. Excellence, then, is not an act, but a habit. – Aristotle.' In an early draft of his now-famous commencement speech at Stanford, this was among the opening remarks:

> First, when I was around your age I made the public statement 'Don't trust anyone over 30.' Of course I meant it at the time. Now I am 50 years old, and it's funny how, when you get to be my age, you begin to see more value in experience.

Without his mid-career challenges, isolations, and struggles, he would never have been able to achieve what he did during his second tenure at Apple. We saw in Chapter 4 that entrepreneurs are more likely to succeed in middle age after learning from a period of setbacks. This is exactly Jobs's story. Without his second peak, he would be considerably less famous and influential today. As he said at Stanford, intuiting the principles of the competency trap that was discussed in Chapter 8, 'it turned out that getting fired from Apple was the best thing that could have ever happened to me. The heaviness of being successful was replaced by the lightness of being a beginner again.'[10]

Jobs isn't alone in scaling a second summit in his career.

In his book *What You Do Is Who You Are*, entrepreneur and venture capitalist Ben Horowitz recounts how he hired a salesman called Mark Cranney to join the cloud software company Opsware. Opsware was a West Coast start-up, full of young, casual, secular Democrats. Cranney was an East Coast Mormon who wore a suit and a tie. Cranney needed a change. He had reached a ceiling at the firm he worked for but couldn't find a good sales job in Boston. Opsware was his antithesis. He didn't like the beanbag culture. He didn't like California. The company had a bad reputation. And he thought sales wasn't appreciated in start-ups. He was established in one way of living and working and didn't want to change. After some persuasion, he went for the interview. He found a business full of rap music, with no process or coordination. All sorts of people interviewed him with little process transparency. It was everything he had expected – chaos. When Cranney challenged Horowitz about what he perceived as the lack of hierarchy and decision-making, telling him that, with all these people doing whatever they wanted, it was no surprise they had a sales problem, Horowitz shot back: 'Hey, motherfucker! I'm the CEO. I make the decisions.'[11] Cranney saw for the first time that, despite the rap and the T-shirts, there was a culture there he might be able to work with. There was just enough overlap to encourage Cranney that he could find an opportunity for himself there. So this mid-career salesman left behind the culture, place and business style he knew, and went west to join a rambunctious start-up that lacked any sales structure. It worked. Cranney was the dose of process, systems and no-nonsense sales talk that Opsware needed. (The company was later sold to Hewlett-Packard.) This was a sort of late blooming for Cranney. He changed his life. He took a risk. He got out of his comfort zone. It was a new sort of career that he didn't have to go into: because he made that change, he had a wide new set of opportunities. Cranney has subsequently worked in venture capital, become the Chief Operating Officer at a drone company, and worked as a business advisor, all on the West Coast.

Many people's careers start off strong, fade away and then return. This sort of life is often characterized by perseverance and strong self-belief. These late bloomers are prepared to stick to their principles, even if doing so is isolating. This is not an easy path to take, and it requires inner conviction.

Vera Wang is an example of this sort of double-peaking career. She also exhibits almost all the aspects of late blooming discussed so far. Wang was a near-Olympic figure skater as a teenager. Aged nineteen, she changed tracks when she realized she wasn't going to make it to the top. 'I really lost my way when my figure-skating career ended. I was nineteen, and I was in a panic because nothing had played out the way I'd hoped, after years of hard work.'[12] Wang then started on an unplanned career that would prove to be a period of inefficient preparation. As the chaos theory of careers would predict, small events became part of a larger transformation.

She went to college and studied art history, including a year at the Sorbonne, and during her summer vacation she dressed windows at Yves Saint Laurent on Madison Avenue, where she met Frances Stein, a *Vogue* editor. Stein saw Wang's detailed knowledge of fashion and told Wang to call her when she graduated. A combination of luck and preparation got Wang that opportunity: she had been passionate about clothes as a child, going to haute couture shows in Paris with her mother, and she always maintained her deep knowledge of clothes. Two years later, after graduating, Wang called Stein and got a job at *Vogue*. Before they would hire her, though, she had to go to secretarial school and learn to type.[13] This was the first of many ways in which Wang now learned the practical side of business. She soon became one of the magazine's youngest editors. This was her long apprenticeship. 'I always had an eye and *Vogue* made that eye even sharper.' She travelled the world and got to know a series of designers who mentored her, the way the three generals mentored Eisenhower.

When Wang realized, aged thirty-eight, that she wouldn't become Editor in Chief of *Vogue* – and that the wining and dining side of being more senior didn't suit her – she decided to leave. Like Audrey Sutherland, she interrupted herself and made a change. She talked to her father about opening a toy company, but he was uninterested so she looked for positions at established companies. She spent two years in charge of accessories at Ralph Lauren. This showed her how closely related creativity and business are. Designers must be able to manage both the creation of a product and its sale. 'Real artists ship,' as Steve Jobs said.

Wang got married, aged forty, and realized how commoditized and homogeneous the wedding dress market was. So she designed her own dress. This taught her that wedding dresses were not only all very similar but also that they were not designed with older brides or bridesmaids in mind. Due to the stress of being unable to have children, which involved many hospital visits, Wang quit her job at Ralph Lauren. Her father advised her to start a business. She told him she wasn't interested, especially as she felt so depressed about not being able to get pregnant. That, he said, was an advantage. Without an emotional attachment to the business, she would be more likely to succeed. And he had the perfect idea. Bridal dresses.

Encouraged by her father in the idea that running the business could be just as creative as designing the dresses, she started a new career as a designer. This is where Wang benefited directly from a form of luck not

REASONS TO HAVE A MIDLIFE CRISIS

available to many late bloomers: financial privilege. Her father invested millions in her bridal store. Wang's creativity, however, was essential to her success. She made modern, sophisticated dresses from new fabrics that were designed more for members of the wedding party than for the bride. Wang also built her own factory: it was spotless, almost like a pharmaceutical facility, and the dresses were kept away from dirty machinery. Rather than asking about a bride's fantasy wedding, she asked detailed questions about the practicalities, so she could design a dress that worked, matching fantasy to reality.

Wang's background in skating acted as an inefficient preparation for designing clothes. Her breakthrough into evening and daywear came after she designed costumes for the Olympic skater Nancy Kerrigan. It was her first-hand knowledge of skating that meant Wang was able to think about every turn and contour the costume would have to accommodate. Wang started late as a designer, but her unplanned career meant that she had a unique set of skills which allowed her to get global recognition. She got the opportunity to design for Kerrigan because she had maintained her skating network from more than twenty years earlier. Skating also taught Wang a more general lesson: 'It teaches you discipline. It gives you the joy of self-expression. There's speed; there's movement; and when you fall down, you pick yourself up and try again. It's a good metaphor for life.'[14]

It's a stretch to say that Wang had a midlife crisis when she left *Vogue* – but it is true that instead of waiting out a period in her career that wasn't working, she made a dramatic change. As with her move away from skating, this allowed her to put her previous experience into a new context. It was through inefficient preparation, an unplanned career, networking, and immersing herself in new cultures that Vera Wang turned a midlife slump into a new career.[15] When the *Harvard Business Review* asked her why she decided to start her own business aged forty, she replied:

Is that old? Perhaps I would have preferred to start off at 20 or 30, but I don't think I would have been anywhere near equipped to know what it takes to be in business. Even at 40, I wasn't entirely sure I should be doing it. It wasn't an era for start-ups. I'd always felt I should learn and earn, and I'd already had two incredible careers working for others... Still, I didn't feel very qualified or secure. I never thought I deserved to found a company. I'd been on the artistic side – pictures and styling and *Vogue* and responsible for the design of 18 lines of accessories at Ralph. To think I could start, and run, and sustain a business? I knew how hard it was.[16]

As we saw earlier, this sort of transformation starts with a moment of inspiration that has to be worked out over months, years, perhaps a lifetime. As Robin Hanson said when I interviewed him:

If you are constructing yourself, methodically, steadily over a lifetime and improving yourself... [or] you are working at something and building something in yourself, your insight, your observations, your self control, whatever it is, then you might have a plausible hope that this self you've constructed will eventually be useful for something.[17]

Longer life expectancies mean more and more people will need to change their careers and think about this process of transforming themselves. In *The 100 Year Life*, economist Lynda Gratton and psychologist Andrew J. Scott have written that the old three-part career model of education–work–retirement is being replaced with a five-part model where the work phase starts with a phase of exploration and where periods of work (involving challenge and growth) are then punctuated with periods of transition.[18] This sort of life is based on the concept of transformation: we will not do one thing for our whole career. More of us work independently, have freelance or portfolio careers, change industries, change specialisms. Being a late bloomer is no longer going to be such a minority pursuit.

As Gratton and Scott write, this also changes how you establish your professional reputation. Careers with more stages and more transitions are more complicated to assess than the old three-part model, where specialist skills were more easily identifiable and measurable. As we saw in the network chapter, the culture you are part of is an important factor in how you receive influence – but it is also a key way in which you are assessed and rated. Business culture creates incentives: we act the way others around us act. So companies are looking to hire people who can contribute to and create the right culture. As economist Ryan Avent says, 'The shared understanding of what the firm does is more valuable than the machines it uses or the patents it holds.'[19] This should create many more opportunities for late bloomers as people will be able to take their learnings from one sort of company or industry and apply them somewhere else. Steve Jobs's success in both computers and entertainment is going to look less and less unusual.

I said earlier that the happiness U-bend was well established. It is also well contested – as is the idea of a midlife crisis. Some people think the U-bend applies only to people on low incomes. Others find no evidence for it. A 2019 paper showed that many happiness researchers, 'rely on the assumption that all individuals report their happiness in the same way'. That's quite an assumption. That paper also found that, once you remove any assumptions about the way happiness is distributed, you can find many different patterns, depending on the assumptions you make. If you assume happiness has a normal distribution, like a bell curve, you find the U-bend. But if you don't assume that, you see that there is no real ranking of age groups by average happiness. When you look at all age brackets on a four-point happiness scale, you find people of all ages at all points on the scale. There's a lot of variation in how happy people feel by age. Indeed, there's so much of that sort of variation that many different distributional assumptions can fit the data, and they all give you a different story.[20]

Similarly, psychologists can be sceptical of the midlife crisis, especially the idea from psychotherapy that we all freak out about death as we reach middle age. And it is easy enough to find exceptions, especially among the subjects of this book, as we shall see. Did Julia Child have a midlife crisis or a moment of inspiration? Samuel Johnson didn't write his dictionary out of mortal agony (although that did plague him) but because his talents were absorbed into a commercial network. Ray Kroc didn't build McDonald's into a global empire as an alternative to buying a sports car: he was finally realizing a long-held ambition after decades of work. Margaret Thatcher's rise to Prime Minister owed more to her own deeply held moral beliefs, long preparation for the job, and the luck of circumstances than to her middle age. The signs of a midlife crisis are conspicuous by their absence in her biography.

However, a recent study of large data sets across many countries has found that middle age comes with U-curves on all sorts of measures of wellbeing. The researchers say, 'Midlife is a time when people disproportionately take their own lives, have trouble sleeping, are clinically depressed, spend time thinking about suicide, feel life is not worth living, find it hard to concentrate, forget things, feel overwhelmed in their workplace, suffer from disabling headaches, and become dependent on alcohol.' The causes of this widespread misery remain unknown. Some evidence suggests primates have a similar wellbeing dip and that this might just be biology. The authors of this recent study say that explanations to do with unmet aspirations are plausible.[21] People often expect to be happy in middle age and unhappy in old age – which, as we have seen, is an error. This might explain the dip: a mismatch between expectations and reality. Some people believe that people get happier in their fifties because they abandon unmet aspirations.[22] That might work for some people, but not for everyone. Giving up one set of aspirations is likely to be successful only if they are replaced with others. Long retirements without any goals or aspirations don't sound very rewarding or fulfilling.

We don't all follow a smooth U-shaped happiness curve: as with cognitive decline, there is great variation. Some people have a more dramatic, more painful V-bend. Others go through a gentle upward slope, starting from a lower point. There are variations between countries, too. In Russia, the U-bend only goes up *after* the point of average life expectancy, a very miserable situation which means most people's lives are a downward slope of unhappiness. In China, the curve doesn't start very high, so it's more of a mild dip and upward slope than a real U.

These variations, between countries and individuals, are similar to novelist Kurt Vonnegut's story arcs.

Vonnegut saw basic patterns in the shapes of novels, biblical stories, myths, and a wide range of narratives. Some follow the U-bend shape, which he called 'Man in Hole' – a story about a man who is doing fine, gets into some sort of problem, and then gets out of it – a classic Hollywood formula. Other patterns include 'Cinderella', where you start off miserable, inch slowly up, step by step, as your fairy godmother provides you with dress, shoes, carriage, and so forth, reach a peak of happiness at the ball, then plummet precipitously down at midnight, only to reach infinite bliss when Prince Charming finds you by means of the missing slipper. Stories from Kafka are more likely to follow the slope we saw in Russia's happiness curve: downward and unremitting. The well-known 'boy meets girl' formula sees someone go from mildly happy to very happy to deep misery and back to very happy. (This is not quite the U-bend because it starts much lower and swings more dramatically.) Think also of a show like *The Sopranos* which has less of a smooth up or down curve, more of a constant fluctuating ambiguity. There are many variations on the happiness U-bend.

Of course, fiction is not real life, and the Vonnegut curves are not based on large data sets of people's experiences. But it is significant that world literature, a repository of observations about human life, has found so much variation in life patterns. Data science research, using 1,300 novels, has shown that the core story arcs that Vonnegut proposed have been measured, albeit with a range of variation.[23] This rich data should be used to supplement the statistics of happiness research. Most people will probably go through some sort of middle-life slump, per the averages, but the actual shape of the curve is not going to be the smooth statistical U-bend. Many people will have a different experience. It isn't provable that the Vonnegut curves are real-life patterns but it makes intuitive sense. Don't you know people whose fortunes turned on a penny, perhaps more than once, whose life started bad and ended worse, or who took a gradual upward journey from unhappiness to happiness? Our lives are more like novels than they are like statistical averages.

Compare the graph we saw earlier of Frank Lloyd Wright's career to Vonnegut's 'boy meets girl' story arc (Figures 12.1 and 12.2).

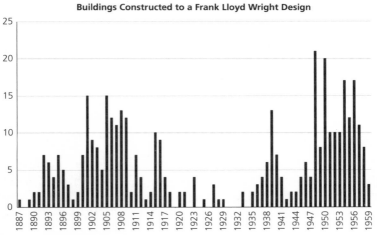

Buildings Constructed to a Frank Lloyd Wright Design

Figure 12.1 Number of buildings constructed to a Frank Lloyd Wright design, 1887–1959
Source: Data for graph taken from William Allin Storrer, *The Architecture of Frank Lloyd Wright: A Complete Catalog*, 3rd edn (University of Chicago Press, 2002).

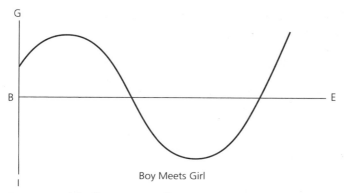

Boy Meets Girl

Figure 12.2 The 'boy meets girl' narrative arc adapted from Kurt Vonnegut, *Palm Sunday* (Vintage Digital, 2010), Kindle edition, p. 625. Drawn by Deepali Agrawal.

This is a crude overlap. We also need to factor in Wright's personal life, which was complicated and fraught – often his personal life seems unable to fit any sort of curve. But there is a falling and rising pattern: Mamah died, Taliesin burned twice, his second marriage was a disaster, his finances were in a hole – in the middle of this he built the Imperial Hotel, re-established Taliesin, and met Olgivanna in 1925, the pivotal year, full of energy and experimentation. And 1925 is right at the bottom of his career curve. It might be a crude overlap, but Wright's personal and professional lives are more suited to a Vonnegut curve than the happiness U-bend.

The variety of curves – and the fact that the midlife slump is temporary – suggests that many people give up their aspirations too early. It's not easy to make the sorts of changes to your life we have discussed in this chapter. But it will be increasingly necessary as we live longer and have different sorts of careers. If you are on a classic U-bend, what feels like permanent malaise is temporary: as Jonathan Rauch says, what is missing in that slump is 'not happiness. It's optimism'.[24] That's not necessarily an argument to accept your life and wait it out. If the happiness U-bend really is nothing to do with you unmet ambitions, then it can still be worth trying to achieve them. And if you are on a different life curve, one more like the Vonnegut patterns, setting new aspirations might be all the more important. It is change that resolves those curves: Vonnegut's story arcs rely on something new happening. If you are living a 'Man in Hole' life or a 'Cinderella', then something needs to happen to move you along the curve. Unlike the U-bend theory, this is not inevitably biology. It requires action. Trying to meet your unmet ambitions is essential to the way these curves work. How else does the man get out of the hole or the boy find the girl? Talking about her late start directing movies, Ava DuVernay said:

> Usually people are going to film school and they're picking up their first camera either in high school or in college years. I was just starting to learn about it at 32 years old. I really think the conversation is about change. Can you change your mind about who you are and what you want to do later in the game?[25]

One thing you hear again and again about the happiness U-bend or the midlife crisis is that acceptance makes people happier as they age. Give up your ambitions and be at peace. But the variations in life patterns and the fact that midlife (un)happiness is more of a biological phase than a reflection of your abilities suggest that some people should *not* accept their lives, but change them. You might *feel* like you are in decline, but in reality you are more likely to be in a phase where you lack optimism for biological reasons. Under those conditions, accepting sounds like giving up for the wrong reason. We wouldn't advise teenagers with decades ahead of them to simply accept their lives and be happy – we shouldn't be advising that to the middle aged either. You might need to accept the loss of a dream in one area to pursue ambitions somewhere else. But not necessarily.

The world is full of people who make mid-career shifts and are all the better for them. Susan Ferugio became a web developer aged fifty-one after a career as a financial risk analyst, a stay-at-home mother and a marketing consultant.[26] Rosalind Arden studied art history before producing science documentaries for television. She got a PhD in behavioural genetics late in her career and is now a research fellow at the LSE. Jenny Hibbert is now a well-known photographer with an exhibition touring the UK. She has travelled all over the world and photographed brown bears in Finland, Kazakhs in Mongolia, and landscapes in Wales. But she didn't buy her first digital camera until she was sixty-two. She had used film before, but only got serious later on: 'I was going through a really messy divorce. Any divorce is a nightmare. It kind of took my mind off everything so I threw myself into photography.'[27] Eric Yuan founded Zoom aged forty-one.[28] Yuan spent fourteen years as a corporate employee and left to start a company when his idea for Zoom was rejected by his employer, Cisco Systems. If they had said yes, he would still be a corporate executive, not a billionaire.[29] Ion Țiriac was a child ping-pong champion in Romania. In his twenties, he competed in ice hockey at the 1964 Winter Olympics and then switched to tennis. Six years later, he won the men's doubles in the French Open, aged thirty-one. After a career as a top-ten tennis player, he became a coach and talent spotter. He discovered Boris Becker. In the 1980s and 1990s, he became a late-blooming businessman in post-Soviet Romania, setting up the country's first private bank. As well as founding the bank, Țiriac was an agent for Siemens and Mercedes-Benz and had a stake in a freight business at Bucharest airport.[30]

Economist Robin Hanson is now a tenured professor with a successful career as an economist. It was not always so. Aged thirty-four, with two small children to support, he left his job in a research lab and started a PhD. There was nothing wrong with his life. Although his job was not very senior, 'I was decently paid and we had children, a stable life.' But, as Robin says, 'I just kept feeling itchy that I had this big potential in life and I wanted to realize it.' He admits that he made the change not due to any revelation: 'It was more desperation

I would think than inspiration.' In his words, he rolled the dice. He felt he had no other choice.[31]

Robin is a classic example of the late bloomers Duhigg saw at his reunion. He didn't have a bad job. He hadn't failed. But it wasn't what he wanted. It wasn't making full use of his potential. Thirty-four might seem early for a midlife crisis (not, I think, that Robin would call it that) but it was late for Robin's ambitions. He had spent the previous decade attending lectures in graduate school on the side of his job, looking for a way forward. He leaned into his crisis – precipitated it, in fact – and made it highly productive. In this way, he created a second career for himself.

•••

What we learned about cognitive decline is a key factor to the way people think about their middle age. Just as believing in your own cognitive decline is a major impediment to staying productive, simply accepting your circumstances is a barrier to midlife transformation. Having a midlife crisis doesn't have to mean embarrassing your children – it can be a way of preparing yourself for the final third of your career.

The journalist Lucy Kellaway gave up her lucrative, high-status career as a writer at the *Financial Times* to train as a maths teacher in her late fifties. It was gruelling but her stamina, attitude and inexhaustible energy meant she was successful. There was no cognitive challenge. Indeed, she discovered huge reserves of enthusiasm, engagement and learning potential in herself. She plans to keep teaching until she is seventy-five. Simultaneously, she set up a charity called Now Teach that recruits people with career experience who want to spend the final stage of their working life as teachers. Over five hundred people with an average twenty-six years' work experience have now retrained as teachers with Now Teach.[32] Kellaway has worked with lawyers, bankers, consultants, civil servants and many others who made the change. Her conclusion:

It's not that you can't teach an old dog new tricks. You absolutely can. What is hard is getting the dog to unlearn its old ones. It was this unlearning of decades of experience of working at other things that proved hard for almost all of us, and was the undoing of a few.[33]

This is supported by research. There are some specific things that you need to learn early. The way ballerinas turn their ankles must be developed while bone calcification is still in progress. Early training changes the brain mapping of musicians, and intense practice changes myelin production in relevant areas of the brain. Similarly, learning a language is much harder later in life. You can still learn to play instruments and speak languages as you age, though it gets more difficult. For most things, youth is a strong advantage, not a necessity. Sometimes as children we acquire 'flawed fundamentals' – that is, we learn the basics wrong – and this hampers us later on. That is what Kellaway was talking about when she said the hardest thing was unlearning old tricks. Adults also routinely underestimate the time required for practice and often lack that time. They are more likely to sustain mediocre performance than to seek out the training and coaching that professionals get.[34]

Kellaway's experience was that people who had not previously made a career transition found it difficult not to learn new things but to get out of old habits. Cognitive decline and middle-age malaise played no role in these people's experience: it was a question of attitude. In her excellent memoir about her experience, Kellaway emphasizes again and again the role of attitude and belief in these sorts of transformations. Once she left the boredom and routine of her old job and started teaching, Kellaway became obsessed with her work and engaged with it in a way she hadn't been for many years. Indeed, at one point she says, 'Never have I been this engaged with anything in my professional life.'[35] Part of what made the change so rewarding was her age. Kellaway no longer worried about being bad at something, no longer fretted about office politics, no longer felt the drudgery of her work. Her life stage – children grown up, marriage over, financial pressures easier – gave her the freedom to change her work, and to enjoy it and pursue it with the determination we normally associate with an ambitious graduate.

Kellaway was practising what Josh Waitzkin – who is both a former chess and tai chi champion – calls investment in loss. In order to be good at something, you must 'give yourself to the learning process'.[36] Waitzkin learned this idea from tai chi, which he took up once he decided to leave professional chess. In order to become proficient at tai chi, you must learn not to resist. Fearing loss, succumbing to pressure, can numb the mind: this was what Waitzkin had learned from the pressures of chess. Once you get into a loop of wanting to win and resisting failure, you cannot learn from errors. Resistance blocks the mind. 'It is essential,' he says, 'to have a liberating incremental approach that allows for times when you are not in a peak performance state... Great ones are willing to get burned time and again as they sharpen their sword in the fire.' He gives the example of Michael Jordan who made more last-minute game-winning shots than any other NBA player in history – but also more last-minute game-losing shots. 'He was willing to look bad on the road to basketball immortality.'[37] Investing in loss is another way of talking about the competency trap we saw in Chapter 8. People who don't believe age matters, who are prepared to invest in loss, are more able to turn the natural changes of middle age into an opportunity to do something new with the final third of their life.

Believing you have gone through cognitive decline is a common feature of middle-age malaise. It comes up again and again in the interviews Jonathan Rauch conducted for *The Happiness Curve*. But it is the belief, not the reality, that causes the problem. If you believe you have gone through cognitive decline, that you are somehow less capable of learning something new in your fifties than your twenties, you are less able to invest in loss. We all have visions of what the final stage of life could be like – and our expectations of middle age influence those visions.

There was recently a TikTok trend for 'coastal grandmothers', started by Lex Nicoleta. This is an aesthetic based in the movies of Nancy Myers (such as the 2003 romcom *Something's Gotta Give*). The coastal grandmother trend takes the chic minimalism of someone like Helen Hunt or Diane Keaton and creates a lifestyle for young people out of it. Although superficially this represents a revival of chinoiserie, sixties music and reading by the fire, it shows us something about what it is that we actually admire about older people. We are very used to people in their sixties and seventies taking up new hobbies, staying physically fit, having good taste in clothes and vases, even having exciting romantic lives such as in Myers's movies, but the idea that someone of that age can be just as intellectually creative, inventive, or accomplished as a younger person has less cache. Coastal grandmother represents, above all, a lifestyle. As Olivia Marcus said, 'If you've ever felt the desire to take a long solo walk on the beach in a button-down and a woven hat – there's no question that you're a coastal grandmother through and through.'[38]

As journalist Farrah Storr writes, the coastal grandmother is an illusion. 'She is an idea of a person. Someone enlightened. With hours of free time. Someone liberated from the 24-7 hustle and the social media anxiety that plagues us deep into the night.' This trend idolizes certain aspects of certain sorts of ageing, late-life accomplishment not often among them. It is about aspiring to the luxury of simplicity. But, as Storr says, 'Simplicity is built upon layers of hard graft. It is earned over time through experience and trial.'[39]

Coastal grandmother doesn't endorse the idea of cognitive decline but it hardly sets out an optimistic vision of what can be achieved with age rather than simply enjoyed from it. Think of the sitcom *Grace and Frankie*. The really daring thing there is not that the couples divorce and start living in a way that is true to themselves – that is almost cliche at this point. No, the really daring thing is that the two women set up a sex-product company in their seventies. The sex part creates some humour and plotlines, but there is real tension about the role of a woman in her seventies as CEO. This is the real cultural frontier for grandmothers: we need to believe in their business capabilities with the same fervour that we admire their chintz, hydrangeas and sex lives.

Just as we believe coastal grandmothers can be stylish we need to take seriously the idea that they could be businesspeople, scientists, or inventors. There are many such examples. Veta Jacqulin Talmadge joined the Peace Corps aged eighty and worked in Lesotho in Africa. 'I thought, Hey, why not! Songwriter Phil Ochs said it well in the song "When I am gone": "I can't do it when I'm gone, so, I guess I'll have to do it while I'm here."'[40] For many later bloomers, you have to do what you have to do. As Kenichi Horie said, after sailing solo across the Pacific aged eighty-three, 'I didn't think I'd be sailing at 83 but I'm still healthy and I didn't want to miss this chance. Challenges are exciting so I'd like to keep trying.'[41]

These are all examples of what economists Lynda Gratton and Andrew J. Scott call the explorer stage of life. As we age the old three-stage model of education–work–retirement is giving way to a new model where periods of work are broken up by periods of exploration. We are simply living too long, and the world is changing too much, for the old model to be sustainable. Gratton and Scott see three prime periods of exploration: your twenties, your forties and your seventies.[42] What matters in this new age of long fruitful living is not just your cognitive test scores but your willingness to keep going and keep changing, to make the most of your midlife transitions.

Conclusion: be your own interruption

'We talked about growing old gracefully, and Elsie, who's seventy-four,
Said, 'A) it's a question of being sincere,
And B) If you're supple, you've nothing to fear.'

Noël Coward, 'I Went to a Marvellous Party'

One submerged but continuous theme of this book has been hard work. Some talents are discovered in a flash of brilliance, but all talents must be patiently worked at to keep shining. None of the people I have discussed made their accomplishments without significant effort, often at the cost of some other aspect of their life. Even the strongest natural talent must be worked into achievement – sometimes forced – the way gold is shaped and smoothed to become jewellery. This can make late blooming a slow and difficult process that only begins with finding your talent.

As we saw in Chapter 8 and the discussion of transformation, many stories of late blooming are not especially dramatic. The French Renaissance philosopher Michel de Montaigne withdrew from public life in 1571 aged forty to spend his remaining years writing essays. His midlife crisis sparked a new literary genre and contributed to a philosophical movement: he became a precursor of the Enlightenment. But it mostly involved sitting in an attic study writing essays based on his decades of immersive reading. You do not have to be Montaigne to discover your talent and work at it.

That spirit lurks in so many more ordinary lives. In the decade I spent as a talent brand consultant conducting interviews and focus groups with employees in global companies, I spoke to hundreds of people in jobs ranging from cleaning and janitorial work to technicians, bankers and executives, and I dealt with organizations from charities to start-ups to global bankers. I was constantly surprised at how much some people loved their work. But I also met many people who felt trapped, dispirited, stagnant.

The people who stayed with me were the ones who felt ignored, who had joined a company with the dream to help to build something, change something, do something useful, but who ended up feeling like their work wasn't worthwhile. They were often not just grumpy (and occasionally angry), but sad. The burdens of lost time, eroded skills, and something inside that yearns to be unforgotten are not only applicable to the tragedy of unemployment, but they are also all too real for people whose work feels insignificant. These lost souls need some direction. Some of them need to find their talent.

But what *is* talent? When Noël Coward went on Dick Cavett's American talk show in 1970, Cavett asked him, 'What is the word for when one has terrific prolific qualities?' The maestro snapped back, deadpan: 'Talent.' We think we know talent when we see it, a form of innate ability that leads to accomplished excellence. In business, recruitment is now routinely known as 'talent attraction'. In this sense, 'talent' often describes high or exceptional professional ability.

There's a broader definition. Samuel Johnson defined talent as: 'Faculty; power; gift of nature. A metaphor borrowed from the talents mentioned in the holy writ.' The 'holy writ' Johnson refers to is the famous Parable of the Talents in the gospels of Matthew and Luke. In it, a master gives talents (coins) to three servants. Two of them invest the money and return with more. The third servant buries the talent to keep it safe and returns with the same amount of money that he was given. The master is angry and casts the servant 'into the outer darkness, where there will be weeping and gnashing of teeth'. His sin was not that he failed to make as much money as the others, but that he did nothing with the gift (or talent) he had been given.

We can think of this cultivation of talents as the pursuit of excellence. This is the ancient Greek concept of *areté*. *Areté* means reaching your full potential as a person; it is the virtue of making the most of your talents. The word *areté* means 'virtue' as well as 'excellence'. Virtue in this sense is about accomplishment. It is virtuous to use your talents, and being excellent at something is a form of virtue.

As humanities scholar Richard Hooker wrote, 'The man or woman of *areté* is a person of the highest effectiveness; they use all their faculties: strength, bravery, wit, and deceptiveness, to achieve real results.'[1] Aristotle gave the example of a horse whose excellence is to run and carry a rider, or an eye whose excellence is to see. These are the virtues of the horse and the eye – in the same way, a person's virtue will be to 'perform his characteristic activity well'.[2]

Areté therefore does not denote particular sorts of capability. Rather, it focuses on the excellence of doing whatever you do best, of using your talents. You can have a talent for anything. There are canonical virtues, outlined in major philosophical and religious traditions, but different disciplines prioritize different virtues. The science blog *SlimeMoldTimeMold* has even recommended 'carefreeness' and 'arrogance' as scientific virtues.[3] All of the late bloomers studied here have cultivated their own particular virtues. This is what the neuroscience, psychology, and sociology could not tell us: we each have to cultivate our own talent.

We all have some set of talents that we can perform well. You do not have to be Noël Coward to have faculties or abilities you can refine and use to 'achieve real results'. There is great virtue in working at what we are good at, in following our talents and abilities. We can all do more to reach our full potential. The parable of the talents is about all of us – it poses the question, are you cultivating your virtues? What we saw in the stories of Margaret Thatcher and Audrey Sutherland, of Frank Lloyd Wright and Ray Kroc, was *areté* in action.

•••

This cultivation can be laborious. Achieving *areté* – or excellence – is hard work. Talents do not exist fully formed waiting to find the right opportunity. That is the mistake Mr Micawber makes in *David Copperfield*. The Micawbers are always talking about the way Mr Micawber's talent isn't appreciated, the way he will prosper as soon as he finds a suitable outlet for his talents, that *something will turn up*, but they never talk about cultivating those talents (whatever they might be), never about the hard work involved. In contrast, David Copperfield becomes a successful writer by apprenticing himself to a dictionary writer, learning shorthand, working hard on his drafts, and spending more than twelve hours a day at work. You must find the right combination of natural ability and lucky opportunity but then you must *work*.

This is well demonstrated by the late bloomer Malcolm X (1925–65). When he was fifteen, a teacher told Malcolm that, as a Black boy, he would never be able to become a lawyer. This was a moment of realization – he would never be accepted as an equal. He realized that, even though he was one of the smartest students in the class, being Black meant he had far fewer options for success. 'It was then that I began to change – inside.'[4] He refocused his attentions away from study. As his biographer Manning Marable has written, 'Malcolm's grades plummeted and his turbulence increased.' He was sent, aged fifteen, to live with his sister. Looking back years later, he saw this through religious eyes, as a moment of transformation. Had he stayed in that town, he would have ended up in a 'menial job', following the path of other Black boys held down by the system. As it was, he was about to begin what Marable called 'his first major reinvention'.[5]

For the next five years, Malcolm Little became a hustler. Dancing, wearing fashionable zoot suits, seducing women, smoking marijuana and selling drugs were his main preoccupations. He fell in with a bad crowd and began committing robberies. The latest research suggests that Little exaggerated his criminal activities in his autobiography and that, as one of his friends put it, 'He was never no big time racketeer or thug.'[6] Certainly, though, he burglarized nightspots in a petty way, was drinking heavily and was taking drugs. He was unemployed and drifted. In 1945, he was arrested in Detroit after robbing a man at gunpoint. He then fled the jurisdiction to Boston,[7] where he had previously lived with his sister. Now he fell back in with the old crowd, a man named Shorty Jarvis, and together they established a gang to burgle houses. They were caught, he was charged with illegal possession of a firearm, and because he had been with a white woman the trial was racially motivated – Malcolm and Shorty got significantly tougher jail sentences than was usual because the lawyers and judge were prejudiced against interracial relationships. His own defence attorney was angry that Malcolm had been associating with white women. Aged twenty, he was sentenced to between six and eight years in jail.

The first year or so of his seven years in prison was a crushing experience. At first, with nothing else available, he got high on nutmeg. Looking back, he had memories of 'cursing guards, throwing things out of my cell, baulking in the lines, dropping my tray in the dining hall, refusing to answer my number'.[8] All of this got him solitary confinement where 'I would pace for hours like a caged leopard'. Eighth grade was the last time he had studied anything 'that didn't have some hustle purpose'. That started to change. A fellow prisoner named Bimbi was famed among the inmates for his absorbing talks about all manner of subjects. Listening to him, Malcolm learned about Thoreau, atheism, the history of Concord, but mostly he saw someone who could 'command total respect... with his words'. One day, Bimbi told Malcolm he had some brains and ought to use them.[9] So he did.

He began correspondence courses, slowly learning to write and to master basic grammar. He moved on to Latin. He was moved to Concord prison, and there was influenced by his brother's conversion to Islam. Don't eat any more pork and stop smoking, advised his brother and 'I'll show you how to get out of prison'. Then his sister managed to get him transferred to another prison, nearly halfway through his sentence, where he had far more freedom. Here there was a library. His brother visited him in this prison, talked to him about Allah, and told him that white people were the devil. His brother also talked to him about Elijah Muhammad, leader of a Black nationalist Islamic sect called the Nation of Islam. Muhammad visited Malcolm's family who spread his influence to Malcolm in jail. Soon Malcolm began writing to Muhammad.

Now Malcolm reached the limit of his abilities. 'At least twenty-five times I must have written that first one-page letter to him... I was trying to make it both legible and understandable.'[10] Marable notes that targeting depressed, isolated prisoners was a strategy of Elijah Muhammad and the Nation of Islam, which focused its efforts on alcoholics, addicts, and prostitutes. And this was one of many significant conversions Malcolm X underwent in his life. But, writing those letters inspired him to continue his self-education. Frustrated that he could not express what he thought in his letters, he went to the prison library. For the first two days, he browsed the dictionary, amazed at the existence of so many words. To get himself started, he began to copy them out. On the first day, he copied down the first page of the dictionary and read it back to himself out loud. 'I was so fascinated that I went on.' He claimed to have copied the entire dictionary.

Malcolm's expanding vocabulary meant he could read more widely. He was, as so many people are when they discover reading, utterly hooked. He crept out of bed at night and read by a small crack of light that reached his cell floor, sneaking back to bed once an hour as the guard passed. In this painstaking way, Malcolm Little spent years educating himself. As Marable writes:

> He consciously remade himself into Gramsci's now famous 'organic intellectual,' creating the habits that, years later, would become legendary. His powers of dedication and self-discipline were extraordinary, and directly opposite to the wayward drifting of his early youth. The trickster disappeared, the clowning side of disobedience, leaving the wilful challenger to authority.[11]

Malcolm gave himself an extraordinary education: Herodotus, Kant, Nietzsche, H. G. Wells's *History of the World*, W. E. B. Du Bois's *Souls of Black Folk*, Gregor Mendel's *Findings in Genetics*, J. A. Roger's *Sex and Race*, Will Durant, Mahatma Gandhi, and so on. He was profoundly affected by history – 'I never will forget how shocked I was when I began reading about slavery's total horror.'[12] He had gone into prison hardly able to write a letter and would emerge on the path to becoming an orator, a leader, and a preacher. When he left prison, he bought a watch. Time was precious to him now, and he was going to continue his hard work exhaustively.

Through this mental labour, Malcolm X developed his *areté* – the nature of his excellence was political and religious, which made him a divisive figure. What is beyond dispute is that the young man who went to jail was very different from the one who came out seven years later. He became the most influential preacher in the Nation of Islam, recruiting many converts, opening temples and, at the age of thirty-two, becoming the Nation's national representative. In his late thirties, he was a national figure, a prominent voice in civil rights debates, and a person of powerful controversy. Personal differences and a growing rivalry between Malcolm and Elijah Muhammad meant that, when Malcolm X said of John F. Kennedy's death it was a case of the chickens coming home to roost, Muhammad took the chance to throw Malcolm out of the Nation. Malcolm X changed his mind about white people being devils and was undergoing another transformation towards more orthodox Islam and less radical politics, albeit still advocating violence. Malcolm X was assassinated aged thirty-nine. His legacy in political and popular culture remains enormous, in music, film, and political discourse.[13] Without the hard work he undertook in prison, this legacy would have been unthinkable for the young man who dropped out of school.

•••

The lesson of *areté* is not just that we must cultivate our own virtues. We also saw in those profiles that it is difficult to discover *areté* in others without getting to know them well. It will take a new and different sort of assessment to get beyond appearances and discover the late bloomer within. So, how do we identify late bloomers?

First, we must dispense with preconceptions. Cognitive decline is not as certain as we think. Learning new habits is not as hard as unlearning old ones. People who simply keep going, who are not going to make less effort, or be less interested, just because they have security or status, be it tenure, seniority, a financial cushion, whatever, are more significant. Plenty of people retire and take up new activities like travel or golf. What is unusual are the people still working on something. Penelope Fitzgerald started writing novels aged sixty partly because she never gave up her intellectual interests: reading literature critically to teach it, learning languages, travelling, going to the opera. The ones who keep going are the ones to watch.

Second, therefore, look for motivation, which will often be non-obvious. Would anyone say Samuel Johnson had motivation? He was indolent, inconsistent, self-absorbed, moody, and frequently idle. But he was obsessive. His friend Robert Dodsley knew this about him and so knew he would be a good dictionary writer. You need to uncover what people do in secret or what they just do, irrespective of circumstances. Fields Medal winner June Huh didn't start taking maths seriously until the end of college: he had wanted to become a poet. He then became so obsessive about maths he lived on frozen pizza so as not to waste time cooking or thinking about food. Katalin Karikó tolerated grant application rejections for years and a demotion before she achieved success with the COVID mRNA vaccine. Edward Jenner was a very observant person. No one believed his discoveries about cuckoos, but it was a signal of the ability he would use to have his breakthrough insight about vaccines. Look at what people persist at, not what persistently happens to them.

Third, look for people who could be great *again*. Lots of people thought Steve Jobs was a spent case after he was fired from Apple. But he retained an aura of intrigue which he later lived up to, quite spectacularly. The same is true of Frank Lloyd Wright, who was thought to be finished before he worked on Fallingwater. He would go on to design the Guggenheim and many other major innovative projects. It was easy for Wright's mentor, Louis Sullivan, to see Wright's talents as a young man: when Wright was in his sixties, others couldn't see the same thing. People who have been great can be great again is a heuristic worth keeping in mind, no matter how 'over' they seem to be. Then there are people who achieved fantastic but not fame-worthy things when they were young, like Vera Wang. Michelangelo did almost no painting for a fifteen-year period in his forties and fifties. He then produced *The Last Judgment*.

Fourth, look for lack of context, changing context, or for people who are open to influences. The movie director Ava DuVernay didn't pick up a camera until she was thirty-two. 'I never thought that I could actually make a film,' she said, 'I had no context for that until I was on sets working as a publicist.'[14] How much can be achieved simply by enabling people to sample the world more broadly, mid-career? The memoirs of Frederick Douglass, Harriet Jacobs and Malcolm X all contain a moment when they realized what it meant to live under slavery or racism. Until then, they had no idea about their own context, despite the fact that they were living in a very obviously (to us) oppressed situation. Once they saw it all again in different terms, their lives began to be transformed.

Fifth, find people who really do believe age is only a number, who aren't going to be what other people expect them to be. We are very used to people in their sixties and seventies taking up new hobbies, staying physically fit, having exciting romantic lives – but the idea that someone of that age can be just as creative, inventive, or accomplished as a younger person has less cache. Yitang Zhang, who made significant progress towards solving the twin prime conjecture aged fifty-five, and has made progress on another famously complex problem in his sixties, was asked about his age by a journalist and said, 'I don't care so much about the age problem. I don't think there is a big difference. I can still do whatever I like to do.' How many people would quit their job aged sixty to kayak 800 kilometres of the Alaskan coastline like Audrey Sutherland did? One big reason she made that decision (and kept going back for twenty years) was that she was guided by herself, not by what other people expected of her. Many late bloomers balance strong self-direction with the ability to take on the right sort of influences.

The main objection people could make to this book is that it is too selective. Anyone can take a group of late bloomers who *did* succeed and draw conclusions. But that isn't reliable. What about all the late bloomers who failed? Look at the existing data on achievement and it is clear. Not that many people do in fact flourish later in life. This book is optimistic moonshine in the face of that experience.

But what if that data is measuring not an undeniable fact of reality but the culture we happen to live in? I spoke recently to an economist at a party. When we discussed examples of mathematicians and scientists who bloomed late, he responded that the distribution – that is, the number of people who bloom 'late' relative to the average – shows that many more people do their best work in the first half of their life. The median age is relatively low. But that measure only shows what has happened. Can we know what might happen if our culture changed?

This book cannot prove that many more mathematicians and scientists could do their best work after fifty. But it can show that it's much more possible than we believe and inspire more people to try. What if we could change our attitude and, in so doing, change our lives? When economist Stephen Dubner ran a large online experiment to have people make major life decisions – about their jobs and mortgages and love lives – based on a coin toss, the ones who came up heads for change tended to be happier. Change may be daunting but it is good. If we expect more of ourselves, who knows what we might be able to achieve. 'With the exercise of self-trust,' said Emerson, 'new powers shall appear.'[15]

Appearances can be deceptive. We simply don't know how many people *could* be late bloomers, given the opportunity. To discover late bloomers, we need to get to know people. The usual measures of success, ability, achievement or talents do not work as well. We saw in the biographical profiles that measuring late bloomers by results is not helpful: everything we have learned we learned from the late period before the success. As writer, critic, and scholar Walter Pater said, our priority is 'not the fruit of experience, but experience itself'. Once we know what it was like to *become* a late bloomer, we can live differently.

Pater wrote that line in a lively and compelling essay at the end of his little book *The Renaissance*. He warned against forming habits, as they can lead to listless, conventional lives. He recoiled from the constraining nature of bourgeois life and sought to awaken his readers to the wonders of lived experience. In this way, by being open to wonder, he believed we could become vitally alive. 'To burn always with this hard, gemlike flame, to maintain this ecstasy, is success in life.'[16] Great passion, he believed, would give a deeper sense of life. This was challenging, to say the least, in Victorian Oxford, where Pater worked, a place of huge moral restraint and timidity. It seems much more normal and acceptable to us. But how many of us actually live like this? How many of us could?

However old you are, whatever your status relative to your peers, life is waiting for you. It is not too late to pursue change, to seek a different life, a better world. Remember, late bloomers are often spurred to start by some interruption. This book shows that *you can be your own interruption*. Ask yourself as Audrey Sutherland did, 'What part of my goal can I achieve now? What can I do now to achieve my goal later?'[17] Making these changes, however they occur, is vitally important: 'Impossible is it for persons to be changed when the days they have still to live stay so much the same,' as Elizabeth Bowen wrote in *A World of Love*.

Go! Change your days. Burn with a hard gemlike flame.

ACKNOWLEDGEMENTS

Without a grant from the Emergent Venture fund, administered by Tyler Cowen, this book would not have been written. My special thanks to Tyler for his sustained support and interest in this book and his forbearance with my requests.

Samuel Johnson, the hero at the heart of this book, once said that in order to write a book a man must turn over half a library: the staff of the London Library have been a friendly and efficient part of that process for me. Not to mention all the good people who sold me cheap books online. My thanks also to everyone who runs archives, especially those with digitized materials or those who are willing to send digital copies of material. Andrew Riley at Churchill College was especially helpful for my work on Margaret Thatcher.

Many of the people I am thanking have assistants who organized meetings, processed paperwork, kept things moving – many thanks for their work, especially to Camey, Sydney, Augustus.

Making this into a saleable book and finding a publisher relied on the generous and persistent efforts of my agent Toby Mundy and his meticulous, attentive colleague Elena Steiert. At John Murray, I have been fortunate to work with the affable and encouraging Jonathan Shipley, who I am pleased to know, as well as his colleague Jenny Campbell.

While I was working on this book, ChatGPT was released, and then GPT-4. None of this book is written by GPT, but it was an invaluable research tool and proofreader, and was one of the early readers of the manuscript; at all stages it offered sensible insights with great swiftness. Many thanks to everyone at OpenAI for making such a remarkable tool available.

Innumerable people have given me ideas, had long conversations with me, and suggested examples of late bloomers, several of whom are mentioned in the book. I am especially grateful to Adaobi Adibe, Will Orr-Ewing, Tyrique King, Jeremy McNeil, Zhengdong Wang, Uri Bram, Matt Clifford, and Arnaud Schenk. They all made me think differently, recommended books, showed a deep interest in my project and made themselves useful in diverse ways. I borrowed a phrase from Chris Brown, for which I thank him, with apologies for not making more of it. I am grateful to all the readers of my blog *The Common Reader* and especially to those readers who have emailed me about this project over the last two years. Special thanks to Anna Gat for recommending that I read *Personal History*, Katharine Graham's autobiography. Adam Morris was the one who told me I should write about this topic in the first place.

When I visited Wisconsin on the trail of Frank Lloyd Wright, I was given a marvellous tour of the Annunciation Greek Orthodox Church by Elizabeth Lumb and was privileged to join the congregation for part of a service one evening. Nicholas Hayes and his wife Angela gave me a tour of their impeccably restored home, the Elizabeth Murphy House, and I enjoyed our conversations about Wright very much; Nicholas also gave me a tour of the local area, and some of Russell Barr Williams's brazen imitations of Wright's work. Bill Martinelli kindly showed me the Jacobs First House. Taliesin is well run by its staff and volunteers, and our tour was in-depth and enthusiastic: the same is true of the Monona Terrace. In Milwaukee, I received splendid hospitality from Jane and Christina.

Researching Audrey Sutherland's life I was dependent on the help and co-operation of her son Jock, her daughter Noelle, her friends Sanford Lung, Neil Frazer, and Jim Kraus, and her editor, John Dutton. I am grateful to them all for their time. For my work on Penelope Fitzgerald, I was very appreciative of the involvement of her son-in-law, Terence Dooley, and her editor, Stuart Proffitt. I am only sorry Penelope's section could not have been longer.

So many people read chapters, gave me insightful comments, reviewed work, and answered my queries. Even one short email response is often very helpful. (Several people responded politely, helpfully and at length to far more of my enquiries.) These include: Charles Moore, Hollis Robbins, Michael Farrell, Ian Deary, Rohit Krishnan, Helen Lewis, Jay Belsky, Rebecca Weir, Eric Gilliam, Meryl Westlake, Agnes Callard, Kenneth Roman, Daniel Cook, Aubrey Scanlan, Kieran Setiya, Paul Graham, Jerker Denrell, Mischa von Krause, Byrne Hobart, Alan Kay, Dean Keith Simonton, Jenny Hibbert, Scott Sumner, Blake Scholl, Jim Bright, Susan Charles, David Galenson, Ted Underwood, Karthik Rajkumar, Pierre Azoulay, and Timothy Bond. Alex Sidles from Paddling Forum helped me find old articles about Audrey Sutherland. David Harbottle retrieved academic papers I couldn't access. Several people agreed to be interviewed, which was a great help, including Robin Hanson, Noah Smith, and Sarah Harkness. God bless all people who respond promptly to their emails.

So many of the ideas in this book have roots in the opportunities my parents worked hard to provide for me. My mother was an inspiration as a late bloomer herself. Most importantly of all, I was privileged to have the love and support of my wife, Catherine, and my children, Penny and Alfred, who have heard enough about late bloomers.

ENDNOTES

INTRODUCTION

1. Ralph Waldo Emerson, 'Self-reliance', in *Nature and Selected Essays*, ed. and intro. Larzer Ziff (Penguin, 2003).

2. Lu Liu, Nima Dehmamy, Jillian Chown, C. Lee Giles, and Dashun Wang, 'Understanding the Onset of Hot Streaks across Artistic, Cultural, and Scientific Careers', *Nature Communications* 12:1 (2021), p. 5392, https://doi.org/10.1038/s41467-021-25477-8

3. Lu Liu, Nima Dehmamy, Jillian Chown, C. Lee Giles, and Dashun Wang, 'Supplementary Information for Understanding the Onset of Hot Streaks across Artistic, Cultural, and Scientific Careers', Supplementary Note 3.1, p. 21.

4. Warren Bennis and Patricia Ward Biederman, *Organizing Genius: The Secrets of Creative Collaboration*, rev. edn (Perseus Books, 1998), p. 8.

5. Walter Pitkin, *Life Begins at Forty* (McGraw-Hill, 1932), Kindle edition.

6. https://ourworldindata.org/life-expectancy#:~:text=The%20United%20-Nations%20estimate%20a,life%20expectancy%20of%2072.3%20years [accessed 13 September 2023].

7. Pitkin, *Life Begins at Forty*.

8. https://www.ons.gov.uk/employmentandlabourmarket/peopleinwork/employmentandemployeetypes/timeseries/lf2v/lms [accessed 13 September 2023].

9. Connie Goldman, 'Late Bloomers: Growing Older or Still Growing?', *Generations: Journal of the American Society on Aging* 15:2 (Spring 1991), pp. 41–4.

10. Jimmy Carter, *The Virtues of Aging*, reissue edn (Balantine Books, 1998), p. 11.

11. Michel de Montaigne, 'On Age', *The Complete Essays*, trans. M. A Screech (Penguin, 1993).

12. John 9:4 KJV.

13. Shane Snow, 'These Are the Ages When We Do Our Best Work', *Fast Company*, 18 April 2016, https://www.fastcompany.com/3058870/these-are-the-ages-when-we-do-our-best-work [accessed 23 September 2023].

14. Pitkin, *Life Begins at Forty*.

15. Bronnie Ware, *The Top Five Regrets of the Dying: A Life Transformed by the Dearly Departing* (Hay House, 2012).

16. Ruth Wilson, *The Jane Austen Remedy: It Is a Truth Universally Acknowledged That a Book Can Change a Life* (Allison & Busby, 2022).

17. Gerald Stratford, *Big Veg* (Headline, 2021).

18. https://www.youtube.com/watch?v=up9wfFpUUaM

19. https://www.trumanlibrary.gov/library/research-files/longhand-note-harry-s-truman?documentid=3&pagenumber=13 [accessed 13 September 2023].

20. Benjamin Lee, 'Viola Davis: "I stifled who I was to be seen as pretty. I lost years"', *Guardian*, 20 October 2018, available at https://www.theguardian.com/film/2018/oct/20/viola-davis-stifled-who-was-lost-years-the-help [accessed 13 September 2023].

PART ONE: MEANDERING CAREER PATHS

1. Katharine Graham's transformation to Mrs Graham, CEO

1. Katharine Graham, *Personal History* (Knopf, 1997), p. 91.

2. Ibid., p. 33.

3. Katharine Graham, 'Learning by Doing', *Bulletin of the American Academy of Arts and Sciences* 42:8 (May 1989), pp. 37–53 (p. 39).

4. Merlo J. Pusey, *Eugene Meyer* (Knopf, 1994), pp. 193–4.

5. Ibid., p. 196.

6. Ibid., p. 330.

7. Graham, *Personal History*, p. 40.

8. Graham, 'Learning by Doing', p. 44.

9. Graham, *Personal History*, p. 42.

10. Ibid., p. 44.

11. Ibid., p. 49.

12. Ibid., p. 51.

13. Pusey, *Eugene Meyer*, p. 242.

14. Pusey, *Eugene Meyer*, p. 248.

15. Graham, *Personal History*, p. 59.

16. Ibid., p. 72.

17. Ibid., pp. 86, 87.

18. Ibid., p. 82.

19. Pusey, *Eugene Meyer*, p. 333.

20. Graham, *Personal History*, p. 113.

21. Deborah Davis, *Katharine the Great: Katharine Graham and Her* Washington Post *Empire* (Harcourt, 1979), p. 120.

22. David Halberstam, *The Powers That Be* (Chatto & Windus, 1979), p. 158.

23. Graham, *Personal History*, p. 126.

24. Ibid., p. 130.

25. Ibid., p. 137.

26. Carol Felsenthal, *Power, Privilege and the* Post: *The Katharine Graham Story* (Seven Stories, 1993), p. 105.

27. Halberstam, *The Powers That Be*, p. 164.

28. Graham, *Personal History*, p. 139.

29. Halberstam, *The Powers That Be*, p. 171.

30. Graham, *Personal History*, p. 140.

31. Ibid., pp. 147–8.

32. Graham, 'Learning by Doing', p. 41.

33. Graham, *Personal History*, p. 181.

34. Ibid., p. 343.

35. Ibid., pp. 92, 93.

36. Graham, *Personal History*, p. 149.

37. Halberstam, *The Powers That Be*, p. 175.

38. Pusey, *Eugene Meyer*, p. 334.

39. Ibid., p. 341.

40. Felsenthal, *Power, Privilege and the* Post, p. 100.

41. Graham, *Personal History*, p. 152.

42. Ibid., p. 159.

43. Ibid., p. 151.

44. Ibid., pp. 162–3.

45. Felsenthal, *Power, Privilege and the* Post, p. 109.

46. Davis, *Katharine the Great*, p. 114.

47. Ibid., p. 115.

48. Pusey, *Eugene Meyer*, p. 359.

49. Graham, *Personal History*, p. 175.

50. Pusey, *Eugene Meyer*, p. 357.

51. Graham, *Personal History*, p. 167.

52. Felsenthal, *Power, Privilege and the* Post, p. 108.

53. Graham, *Personal History*, p. 178.

54. Pusey, *Eugene Meyer*, p. 393.

55. Ibid.

56. Felsenthal, *Power, Privilege and the* Post, p. 95.

57. Elizabeth Pope Frank, 'Vassar's Most Powerful Alumna: Katharine Meyer Graham '38', *Vassar Quarterly* 74:3 (1 March 1978), pp. 6–9.

58. Graham, *Personal History*, p. 173.

59. Pusey, *Eugene Meyer*, p. 272.

60. Halberstam, *The Powers That Be*, p. 190.

61. Graham, *Personal History*, p. 187.

62. Ibid., p. 180.

63. Ibid.

64. Pusey, *Eugene Meyer*, p. 366.

65. Graham, *Personal History*, pp. 181–2.

66. Davis, *Katharine the Great*, p. 146.

67. Halberstam, *The Powers That Be*, p. 193.

68. Ibid., p. 302.

69. Ibid., p. 303.

70. Ibid., p. 305.

71. Graham, 'Learning by Doing', p. 44.

72. Davis, *Katharine the Great*, p. 145.

73. Halberstam, *The Powers That Be*, p. 306.

74. Ibid., pp. 306–7.

75. Graham, *Personal History*, p. 231.

76. Ibid., p. 237.

77. Halberstam, *The Powers That Be*, pp. 308–9.

78. Graham, *Personal History*, p. 243.

79. Halberstam, *The Powers That Be*, p. 311.

80. Graham, *Personal History*, p. 245.

81. Ibid., p. 246.

82. Pusey, *Eugene Meyer*, p. 394.

83. Graham, *Personal History*, p. 213.

84. Ibid., p. 214.

85. Ibid., p. 215.

86. Ibid., p. 278.

87. Ibid., pp. 283–4.

88. Ibid., p. 301.

89. Ibid., p. 302.

90. Ibid., p. 307.

91. Ibid., p. 308.

92. Ibid., p. 317.

93. Ibid., p. 315.

94. Ibid., p. 320.

95. Ibid., pp. 328–9.

96. Ibid., pp. 330, 331.

97. Ibid., p. 339.

98. Ibid., p. 340.

99. 'Katharine Graham', *New York Times*, 18 July 2001, Section A, p. 22.

100. Tom Kelly, *The Imperial Post: The Meyers, the Grahams and the Paper that Rules Washington* (William Morrow, 1983), p. 133.

101. Graham, 'Learning by Doing', p. 43.

102. Graham, *Personal History*, p. 336.

103. Frank, 'Vassar's Most Powerful Alumna'.

104. 'Katharine Graham', *New York Times*, 18 July 2001, Section A, p. 22.

105. Alice Schroeder, *The Snowball: Warren Buffett and the Business of Life* (Bloomsbury, 2008), p. 401.

106. Ibid., p. 378.

107. Graham, *Personal History*, p. 82.

108. Schroeder, *The Snowball*, p. 400.

109. Ibid., pp. 403, 424.

110. Graham, 'Learning by Doing', p. 45.

111. Harry Rosenfeld, *From Kristallnacht to Watergate: Memories of a Newspaperman* (Excelsior, 2013), p. 172.

112. Randall Frost, 'Graham, Katharine Meyer (1917–2001), Newspaper Publisher', *American National Biography*, 1 December 2003, https://www-anb-org.lonlib.idm.oclc.org/view/10.1093/anb/9780198606697.001.0001/anb-9780198606697-e-1603493 [accessed 13 September 2023].

113. Graham, 'Learning by Doing', p. 48.

114. Pusey, *Eugene Meyer*, p. 395.

115. David Remnick, 'Citizen Kay: The Most Imposing Woman in Journalism Delivers an Unexpectedly Confessional Autobiography', *New Yorker*, 12 January 1997.

116. Wayne Robbins, 'Remembering Kay', *Editor and Publisher*, 23 July 2001.

117. Graham, *Personal History*, p. 342.

118. Kelly, *Imperial Post*, p. 164.

119. Ibid., p. 153.

120. Ibid., p. 115.

121. Remnick, 'Citizen Kay'.

122. *Aphra: The Feminist Literary Magazine*, Winter 1973–4, p. 53.

123. Kelly, *The Imperial Post*, p. 198.

124. Ibid., pp. 197–207.

125. Todd J. Shields, 'Katharine Graham: The Business Woman', *Editor and Publisher*, 23 July 2001.

126. Rosenfeld, *From Kristallnacht to Watergate*, pp. 107, 268.

127. Kelly, *The Imperial Post*, p. 243.

2. Inefficient preparation

1. Tom Wujec, 'Build a Tower, Build a Team', *TED Talks*, 22 April 2010, https://www.youtube.com/watch?v=H0_yKBitO8M

2. Daniel McGinn, 'Life's Work: An Interview with Jerry Seinfeld', *Harvard Business Review*, January–February 2017, p. 172, https://hbr.org/2017/01/lifes-work-jerry-seinfeld [accessed 22 June 2022].

3. David Epstein, *Range: How Generalists Triumph in a Specialized World* (Macmillan, 2019), p. 77.

4. Rachel Reeves, *Women of Westminster: The MPs Who Changed Politics* (Bloomsbury, 2019), p. 136.

5. Tyler Cowen and Daniel Gross, *Talent: How to Identify Energisers, Creatives, and Winners around the World* (Nicholas Brealey, 2022), p. 121.

6. Alexandra Stevenson and Matthew Goldstein, 'John Paulson's Fall From Hedge Fund Stardom', *New York Times*, 1 May 2007, available at https://www.nytimes.com/2017/05/01/business/dealbook/john-paulsons-fall-from-hedge-fund-stardom.html [accessed 28 October 2023].

7. Gregory Zuckerman, *The Greatest Trade Ever: The Behind-the-Scenes Story of How John Paulson Defied Wall Street and Made Financial History* (Crown, 2010), pp. 35–6.

8. Ibid., p. 54.

9. Ibid., p. 105.

10. Mae Laborde obituary, *Legacy.com*, https://www.legacy.com/us/obituaries/latimes/name/mae-laborde-obituary?n=mae-laborde&pid=155438078&fhid=11022 [accessed 23 September 2023].

11. Jane Sturges and Catherine Bailey, 'Walking Back to Happiness: The Resurgence of Latent Callings in Later Life', *Human Relations*, 11 April 2022, p. 17, https://doi.org/10.1177/00187267221095759

12. Ibid., p. 19.

13. Ibid., p. 23.

14. Ibid., p. 24.

15. Shoshana R. Dobrow, Hannah Weisman, and Jennifer Tosti-Kharas, 'Calling and the Good Life: A Meta-Analysis and Theoretical Extension', *Administrative Science Quarterly* 68:2 (2023), pp. 508–50.

16. Bryan J. Dik and Ryan D. Duffy, 'Calling and Vocation at Work: Definitions and Prospects for Research and Practice', *The Counseling Psychologist* 37:3 (2009), pp. 424–50.

17. Chris Gardner, *The Pursuit of Happyness* (Amistad, 2006), p. 168.

18. Ibid., p. 193.

19. Ibid., p. 197.

20. Ibid., p. 214.

21. Ibid., pp. 152–3.

22. Valentine Cunningham, 'Suffocating Suffolk', *Times Literary Supplement*, 17 November 1978, p. 9.

23. Philip Hensher, 'Perfection in a Small Space', *Spectator*, 21 October 2001, p. 51, http://archive.spectator.co.uk/article/21st-october-2000/51/books [accessed 6 July 2022].

24. Dean Flower and Linda Henchey, 'Penelope Fitzgerald's Unknown Fiction', *The Hudson Review* 61:1 (Spring 2008), pp. 47–65.

25. Hugh Adlington, *Penelope Fitzgerald* (Liverpool University Press, 2018).

26. Arthur Lubow, 'An Author of a Certain Age', *New York Times*, 15 August 1999, section 6, p. 30.

27. Hermione Lee, *Penelope Fitzgerald: A Life* (Chatto & Windus, 2013), p. 89.

28. Ibid., pp. 100, 95.

29. Penelope Fitzgerald, *So I Have Thought of You: The Letters of Penelope Fitzgerald*, ed. Terence Dooley, Penelope Fitzgerald to Richard Ollard, 5 October 1989, p. 409.

30. Peter Lennon, 'Men Are Such Hopeless Creatures, Life's Just Too Much for Them', *Guardian*, 13 April 1998, pp. 10–11.

31. Terence Dooley, 'Introduction', in Fitzgerald, *Letters*, p. xv.

32. Fitzgerald, *Letters*, Penelope Fitzgerald to Mayliss Conder, 5 January 1977, pp. 175–6.

33. Ibid., Penelope Fitzgerald to J. Howard Woolmer, 29 November 1978, p. 331; Terence Dooley, 'Introduction', in Fitzgerald, *Letters*, p. xxxvi.

34. Lee, *Penelope Fitzgerald*, p. 226.

35. Fitzgerald, *Letters*, Penelope Fitzgerald to Richard Ollard, 20 November 1980, p. 382.

36. Lee, *Penelope Fitzgerald*, p. 234.

37. Ibid., p. 236.

38. Fitzgerald, *Letters*, Penelope Fitzgerald to Tina Fitzgerald, 15 April 1965, p. 37.

39. Penelope Fitzgerald, *Human Voices* (Fourth Estate, 2010), p. 106; Fitzgerald, *Letters*, Penelope Fitzgerald to Richard Ollard, 29 February 1980, p. 378.

40. Terence Dooley, 'Introduction', in Fitzgerald, *Letters*, p. xxvi.

41. A. S. Byatt, 'Preface', in Fitzgerald, *Letters*, p. x.

42. Fitzgerald, *Letters*, Penelope Fitzgerald to Alberto Manguel, 14 September 1998, p. 475; Lennon, 'Men Are Such Hopeless Creatures', pp. 10–11.

43. Wendy Lesser, 'Penelope', in *On Modern British Fiction*, ed. Zachary Leader (Oxford University Press, 2002), pp. 107–25.

44. Lee, *Penelope Fitzgerald*, p. 197.

45. Ibid., p. 198.

46. Fitzgerald, *Letters*, Penelope Fitzgerald to Richard Ollard, 20 February 1980, p. 376.

47. Ibid., Penelope Fitzgerald to Francis King, 28 October [c. 1998], p. 292.

48. Ibid., Penelope Fitzgerald to Chris Carduff, 5 December 1999, p. 514.

49. Ibid., Penelope Fitzgerald to Chris Carduff, 15 March 2000, p. 517.

50. Ibid., Penelope Fitzgerald to Richard Ollard, 25 February 1981, p. 383.

51. Fitzgerald, *Human Voices*, pp. 94, 155.

52. Penelope Fitzgerald, *The Bookshop* (Fourth Estate, 2014), p. 37.

53. Fitzgerald, *Letters*, Penelope Fitzgerald to Hugh Lee, 14 May 1978, p. 23.

54. Lee, *Penelope Fitzgerald*, p. 214.

55. Fitzgerald, *Letters*, Penelope Fitzgerald to Tina Fitzgerald, 11 November 1968, p. 61.

56. Archibald Colquhoun, 'Translator's Note', in Giuseppe di Lampedusa, *Two Stories and a Memory* (Collins & Harvill, 1962), pp. 17–20.

57. Frank Kermode, 'The Duckworth School of Writers', *London Review of Books* 2:22 (20 November 1980).

3. Ray Kroc's long apprenticeship

1. Ray Kroc, with Robert Anderson, *Grinding It Out: The Making of McDonald's*, reissue edn (St Martin's Press, 1977), p. 71.

2. Ibid., pp. 9–10.

3. Ibid., p. 46.

4. John A. Jakle and Keith A. Sculle, *Fast Food: Roadside Restaurants in the Automobile Age* (Johns Hopkins University Press, 1999), p. 149.

5. David W. Galenson, *Old and Young: The Two Life Cycles of Artistic Creativity* (Princeton University Press, 2006), pp. 4–5.

6. Quoted in David Galenson, *Old Masters and Young Geniuses* (Princeton University Press, 2008), p. 106.

7. Galenson, *Old and Young*, p. 126.

8. Quoted in S. Baker and G. M. Campbell, *The Complete Idiot's Guide to Project Management* (Alpha Books, 2003), p. 236.

9. David Ogilvy, *Confessions of an Advertising Man* (Southbank Publishing, 2011), p. 69.

10. Kroc, *Grinding It Out*, p. 51.

11. Ibid., pp. 18–38.

12. Ibid., pp. 50–8.

13. Ibid., p. 63.

14. Kenneth N. Gilpin, 'Richard McDonald, 89, Fast-Food Revolutionary', *New York Times* 16 July 1998, section A, p. 27, https://www.nytimes. com/1998/07/16/business/richard-mcdonald-89-fast-food-revolutionary.html [accessed 21 October 2022].

15. Joel Stice, 'The Tragic Real-Life Story of the McDonald Brothers', *Mashed*, 27 October 2020, https://www.mashed.com/147897/the-tragic-real-life-story-of-the-mcdonald-brothers/ [accessed 21 October 2022].

16. Daniel Bates, 'Exclusive: How McDonald's "Founder" Cheated the Brothers Who Really Started Empire out of Hundreds of Millions, Wrote Them Out of Company History – And Left One to Die of Heart Failure and the Other Barely a Millionaire', *Daily Mail*, 5 May 2015, https://www.dailymail.co.uk/news/article-3049644/How-McDonald-s-founder-cheated-brothers-REALLY-started-empire-300m-wrote-company-history-left-one-die-heart-failure-barely-millionaire.html [accessed 21 October 2022].

17. Ibid.

18. Dave Batty and Chris Johnston, '*Social Network* "made up stuff that was hurtful", says Mark Zuckerberg', *Guardian*, 8 November 2014, https://www.theguardian.com/technology/2014/nov/08/mark-zuckerberg-social-network-made-stuff-up-hurtful [accessed 21 October 2022].

19. Josh Ozersky, *The Hamburger: A History* (Yale University Press, 2008), pp. 26, 28.

20. Philip Langdon, *Orange Roofs, Golden Arches: The Architecture of American Chain Restaurants* (Knopf, 1986), p. 30.

21. Kroc, *Grinding It Out*, p. 90.

22. Jakle and Sculle, *Fast Food*, pp. 27–58.

23. Ronald L. McDonald, *The Complete Hamburger: The History of America's Favorite Sandwich* (Birch Lane Press, 1997), p. 37.

24. Jakle and Sculle, *Fast Food*, pp. 101–2.

25. Ozersky, *The Hamburger*, pp. 35–6.

26. Eric Schasser, *Fast Food Nation: What the All-American Meal is Doing to the World* (Allen Lane, 2001), p. 41.

27. Ozersky, *The Hamburger*, pp. 46–8.

28. John F. Love, *McDonald's: Behind the Arches* (Bantam, 1995), p. 61.

29. Quoted in Galenson, *Old and Young*, p. 98.

30. Kroc, *Grinding It Out*, p. 101.

31. Love, *Behind the Arches*, p. 7.

32. Galenson, *Old and Young*, p. 7.

33. Paul D. Paganucci, 'Preface', in *Grinding It Out*, p. 3.

34. Galenson, *Old and Young*, p. 15.

35. David Halberstam, *The Fifties* (Fawcett, 1994), pp. 155–60.

36. Ozersky, *The Hamburger*, p. 57.

37. Kroc, *Grinding It Out*, p. 72.

38. Ibid., p. 10.

39. Halberstam, *The Fifties*, p. 164.

40. Ibid., p. 22.

41. Ibid., p. 80.

42. Galenson, *Old Masters and Young Geniuses*, p. 13.

43. Kroc, *Grinding It Out*, p. 10.

44. Ibid., p. 15.

45. Halberstam, *The Powers That Be*, p. 166.

46. Kroc, *Grinding It Out*, p. 50.

47. Ibid., p. 48.

48. Ibid., p. 87.

49. J. Anthony Lukas, 'As American as a McDonald's Hamburger on the Fourth of July', *New York Times*, 4 July 1971, Section SM, p. 4.

50. Amity Shlaes, *Coolidge* (HarperCollins, 2013), p. 8.

51. Schasser, *Fast Food Nation*, pp. 13–23.

PART TWO: WHEN FATE INTERVENES

4. Intentionally unplanned careers and being ready for luck

1. Charles Duhigg, 'Wealthy, Successful, and Miserable', *New York Times Magazine*, 21 February 2019, https://www.nytimes.com/interactive/2019/02/21/magazine/elite-professionals-jobs-happiness.html [accessed 13 September 2023].

2. Yang Wang, Benjamin F. Jones and Dashun Wang, 'Early-Career Setback and Future Career Impact', *Nature Communications* 10 (2019), p. 4331, https://doi.org/10.1038/s41467-019-12189-3

3. Amity Shlaes, *Coolidge* (HarperCollins, 2013), pp. 54, 76.

4. Richard Wiseman, *The Lucky Factor: The Scientific Study of the Lucky Mind* (Arrow, 2004), p. 48.

5. Wiseman, *The Lucky Factor*, pp. 55, 60.

6. Paul Graham, 'How to Do Great Work', July 2023, http://paulgraham.com/greatwork.html#f5n

7. Jacqueline S. Thursby, 'Angelou, Maya (4 Apr. 1928–28 May 2014), Writer, Performer, and Activist', *American National Biography*, 29 November 2018, https://www-anb-org.lonlib.idm.oclc.org/view/10.1093/anb/9780198606697.001.0001/anb-9780198606697-e-00700 [accessed 18 November 2022].

8. Samuel Johnson, 'Poetry Debased by Mean Expressions. An Example from Shakespeare', *Rambler* No. 168, 26 October 1751, https://www.johnsonessays.com/the-rambler/no-168-poetry-debased-by-mean-expressions-an-example-from-shakespeare/ [accessed 18 November 2022].

9. Wiseman, *The Lucky Factor*, p. 57.

10. James Austin, *Chase, Chance, and Creativity: The Lucky Art of Novelty* (Columbia, 1978), p. 71.

11. Ibid., pp. 73–7.

12. Ibid., p. 75.

13. Ibid., p. 92.

14. Jim E. H. Bright and Robert G. L. Pryor, *The Chaos Theory of Careers: A New Perspective on Working the 21st Century* (Routledge, 2011); Jim E. H. Bright and Robert G. L. Pryor 'The Chaos Theory of Careers: A User's Guide', *The Career Development Quarterly* 53:4 (2005), pp. 291–305.

15. Jim E. H. Bright and Robert G. L. Pryor, 'The Chaos Theory of Careers', *Australian Journal of Career Development* 12:3 (2003), pp. 12–20.

16. Seneca, 'Letter LXXXIII', *Letters from a Stoic*, trans. Robin Campbell (Penguin, 2004), p. 140.

17. Jim E. H. Bright and Robert G. L. Pryor, 'The Value of Failing in Career Development: A Chaos Theory Perspective', *International Journal for Educational and Vocational Guidance* 12 (2012), pp. 67–79.

18. Jayna Cooke, 'Own Your Happyness: A Q&A With Chris Gardner', *Forbes*, 15 March 2017, https://www.forbes.com/sites/jaynacooke/2017/03/15/own-your-happyness-a-qa-with-chris-gardner/?sh=513d9c201b27 [accessed 23 September 2023].

19. Ibid.

20. Audrey Sutherland, *Paddling My Own Canoe* (University of Hawaii, 1978; Patagonia, 2018), p. 165.

21. Harry Lambert, 'Dominic Cummings: The Machiavel in Downing Street', *New Statesman*, 25 September 2019, https://www.newstatesman.com/politics/uk/2019/09/dominic-cummings-machiavel-downing-street

22. https://www.conservativehome.com/thetorydiary/2014/05/a-profile-of-dominic-cummings-friend-of-gove-and-enemy-of-clegg.html [accessed 23 September 2023].

23. https://www.theguardian.com/politics/2019/jul/26/dominic-cummings-a-career-psychopath-in-downing-street [accessed 23 September 2023].

24. Lambert, 'Dominic Cummings'.

25. Marshall Sella, 'You Have a Cold Heart, Degas!', *New York Times*, 26 January 1997, Section 6, p. 22, https://www.nytimes.com/1997/01/26/magazine/you-have-a-cold-heart-degas.html [accessed 23 June 2022].

26. Aamna Mohdin, 'Art Historian Sister Wendy Beckett Dies Aged 88', *Guardian*, 26 December 2018, https://www.theguardian.com/tv-and-radio/2018/dec/26/art-historian-sister-wendy-beckett-dies-aged-88 [accessed 23 June 2022].

27. Sister Wendy Beckett in Conversation with Bill Moyers, 1997.

28. Robert D. McFadden, 'Sister Wendy Beckett, Nun Who Became a BBC Star, Dies at 88', *New York Times*, 26 December 2018, Section B, p. 12, https://www.nytimes.com/2018/12/26/obituaries/sister-wendy-beckett-dead.html [accessed 23 June 2022].

29. 'At Wimbeldon with: Ion Tiriac, Tennis's Grandest Bad Boy', *The New York Times*, 24 June 1993, https://www.nytimes.com/1993/06/24/garden/at-wimbledon-with-ion-tiriac-tennis-s-grandest-bad-boy.html [accessed 23 September 2023].

30. Pierre Azoulay, Benjamin F. Jones, J. Daniel Kim, and Javier Miranda, 'Age and High-Growth Entrepreneurship', *AER: Insights* 2:1 (2020), pp. 65–82 (p. 76), https://doi.org/10.1257/aeri.20180582

31. Frederick Gieschen, 'Julian Robertson: Lessons from the Tiger Who Was a Wolf', *Neckar Substack*, 4 September 2022, https://neckar.substack.com/p/the-tiger-that-was-a-wolf-lesosns?nthPub=1351 [accessed 28 October 2023].

32. Giacomo Tognini, 'Budget Billionaire: How Frontier Airlines Chairman Bill Franke Rode Low Fares to the Forbes List', *Forbes*, 6 April 2022, https://www.forbes.com/sites/giacomotognini/2022/04/06/budget-billionaire-how-frontier-airlines-chairman-bill-franke-rode-low-fares-to-the-forbes-list/ [accessed 28 October 2023].

33. Azoulay et al., 'Age and High-Growth Entrepreneurship', p. 67.

34. Ibid., p. 73.

35. Ibid., p. 74.

36. Ibid., p. 72.

37. Francine Lafontaine and Kathryn Shaw, 'Serial Entrepreneurship: Learning by Doing?', Working Paper 20312, http://www.nber.org/papers/w20312, July 2014.

38. Jessica Livingston, *Founders at Work: Stories of Start-ups' Early Days* (Apress, 2007), pp. 191–5.

39. Azoulay, 'Age and High-Growth Entrepreneurship', p. 78.

40. C. Mirjam Van Praag and Hans Van Ophem, 'Determinants of Willingness and Opportunity to Start as an Entrepreneur', *Small Business: Critical Perspectives on Business and Management*, ed. D. J. Storey (Routledge, 2000), pp. 38–62.

41. David Blanchflower and Andrew Oswald, 'What Makes a Young Entrepreneur?', NBER Working Paper No. 3252, February 1990, https://www.nber.org/system/files/working_papers/w3252/w3252.pdf [accessed 28 October 2023].

42. Catherine Perloff, 'How David Duffield Took 20 Years and Four Startups to Develop the Corporate Culture Behind His Enterprise Software Empire', *Forbes*, 3 November 2019, https://www.forbes.com/sites/catherineperloff/2019/11/03/how-david-duffield-took-20-years-and-four-startups-to-develop-the-corporate-culture-behind-his-enterprise-software-empire/?sh=30c16d003a3e

43. Perloff, 'Duffield'.

44. A. Miguel Amaral, Rui Baptista, and Francisco Lima, 'Serial Entrepreneurship: The Impact of Human Capital on Time to Re-entry', *Small Business Economics* 37 (2011), pp. 1–21, doi: 10.1007/s11187-009-9232-4

45. Irwin N. Gertzog, 'Changing Pathways to the U.S. House of Representatives: Widows, Elites, and Strategic Politicians', in *Women Transforming Congress*, ed. Cindy Simon Rosenthal (University of Oklahoma, 2002), pp. 95–118.

46. Alexander Baturo and Julia Gary, 'When Do Family Ties Matter? The Duration of Female Suffrage and Women's Path to High Political Office', *Political Research Quarterly* 71:3 (2018), pp. 695–709.

47. Gertzog, 'Changing Pathways', pp. 95–118.

48. Wayne King, 'Hayakawa Resists Idea of Dropping Out of Race', *New York Times*, 24 January 1982, Section 1, p. 24.

49. Wallace Turner, 'Hayakawa–Tunney Senate Race a Study in Contrasts', *New York Times*, 24 September 1976, p. 23.

50. Katherine Bishop, 'S. I. Hayakawa Dies at 85; Scholar and Former Senator', *New York Times*, 28 February 1992, Section B, p. 6.

51. Turner, 'Hayakawa–Tunney Senate Race a Study in Contrasts', p. 23.

52. 'Scholar in a Vortex; Samuel Ichie Hayakawa', *New York Times*, 6 December 1968, p. 39.

53. Turner, 'Hayakawa–Tunney Senate Race a Study in Contrasts', p. 23.

54. Wallace Turner, 'Hayakawa Abandons Race for a Second Term in Senator', *New York Times*, 31 January 1982, Section 1, p. 24.

55. King, 'Hayakawa Resists Idea of Dropping Out of Race', p. 24.

56. David McCullough, *Truman* (Simon & Schuster, 1992), pp. 296–7.

57. Stephen E. Ambrose, *Eisenhower, Volume I: Soldier, General of the Army, President Elect, 1890-1952* (George Allen & Unwin, 1984), p. 119.

58. William Lee Miller, *Two Americans: Truman, Eisenhower, and a Dangerous World* (New York: Vintage, 2012), pp. 72–3; Merle Miller, *Plain Speaking: An Oral Biography of Harry Truman* (New York: Berkley Publishing Corporation, 1973), p. 134.

59. Author's interview with Charles Moore, https://commonreader.substack.com/p/charles-moore-interview?s=wdetails

5. Margaret Thatcher: chance favours the prepared mind

1. David Canadine, *Margaret Thatcher: A Life and Legacy* (Oxford University Press, 2017), p. 7.

2. 'Written Interview', *Pionyerskaya Pravda*, Margaret Thatcher Foundation, 10 March 1990, https://www.margaretthatcher.org/document/107894 [accessed 27 June 2022].

3. London School of Economics, Thatcher, The Thatcher Factor/1, 001/3, Interview with Jeffrey Archer, pp. 6, 7.

4. 1949–59 (candidate): Interview with Marjorie Maxse, 1 February 1949, Thatcher MSS (1/1/1), Margaret Thatcher Foundation, https://www.margaretthatcher.org/document/109915 [accessed 27 June 2022]; 1949–59 (candidate): Beryl Cook to J. P. L. Thomas, 1 February 1949, Thatcher MSS (memoirs boxes), Margaret Thatcher Foundation, https://www.margaretthatcher.org/document/109917 [accessed 27 June 2022]; 1949–59 (candidate): Letters of reference, 1 February 1949, Margaret Thatcher Foundation, https://www.margaretthatcher.org/document/109916 [accessed 27 June 2022]; 1949–59 (candidate): Beryl Cook report on Margaret Roberts,

Conservative Party Archive CCO 220/3/11/6, 19 November 1951, Margaret Thatcher Foundation, https://www.margaretthatcher.org/document/111242 [accessed 27 June 2022].

5. Margaret Thatcher to John Hare, 3 January 1955, Thatcher MSS (1/1/1), Margaret Thatcher Foundation, https://www.margaretthatcher.org/document/109935 [accessed 27 June 2022].

6. 1949–59 (candidate): Donald Kaberry Interview with MT, 14 March 1956, Donald Kaberry to Margaret Thatcher 15 March 1956, Thatcher MSS (1/1/1), Margaret Thatcher Foundation, https://www.margaretthatcher.org/document/109938 [accessed 27 June 2022].

7. Rachel Reeves, *Women of Westminster: The MPs Who Changed Politics* (Bloomsbury, 2019), p. 79.

8. 'Extract from Report on Candidates Interviewed by Maidstone Division', Thatcher MSS (1/1/1), 18 March 1958, Margaret Thatcher Foundation, https://www.margaretthatcher.org/document/109943 [accessed 28 June 2022].

9. 'Extract from Memo Miss Harris to Mr. Kaberry', 15 July 2022, Thatcher MSS (1/1/1), Margaret Thatcher Foundation, https://www.margaretthatcher.org/document/109944 [accessed 28 June 2022].

10. Margaret Thatcher to Donald Kaberry, 18 August 1958, Thatcher MSS (1/1/1), Margaret Thatcher Foundation, https://www.margaretthatcher.org/document/109946 [accessed 28 June 2022].

11. Margaret Thatcher to Donald Kaberry, 16 March 1956, Thatcher MSS (1/1/1), Margaret Thatcher Foundation, https://www.margaretthatcher.org/document/109939 [accessed 28 June 2022].

12. 'Reports Received from Central Office Area Agents on Parliamentary Candidates: Finchley – Mrs Margaret Thatcher', 1 November 1959, Thatcher MSS (1/1/1), Margaret Thatcher Foundation, https://www.margaretthatcher.org/document/109947 [accessed 28 June 2022].

13. Tony Shrimsley, 'Margaret: First Woman Chancellor?', *Sun*, 10 April 1970, Margaret Thatcher Foundation, https://www.margaretthatcher.org/document/101809 [accessed 28 June 2022].

14. Russell Lewis, *Margaret Thatcher: A Personal and Political Biography* (Routledge & Kegan Paul, 1975), p. 4.

15. Charles Moore, *Margaret Thatcher: The Authorized Biography. Volume 1: Not for Turning* (Penguin, 2014), p. 185.

16. Luke Blaxill and Kaspar Beelen, 'A Feminized Language of Democracy? The Representation of Women at Westminster since 1945', *Twentieth Century British History* 27:3 (September 2016), pp. 412–449, https://doi.org/10.1093/tcbh/hww028

17. Margaret Thatcher, 'Interview for Finchley Times', 9 December 1966, Margaret Thatcher Foundation, https://www.margaretthatcher.org/document/101297 [accessed 21 June 2022]

18. Giles Scott-Smith, '"Her Rather Ambitious Washington Program": Margaret Thatcher's International Visitor Program Visit to the United States in 1967', *Contemporary British History*, November 2003, pp. 65–86, doi: 10.1080/13619460308565458

19. Author's interview with Charles Moore, https://commonreader.substack.com/p/charles-moore-interview?s=wdetails

20. Dean Keith Simonton, *Genius, Creativity, & Leadership: Historiometric Enquiries* (Harvard University Press, 1984), p. 65.

21. Jon Agar, 'Thatcher, Scientist', *Notes and Records of the Royal Society*, 22 June 2011, DOI:10.1098/rsnr.2010.0096, Margaret Thatcher Foundation, https://www.margaretthatcher.org/document/112774 [accessed 24 June 2022], p. 10.

22. Ibid., p. 12.

23. Agar, 'Thatcher, Scientist', p. 12.

24. Ibid.

25. Martin Gilbert, *In Search of Churchill* (HarperCollins, 1995), p. 266.

26. London School of Economics, Thatcher, The Thatcher Factor/1, 002/2, Interview with Lord Carrington, p. 4.

27. Author's interview with Charles Moore.

28. John Campbell, *Margaret Thatcher: Volume One: The Grocer's Daughter* (Vintage, 2007), p. 265.

29. Author's interview with Charles Moore.

30. Shlaes, *Coolidge*, pp. 254–5.

31. Ibid., pp. 277–8.

32. A. J. Baime, *The Accidental President: Harry S. Truman and the Four Months That Changed the World*, reprint edn (Bantam Books, 2020), p. 247.

33. For details of Bonar Law, see Robert Blake, *The Unknown Prime Minister: The Life and Times of Andrew Bonar Law, 1858–1923*, reprint edn (Faber & Faber) and R. J. Q. Adams, *Bonar Law: The Unknown Prime Minister* (John Murray, 1999).

34. Ferdinand Mount, *Cold Cream* (Bloomsbury, 2009), p. 289.

35. Interview, *Daily Mail*, 1 March 1990, Margaret Thatcher Foundation, https://www.margaretthatcher.org/document/107885 [accessed 27 June 2022].

36. Mount, *Cold Cream*, p. 290.

37. Ibid., p. 286.

38. Margaret Thatcher, 'Interview for Finchley Times', 9 December 1966, Margaret Thatcher Foundation, https://www.margaretthatcher.org/document/101297 [accessed 21 June 2022].

39. Charles Stuart Kennedy, 'Interview with William J. Galloway', 28 September 1999, The Association for Diplomatic Studies and Training Foreign Affairs Oral History Project, Library of Congress, pp. 102–4, 136, 142, http://www.loc.gov/item/mfdipbib000406 [accessed 30 June 2022].

40. Margaret Thatcher, TV Interview for Granada TV World in Action, 31 January 1975, Margaret Thatcher Foundation, https://www.margaretthatcher.org/document/102450

41. Ina Zweiniger-Bargielowska, 'Rationing, Austerity and the Conservative Party Recovery after 1945', *The Historical Journal*, 37 (1994), pp. 173–97 (p. 177).

42. Simon Garfield, *Our Hidden Lives: The Remarkable Diaries of Postwar Britain* (Ebury, 2005), p. 251.

43. Zweiniger-Bargielowska, 'Rationing', p. 179.

44. Ibid., pp. 178–9.

45. Ibid., pp. 193–4.

46. David Kynaston, *Austerity Britain, 1945–1951* (Bloomsbury, 2008), p. 385.

47. James Hinton, 'Militant Housewives: The British Housewives' League and the Attlee Government', *History Workshop* 38 (1994), pp. 128–56, http://www.jstor.org/stable/4289322 [accessed 20 June 2022]. There was a sixteen-point swing for middle-class women, compared to seven points overall for women and thirteen points for middle-class men.

48. Ruth Adam, *A Woman's Place, 1910–1975* (Chatto & Windus, 1975), p. 162.

49. Margaret Thatcher, '1950 General Election Address', 3 February 1950, Margaret Thatcher Foundation, https://www.margaretthatcher.org/document/100858 [accessed 21 June 2022].

50. Margaret Thatcher, 'Interview for Finchley Times', 9 December 1966, Margaret Thatcher Foundation, https://www.margaretthatcher.org/document/101297 [accessed 21 June 2022].

51. Margaret Thatcher, '1970 General Election Address', 28 May 1970, Margaret Thatcher Foundation, https://www.margaretthatcher.org/document/101754 [accessed 21 June 2022].

52. Margaret Thatcher, 'Interview for Finchley Times', 1 August 1969, Margaret Thatcher Foundation, https://www.margaretthatcher.org/document/101678 [accessed 21 June 2022].

53. Denis Kavanagh, 'Sir Gordon Reece', *Independent*, 26 September 2001, https://www.independent.co.uk/news/obituaries/sir-gordon-reece-9201156.html [accessed 4 July 2022].

54. Laura Beers, 'Thatcher and the Women's Vote', in *Making Thatcher's Britain*, ed. Ben Jackson and Robert Saunders (Cambridge University Press, 2012), pp. 113–31 (p. 119).

55. Moore, *Margaret Thatcher*, p. 278.

56. Ibid., p. 277.

57. John Kemp, 'Mrs Thatcher's Plans for Retirement', *Pre-Retirement Choice*, January 1975, pp. 13–14, Margaret Thatcher Foundation, https://www.margaretthatcher.org/document/102055 [accessed 24 June 2022].

58. Margaret Thatcher TV Interview for Granada TV World in Action, 31 January 1975, Margaret Thatcher Foundation, https://www.margaretthatcher.org/document/102450

59. Canadine, *Margaret Thatcher*, p. 35.

60. Ibid., p. 75

61. Canadine, *Margaret Thatcher*, p. 16.

62. Moore, *Margaret Thatcher*, pp. 276, 277, 280.

63. Ibid., p. 285.

64. Jean Mann, *Woman in Parliament* (Odhams Press, 1962), p. 31.

65. Bernard Levin, 'The Tories' Best Hope of Salvation', *The Times*, 23 January 1975, p. 16.

66. Bernard Levin, 'Find the Lady Should be the Cry if Tories Want a Change', *The Times*, 28 January 1975, p. 14.

67. Lewis, *Margaret Thatcher*, p. 2.

68. Moore, *Margaret Thatcher*, vol. 1, p. 273.

69. Ibid., p. 268.

70. Ibid., p. 275.

71. Ibid., p. 287.

72. Ibid., p. 291.

73. Ibid., p. 135.

74. Ibid., p. 269n.

75. Bernard Levin, 'Tories Must Look before They Leap into Line behind a New Leader', *The Times*, 16 October 1974, p. 14.

76. Campbell, *Margaret Thatcher*, p. 287.

77. Miriam Stoppard interview, 1985.

78. Ronald Miller, *A View from the Wings* (Weidenfeld & Nicolson, 1993), p. 225.

79. *BBC Question Time*, 11 April 2013, https://www.youtube.com/watch?v=Ae5nEiwz-v0

80. Reeves, *Women of Westminster*, p. 148.

81. Archive (Hailsham MSS), 'MT: Hailsham Diary (Discussion with Peter Carrington) [Serious Doubts about MT & Keith Joseph]', 29 March 1977, Margaret Thatcher Foundation, https://www.margaretthatcher.org/document/111182 [accessed 21 June 2022].

82. Moore, *Margaret Thatcher*, vol. 1, p. 453n.

83. PHS, 'The Times Diary: Professionalism in a Nice Blue Hat', *The Times*, 11 September 1974, p. 14.

84. Paul Routledge, *Public Servant, Secret Agent: The Elusive Life and Violent Death of Airey Neave* (Fourth Estate, 2002), p. 257.

85. George Younger, *1976–1979 Younger Diary*, 4 December 1978, 5 April 1979, Margaret Thatcher Foundation, http://09b37156ee7ea2a93a5e-6db7349bced3b64202e14ff100a12173.r35.cf1.rackcdn.com/Arcdocs/1976-79%20Younger%20diary.pdf [accessed 21 June 2022].

86. David Cannadine, 'Thatcher [née Roberts], Margaret Hilda, Baroness Thatcher (1925–2013)', *Oxford Dictionary of National Biography*, https://doi-org.lonlib.idm.oclc.org/10.1093/ref:odnb/106415

87. Edward Pierce, 'Sir Gordon Reece', *Guardian*, 27 September 2001, https://www.theguardian.com/news/2001/sep/27/guardianobituaries.obituaries [accessed 4 July 2022].

88. Denis Kavanagh, 'Sir Gordon Reece', *Independent*, 26 September 2001, https://www.independent.co.uk/news/obituaries/sir-gordon-reece-9201156.html [accessed 4 July 2022].

89. Mann, *Woman in Parliament*, pp. 35–6.

90. London School of Economics, Thatcher, The Thatcher Factor/1, 001/6, Interview with Tim Bell, p. 3.

91. Reeves, *Women of Westminster*, p. 107; Margaret Thatcher, Interview for *Daily Star*, 27 January 1988, Margaret Thatcher Foundation, https://www.margaretthatcher.org/document/107029 [accessed 19 August 2022].

92. Miller, *A View from the Wings*, pp. 212–13, 219.

93. London School of Economics, Thatcher, The Thatcher Factor/1, 002/10, Interview with Lord Gowrie, p. 10.

94. Campbell, *Margaret Thatcher*, pp. 292, 294.

95. Radek Sikorski, 'A Cold War Angel and a Democratic Miracle', *Daily Telegraph*, 10 April 2013, p. 23.

96. Charles Stuart Kennedy, 'Interview with William J. Galloway'.

97. Moore, *Margaret Thatcher*, p. 223.

98. Miller, *A View from the Wings*, p. 219.

99. Campbell, *Margaret Thatcher*, p. 234.

100. Kelvin MacKenzie, Interview Transcript, *Sun,* 6 November 1989, Margaret Thatcher Foundation, https://www.margaretthatcher.org/document/107430 [accessed 27 June 2022].

101. Moore, *Margaret Thatcher*, p. 26.

102. Ibid., p. 438.

103. Ibid., p. 730.

104. Kelvin MacKenzie, Interview Transcript.

105. London School of Economics, Thatcher, The Thatcher Factor/1, 002/2, Interview with Lord Carrington, p. 32.

106. Campbell, *Margaret Thatcher*, p. 261.

PART THREE: NETWORKS AND INFLUENCE

6. The importance of influential connections

1. Paul Routledge, *Public Servant, Secret Agent: The Elusive Life and Violent Death of Airey Neave* (Fourth Estate, 2002), p. 258.

2. Christopher Leslie Brown, *Moral Capitalism: Foundations of British Abolitionism* (University of North Carolina Press, 2006), pp. 197–200.

3. Niall Ferguson, *The Square and the Tower* (Allen Lane, 2017).

4. Jonah Lehrer, 'A Physicist Solves the City', *New York Times*, 17 December 2010, https://www.nytimes.com/2010/12/19/magazine/19Urban_West-t.html?searchResultPosition=1

5. Karthik Rajkumar, Guillaume Saint-Jacques, Iavor Bojinov, Erik Brynjolfsson, and Sinan Aral, 'A Causal Test of the Strength of Weak Ties', *Science* 377:6612 (16 September 2022); Dashun Wang and Brian Uzzi, 'Weak Ties, Failed Tries, and Success: A Large-Scale Study Provides a Causal Test for a Cornerstone of Social Science', *Science* 377:6612 (15 September 2022), pp. 1256–8.

6. Ferguson, *The Square and the Tower*, p. 96.

7. All details about Van Leeuwenhoek taken from J., Backer, W. Reijnders, K. Krab, J. van Doorn, C. Biemans, and L. Robertson, *Antonie van Leeuwenhoek: Master of the Minuscule* (Brill, 2016).

8. Mihaly Csikszentmihalyi, 'Implications of a Systems Perspective for the Study of Creativity', *Handbook of Creativity*, ed. Robert J. Sternberg (Cambridge University Press, 1999), pp. 313–35 (p. 333).

9. Mihaly Csikszentmihalyi, 'The Systems Model of Creativity and Its Applications', in *The Wiley Handbook of Genius*, ed. Dean Leith Simonton (Wiley-Blackwell, 2014).

10. Csikszentmihalyi, 'Implications of a Systems Perspective for the Study of Creativity', p. 314.

11. Samuel P. Fraiberger, Roberta Sinatra, Magnus Resch, Christoph Riedl, and Albert-László Barabási, 'Quantifying Reputation and Success in Art', *Science*, 16 November 2018, pp. 825–9.

12. Randall Collins, 'Review: Collaborative Circles: Friendship Dynamics and Creative Work by Michael P. Farrell', *Social Forces* 83:1 (September 2004), pp. 433–6 (p. 436).

13. Gino Cattani and Simone Ferriani, 'A Core/Periphery Perspective on Individual Creative Performance: Social Networks and Cinematic

Achievements in the Hollywood Film Industry', *Organization Science* 19:6 (November–December 2008), pp. 824–44.

14. Andrew B. Hargadon, 'Bridging Old Worlds and Building New Ones: Towards a Microsociology of Creativity', p. 16, https://www.researchgate. net/profile/Andrew-Hargadon/publication/253734313_Bridging_old_ worlds_and_building_new_ones_Towards_a_microsociology_of_creativity/ links/54105fa50cf2d8daaad3ca1e/Bridging-old-worlds-and-building-new-ones-Towards-a-microsociology-of-creativity.pdf [accessed 11 September 2023].

15. Emma Brown, 'In the Middle of Somewhere with Ava DuVernay and Emayatzy Corinealdi', *Interview Magazine*, 9 October 2012, https://www. interviewmagazine.com/film/ava-duvernay-emayatzy-corinealdi [accessed 11 September 2023].

16. Malcolm Gladwell, *The Tipping Point: How Little Things Can Make a Big Difference*, new edn (Abacus, 2002).

17. Peter Sheridan Dodds, Roby Muhamad, and Duncan J. Watts, 'An Experimental Study of Search in Global Social Networks', *Science* 301:827 (2003), doi: 10.1126/science.1081058 [accessed 27 October 2022].

18. Nicholas A. Christakis and James H. Fowler, *Connected: The Surprising Power of Our Social Networks and How They Shape Our Lives* (Little, Brown, 2009), pp. 27–9.

19. Otto Kallir, *Grandma Moses* (Harry N. Abrams, 1973), p. 15.

20. Ibid., p. 20.

21. 'Grandma Moses' Daughter, 70', *New York Times*, 16 October 1958, p. 37; 'Grandma Moses Died at Age of 101', *New York Times*, 14 December 1961, pp. 1, 46.

22. Kallir, *Grandma Moses*, p. 25.

23. Ibid., pp. 27, 28.

24. 'Louis Caldor Helped Set Up Grandma Moses in Art World', *New York Times*, 19 June 1973, p. 38.

25. 'L. J. Caldor, "found" Grandma Moses' art', *Bennington Banner*, 19 July 1973, p. 14.

26. 'Painter Grandma Moses Dies at 101', *The Virginian-Pilot*, 14 December 1961, p. 1.

27. 'Grandma Moses Died at Age of 101', *New York Times*, 14 December 1961, pp. 1, 46.

28. Martin Kalfatovic, 'Janis, Sidney (1896–1989), Art Dealer and Collector', *American National Biography*, February 2000, https://www-anb-org. lonlib.idm.oclc.org/view/10.1093/anb/9780198606697.001.0001/anb-9780198606697-e-1701545 [accessed 11 September 2023].

29. 'Grandma Moses at 95', *New York Times*, 7 September 1955, p. 30.

30. Kallir, *Grandma Moses*, p. 34.

31. Ibid., p. 44.

32. Ibid., p. 50.

33. Ibid., p. 65.

34. 'Grandma Moses at 100 Still the Gay Gamin', *Victoria Advocate*, 4 September 1960, p. 25.

35. 'Grandma Moses at 95', *New York Times*, 7 September 1955, p. 30.

36. Kallir, *Grandma Moses*, p. 189.

37. Jane Gross, 'Grandma Moses's Descendants', *New York Times*, 26 November 2008, https://archive.nytimes.com/newoldage.blogs.nytimes.com/2008/11/26/grandma-mosess-descendants/?searchResultPosition=3 [accessed 11 September 2023].

38. 'Grandma Moses at 95', *New York Times*, 7 September 1955, p. 30.

7. Samuel Johnson's years of obscurity

1. Johnson, 'Rambler, No. 47, Tuesday 28 August 1750', in *Selected Essays*, ed. David Womersley (Penguin, 2003), p. 123.

2. James Boswell, *Life of Johnson*, ed. R. W. Chapman (Oxford University Press, 1953, 1970, 1980), November 1784, p. 427.

3. Ibid., p. 1358.

4. Leo Damrosch, *The Club: Johnson, Boswell, and the Friends Who Shaped an Age* (Yale University Press, 2019), p. 10.

5. Samuel Johnson, *The Letters of Samuel Johnson, Volume I: 1731–1732*, ed. Bruce Redford (Princeton University Press, 1992), Samuel Johnson to Edward Cave, 25 November 1734, p. 6 and n.

6. Johnson, *Letters, Vol. I*, Samuel Johnson to Richard Congreve, 25 June 1735, pp. 9–10.

7. James Clifford, *Young Samuel Johnson* (William Heinemann, 1955), p. 141.

8. Lawrence Lipking, *Samuel Johnson: The Life of an Author* (Harvard University Press, 1998), p. 48.

9. William Shaw, *Memoirs of Dr. Johnson* (Oxford University Press, 1974), p. 33.

10. Boswell, *Life*, 17 April 1778, pp. 960–1.

11. Johnson, 'Rambler, No. 45, Tuesday 21 August, 1750', p. 117; 'Rambler, No. 25, Tuesday 12 June, 1750', p. 73; 'Rambler, No. 8, Saturday 14 April, 1750', p. 27.

12. Boswell, *Life*, 17 April 1778, pp. 960–1.

13. Shaw, *Memoirs of Dr. Johnson*, p. 27.

14. Samuel Johnson, *Life of Cowley*, in *Lives of the English Poets*, ed. G. B. Hill (Oxford: Clarendon Press, 1905), p. 2.

15. Lipking, *Samuel Johnson*, p. 50.

16. Boswell, *Life*, 7 April 1778, p. 912.

17. Ibid., 5 April 1776, p. 732.

18. Ibid., 9 April 1778, p. 918.

19. Ibid., Summer 1754, p. 191.

20. Ibid., Summer 1754, p. 193.

21. Hugo M. Reichard, 'Boswell's Johnson, the Hero Made by a Committee', *PMLA* 95:2 (1980), pp. 225–33 (p. 227), https://doi.org/10.2307/462017

22. Clifford, *Young Samuel Johnson*, p. 278.

23. Jack Lynch, 'Generous Liberal-Minded Men: Booksellers and Poetic Careers in Johnson's *Lives of the Poets*', *The Yearbook of English Studies* 45 (2015), pp. 93–108, https://doi.org/10.5699/yearenglstud.45.2015.0093

24. Allen Reddick, *The Making of Johnson's Dictionary, 1746–1773* (Cambridge University Press, 1990), p. 17.

25. Harry M. Solomon, *The Rise of Robert Dodsley* (Southern Illinois University Press, 1996), p. 199.

26. James E. Tierney, 'Robert Dodsley', *Oxford Dictionary of National Biography*, 3 October 2013, https://doi-org.lonlib.idm.oclc.org/10.1093/ref:odnb/7755

27. Peter Burke, *A Social History of Knowledge: Vol II from the Encyclopédie to Wikipedia* (Polity, 2012), p. 24.

28. John V. Pickstone, *Ways of Knowing: A New History of Science, Technology and Medicine* (Manchester University Press, 2000).

29. Johnson, *Letters, Vol. I*, Samuel Johnson to Samuel Richardson, 28 March 1754, p. 79; Samuel Johnson to William Strahan, 22 March 1753, p. 68.

30. William Deward, 'Anecdotes', *Johnsonian Miscellanies: Volume II*, ed. G. B. Hill (Oxford University Press, 1897), p. 303.

31. Pat Rogers, 'Johnson, Samuel (1709–1784), author and lexicographer', *Oxford Dictionary of National Biography*, https://www-oxforddnb-com.lonlib.idm.oclc.org/view/10.1093/ref:odnb/9780198614128.001.0001/odnb-9780198614128-e-14918 [accessed 30 September 2022].

32. Burke, *A Social History of Knowledge*, p. 179.

33. Boswell, *Life*, Samuel Johnson to Francis Barber, 25 September 1770, p. 434.

34. Boswell, *Life*, pp. 45, 44.

35. *The Correspondence and Other Papers of James Boswell Relating to the Making of the Life of Johnson*, 2nd edn, ed. Marshall Waingrow (Edinburgh University Press, 2011), p. 19.

36. Boswell, *Life*, 14 July 1763, p. 304.

37. Ibid., 21 July 1763, p. 315.

38. Ibid., 9 April 1778, 919.

39. Ibid., 14 July 1763, p. 303.

40. Ibid., 12 March 1776, p. 696.

41. Johnson, *Letters*, Samuel Johnson to John Taylor, 10 August 1742, p. 28; Samuel Johnson to Edward Cave, Autumn 1743, p. 34.

42. Samuel Johnson, *Diaries, Prayers, and Annals*, ed. E. L. McAdam, Donald Hyde, and Mary Hyde (Yale Digital Edition of the Works of Samuel Johnson, Series Volume 1), pp. 100–1.

43. Boswell, *Life*, November 1784, p. 1363n.

44. Ibid., 5 August 1763, pp. 331–2.

45. Johnson, *Letters, Vol. I*, Samuel Johnson to Hill Boothby, 31 December 1755, pp. 120–1.

46. Ibid., Samuel Johnson to Andrew Millar, 11 July 1753, p. 72; Samuel Johnson to Thomas Birch, January 1754, p. 77; Samuel Johnson to Thomas Birch, 4 November 1752, p. 65.

47. Hester Lynch Piozzi, *Anecdotes of Dr. Johnson* (Oxford University Press, 1974), p. 87.

48. Boswell, *Life*, Summer 1778, pp. 1001–2.

49. George Steevens, 'Anecdotes of George Steevens', *Johnsonian Miscellanies: Volume II*, ed. G. B. Hill (Oxford University Press, 1897), p. 325.

50. Arthur Murphy, 'Essay on Life and Genius of Samuel Johnson L.L.D.', *Johnsonian Miscellanies: Volume I*, p. 361.

51. Clifford, *Young Samuel Johnson*, p. 119.

52. Boswell, *Life*, 4 April 1778, p. 907.

53. Miss Reynolds, 'Recollections of Dr. Johnson', *Johnsonian Miscellanies: Volume II*, p. 252.

54. Clifford, *Young Samuel Johnson*, p. 150.

55. Fanny Burney, *The Diary of Fanny Burney* (Everyman, 1940), 'Saturday Morning', August 1778, p. 15.

56. Clifford, *Young Samuel Johnson*, p. 66.

57. Ibid., p. 84.

58. Tom Davies, *Memoirs of the Life of David Garrick Esq. Volume I* (Longman, 1808; first published, 1781), pp. 156–7.

59. Boswell, *Life*, 7 August 1755, p. 209.

60. James Clifford, *Dictionary Johnson*, (Heinemann, 1979), p. 147.

61. Thomas Carlyle, 'The Hero as Man of Letters', *On Heroes, Hero-Worship & The Heroic in History*, ed. Michael K. Goldberg, Joel J. Brattin, and Mark Engel (University of California Press, 1993), p. 154.

62. Carlyle, 'Man of Letters', p. 157.

63. Clifford, *Dictionary Johnson*, p. 74.

64. Boswell, *Life*, 1750, p. 149.

65. Clifford, *Dictionary Johnson*, p. 80.

66. William Deward, 'Anecdotes', *Johnsonian Miscellanies: Volume II*, ed. G. B. Hill (Oxford University Press, 1897), p. 423.

67. Johnson, *Letters*, Samuel Johnson to Joseph Warton, 15 April 1756, p. 134.

68. Harriet Kirkley, *A Biographer at Work: Samuel Johnson's Notes for the 'Life of Pope'* (Bucknell University Press, 2002), pp. 164, 233.

69. Clifford, *Young Samuel Johnson*, p. 62.

70. Boswell, *Life*, Thursday 9 April 1778, p. 919. The Bishop's quotation is from Plutarch's *Life of Solon* and in Boswell is printed in ancient Greek.

71. Miss Reynolds, 'Recollections of Dr. Johnson', p. 262.

72. Boswell, *Life*, 7 April 1778, p. 908.

73. Ibid., 20 September 1777, p. 857.

74. Samuel Johnson, *Life of Waller*, in *Lives of the Poets*, ed. John H. Middendorf (Yale Digital Edition of the Works of Samuel Johnson, Series Volume 21), p. 313.

75. Johnson, *Diaries, Prayers, and Annals*, p. 266.

76. Samuel Johnson, *Life of Pope*, in *Lives of the Poets*, ed. John H. Middendorf (Yale Digital Edition of the Works of Samuel Johnson, Series Volume 23), p. 1074.

77. Lawrence Lipking, 'The Death and Life of Samuel Johnson', *The Wilson Quarterly* 8:5 (1984), pp. 140–51 (p. 143), http://www.jstor.org/stable/40257647 [accessed 19 July 2022].

78. Samuel Johnson, 'Rambler No. 60, Saturday 13 October 1750', in *Selected Essays*, ed. David Womersley (Penguin, 2003), p. 131.

79. Samuel Johnson, 'Life of Savage', in *Lives of the Poets*, ed. John H. Middendorf (Yale Digital Edition of the Works of Samuel Johnson, Series Volume 22), p. 851.

80. Johnson, *Letters*, Samuel Johnson to Bennet Langton, 27 June 1758, p. 166.

81. Ibid., Samuel Johnson to John Taylor, 18 November 1756, p. 148.

82. Samuel Johnson, 'Preface', *Johnson on Shakespeare*, ed. Walter Raleigh (Oxford University Press, 1908), pp. 16, 12, 13, 15.

83. Samuel Johnson, 'The Rambler, No. 71 Tuesday 20 November 1750', p. 147; 'The Rambler, No. 49, Tuesday 4 September 1750', p. 124; 'The Rambler, No. 47, Tuesday 28 August 1750, p. 123; 'The Rambler, No. 4, Saturday 31 March 1750, p. 15.

84. Boswell, *Life*, Wednesday 20 March 1776, p. 691; Tuesday 31 March 1778, p. 899; Saturday 23 March 1776, p. 706; Saturday 30 September 1769, p. 405; Wednesday 3 November 1784, p. 1362; Friday 18 April 1783, p. 1224.

85. Johnson, 'Rambler, No. 41, Tuesday 7 August, 1750', p. 115.

PART FOUR: CHANGING AND AGEING

8. Change your circumstances to change yourself

1. Michael P. Farrell, *Collaborative Circles: Friendship Dynamics & Creative Work* (University of Chicago Press, 2001), pp. 2, 7, 11, 12.

2. Warren G. Bennis and Patricia Ward Biederman, *Organizing Genius: The Secrets of Creative Collaboration* (Basic Books, 1997).

3. Farrell, *Collaborative Circles*, p. 14.

4. Ibid., p. 117.

5. Ibid., p. 132.

6. Michael P. Farrell to Henry Oliver, email, 23 April 2022.

7. David Epstein, *Range Widely,* 'A Practical Guide To Building Team Culture (Including Remote-Team Culture)', https://davidepstein.substack.com/p/a-practical-guide-to-building-team-22-08-14

8. https://www.strategy-business.com/article/How-Fearless-Organizations-Succeed

9. Taste for Makers, February 2002, http://www.paulgraham.com/taste.html

10. Pierre Azoulay, Joshua S. Graff, and Zivin Jialan Wang, 'Superstar Extinction', NBER Working Paper 14577, https://www.nber.org/papers/w14577 [accessed 13 September 2023].

11. Pierre Azoulay, Christian Fons-Rosen, and Joshua S. Graff Zivin, 'Does Science Advance One Funeral at a Time?', NBER Working Paper 21788, https://www.nber.org/papers/w21788 [accessed 13 September 2023].

12. Michael Housman and Dylan Minor, 'Toxic Workers', Harvard Business School Working Paper 16-057, https://www.hbs.edu/ris/Publication%20Files/16-057_d45c0b4f-fa19-49de-8f1b-4b12fe054fea.pdf [accessed 13 September 2023].

13. Therese Amabile and Stephen Kramer, 'The Power of Small Wins', *Harvard Business Review*, May 2011.

14. Stefan Wuchty, Benjamin F. Jones, and Brian Uzzi, 'The Increasing Dominance of Teams in Production of Knowledge', *Science* 316 (18 May 2007), pp. 1036–9, https://asset-pdf.scinapse.io/prod/1965631677/1965631677.pdf [accessed 13 September 2023].

15. Michael E. Rose and Co-Pierre Georg, 'What 5,000 Acknowledgements Tell Us about Informal Collaboration in Financial Economics', *Research Policy* 50:6 (2021), https://doi.org/10.1016/j.respol.2021.104236

16. Seth Gershenson, Cassandra M. D. Hart, Joshua Hyman, Constance Lindsay and Nicholas W. Papageorge, 'The Long-Run Impacts of Same-Race Teachers', NBER Working Paper, 25254, http://www.nber.org/papers/w25254 [accessed 13 September 2023].

17. Jerker Denrell, 'Indirect Social Influence', *Science* n.s. 321:5885 (4 July 2008), pp. 47–8; Jerker Denrell and Gael Le Mens, 'Interdependent Sampling and Social Influence', *Psychological Review* 114:2 (2007), pp. 398–422.

18. Shi Pu, Yu Yan and Liang Zhang, 'Do Peers Affect Undergraduates' Decisions to Switch Majors?', Edited Working Paper: 20-246. Retrieved from Annenberg Institute at Brown University: https://doi.org/10.26300/sdbt-4n23

19. J. McGrath Cohoon, 'Toward Improving Female Retention in the Computer Science Major', *Communications of the ACM* 44:5 (2001), pp. 108–14.

20. Michael Kremer and Dan Levy, 'Peer Effects and Alcohol Use among College Students', *Journal of Economic Perspectives* 22:3 (Summer 2008), pp. 189–206.

21. Alex Bell, Raj Chetty, Xavier Jar Avel, Ne Viana Pe Tkova, and John Van Reenen, 'Who Becomes an Inventor in America? The Importance of Exposure to Innovation', https://opportunityinsights.org/wp-content/uploads/2021/12/inventors_summary.pdf [accessed 13 September 2023].

22. Raj Chetty, Matthew O. Jackson, Theresa Kuchler, Johannes Str Oebel, Abigail Hiller, and Sarah Oppenheimer, 'Social Capital and Economic Mobility', https://opportunityinsights.org/wp-content/uploads/2022/07/socialcapital_nontech.pdf [accessed 13 September 2023].

23. Aristotle, *Poetics* IV; John Stuart Mill, *The Subjection of Women*, in *On Liberty, Utilitarianism and Other Essays* (Oxford University Press, 1991, 1998, 2008, 2015), p. 429.

24. Randall Collins, *The Sociology of Philosophies: A Global Theory of Intellectual Change* (Harvard University Press, 1998), p. 6.

25. J. H. Chariker, Y. Zhang, J. R. Pani and E. C. Rouchka, 'Identification of Successful Mentoring Communities Using Network-Based Analysis of Mentor–Mentee Relationships across Nobel Laureates', *Scientometrics* 111:3 (2017), pp. 1733–49, doi: 10.1007/s11192-017-2364-4

26. Transcript: Ezra Klein Interviews Patrick Collison, 27 September 2022, https://www.nytimes.com/2022/09/27/podcasts/transcript-ezra-klein-interviews-patrick-collison.html [accessed 13 September 2023].

27. Michael Rutter, 'Pathways from Childhood to Adult Life', *Journal of Childhood Psychology and Psychiatry* 30:1 (1989), pp. 23–51.

28. Robert J. Sampson and John H. Laub, 'Socioeconomic Achievement in the Life Course of Disadvantaged Men: Military Service as a Turning Point, Circa 1940–1965', *American Sociological Review* 61:3 (June 1996), pp. 347–67.

29. Ibid.

30. Glen H. Elder, Jr., 'The Life Course as Developmental Theory', *Child Development* 69:1 (February 1998), pp. 1–12.

31. Clare Mac Cumhaill and Rachael Wiseman, *Metaphysical Animals: How Four Women Brought Philosophy Back to Life* (Vintage, 2023).

32. Harry Rosenfeld, *From Kristallnacht to Watergate: Memoirs of a Newspaperman* (SUNY Press, 2013), pp. 189–96.

33. Jay Belsky, 'Your Kid is Probably Not an "Orchid" or a "Dandelion" – But Could be Both', *Scientific America*, 15 March 2022.

34. T. Deutsch, 'Child, Julia (1912–2004), Cookbook Author and Television Chef', *American National Biography*, https://www-anb-org.lonlib.idm.oclc.org/view/10.1093/anb/9780198606697.001.0001/anb-9780198606697-e-1603573 [accessed 14 December 2022].

35. L. A. Paul, *Transformative Experiences* (Oxford University Press, 2014), p. 3.

36. Rosenfeld, *From Kristallnacht to Watergate,* p. 106.

37. Katharine Graham, *Personal History* (Knopf, 1997), p. 346.

38. Agnes Callard, *Aspiration* (Oxford University Press, 2018), pp. 47–8.

39. Jerker Denrell and Gaël Le Mens, 'Revisiting the Competency Trap', *Industrial and Corporate Change* 29:1 (2020), pp. 183–205.

40. Quoted in Jerker Denrell and James G. March, 'Adaptation as Information Restriction: The Hot Stove Effect', *Organization Science* 12:5 (September–October 2001), pp. 523–38.

41. Rosenfeld, *From Kristallnacht to Watergate*, p. 176.

42. Isabel Losada, *New Habits: Today's Women Who Choose to Become Nuns* (Hodder & Stoughton, 1999).

9. Audrey Sutherland: live immediately

1. Audrey Sutherland, *Paddling My Own Canoe* (University of Hawaii, 1978; Patagonia, 2018), p. 9.

2. Ibid., p. 14.

3. Ibid., pp. 15–16.

4. Audrey Sutherland, *Paddling North* (Patagonia, 2012).

5. Mage Nichols, 'Audrey Sutherland: The Grande Dame of Inflatable Kayaks', *Sea Kayaker*, October 2004, p. 28.

6. Sutherland, *Paddling My Own Canoe*, p. 15.

7. Dale Hope, 'Patagonia Books Presents an Interview with Audrey Sutherland, Author of Paddling North', https://www.patagonia.com/stories/patagonia-books-presents-an-interview-with-audrey-sutherland-author-of-paddling-north/story-18316.html [accessed 13 September 2023].

8. Sanford Lung to Henry Oliver, email, 2 December 2022; Neil Frazer to Henry Oliver, email, 4 December 2022.

9. Jen A. Miller, 'Overlooked No More: Audrey Sutherland, Paddler of Her Own Canoe', *New York Times*, 6 March 2020, https://www.nytimes.com/2020/03/06/obituaries/audrey-sutherland-overlooked.html

10. Interview with Jock Sutherland, 3 February 2023.

11. Sanford Lung to Henry Oliver, email, 9 December 2022.

12. Linda Daniel, 'Audrey Sutherland Profile', *Sea Kayaker*, Spring 1998.

13. Sanford Lung to Henry Oliver, email, 9 December 2022.

14. Mary McClintok, 'Paddling North, Review', *Sea Kayaker*, October 2012, p. 39.

15. Sutherland, *Paddling My Own Canoe*, p. 28.

16. Ibid., pp. 30–1.

17. Ibid., p. 162.

18. Sutherland, *Paddling North*, p. 11.

19. Ibid., p. 15.

20. Ibid., p. 18.

21. Ibid., p. 23.

22. David Thompson, '7 Fearless Ladies Who Have Mastered Paddling And Living Well', *Paddling Magazine*, Spring 2015, https://paddlingmag.com/stories/water-women-the-pioneer/ [accessed 13 September 2023].

23. Quoted in Nichols, 'Audrey Sutherland: The Grand Dame of Inflatable Kayaks', pp. 22–9.

24. Interview with Neil Frazer, 8 December 2022.

25. Agnes Callard, *Aspiration* (Oxford University Press, 2018), p. 55.

26. https://www.atvbt.com/ngannou/ [accessed 23 September 2023].

27. Callard, *Aspiration*, p. 61.

28. Sutherland, *Paddling My Own Canoe*, pp. 110, 111.

29. Ibid., p. 124.

30. Matt Warshaw, 'Goodbye Sunshine Superman', in *Big Wave: Stories of Riding the World's Wildest Water*, ed. Clint Willis (Thunder's Mouth, 2003), pp. 86–7.

31. Daniel, 'Audrey Sutherland Profile'.

32. Interview with Neil Frazer, 8 December 2022.

33. Interview with Jock Sutherland, 3 February 2023.

34. Lorenn Walker, *Aging with Strength* (Hawaii, independently published, 2012), p. 37.

35. https://www.forbes.com/sites/jaynacooke/2017/03/15/own-your-happyness-a-qa-with-chris-gardner/?sh=513d9c201b27 [accessed 12 September 2023].

36. Walker, *Aging with Strength*, p. 38.

37. Daniel, 'Audrey Sutherland Profile'.

38. R. G. Pryor and J. E. Bright, 'The Chaos Theory of Careers (CTC): Ten Years On and Only Just Begun', *Australian Journal of Career Development* 23:1 (2014), pp. 4–12.

39. Walker, *Aging with Strength*, p. 35.

40. Daniel, 'Audrey Sutherland Profile'.

41. Audrey Sutherland, 'Paddling Hawaii. The Tropical Option', *Sea Kayaker*, Winter 1984, pp. 40–4.

42. Interview with Jim Kraus, 23 February 2023.

43. Interview with Jock Sutherland, 3 February 2023.

44. Interview with Jim Kraus, 23 February 2023.

45. Interview with Jim Kraus, 23 February 2023.

46. John Muir, *The Story of My Boyhood and Youth*, in *Nature Writings* (Library of America, 1997), p. 7.

47. Michael Molloy, *Experiencing the World's Religions* (McGraw-Hill, 2010), p. 562.

48. Richard McMahon, *Adventuring in Hawaii* (Sierra Club Books, 1996), p. 346.

49. Walker, *Aging with Strength*, p. 36.

50. Paul Theroux, 'Hawaii Rough and Smooth', *New York Times*, 20 May 1990, Section 6, p. 28.

51. Alastair Humphreys, 'Audrey Sutherland', YouTube, 24 July 2018, https://www.youtube.com/watch?v=OkUynbpu2sQ [accessed 12 September 2023].

52. Marcus Aurelius, *Meditations*, trans. Gregory Hays (Weidenfeld & Nicolson, 2003), 6.26, p. 74.

53. Dale Hope, 'Patagonia Books Presents an Interview with Audrey Sutherland, Author of *Paddling North*', https://eu.patagonia.com/gb/en/stories/patagonia-books-presents-an-interview-with-audrey-sutherland-author-of-paddling-north/story-18316.html [accessed 12 September 2023].

54. Patricia Hubbard, *The Outdoor Woman: A Handbook to Adventure* (MasterMedia, 1992), p. 39.

55. Sutherland, *Paddling North*, p. 18.

56. Marcus Aurelius, *Meditations*, 4.17, p. 41.

57. Michel de Montaigne, 'On Age', *The Complete Essays*, trans. M. A. Screech (Penguin, 1993).

58. Seneca, *On the Shortness of Life* (Penguin, 2004), p. 13.

10. The more you do, the more you succeed

1. Arthur C. Brooks, 'Your Professional Decline is Coming (Much) Sooner Than You Think', *Atlantic*, July 2019, https://www.theatlantic.com/magazine/archive/2019/07/work-peak-professional-decline/590650/; Arthur C. Brooks, *From Strength to Strength* (Portfolio, 2022).

2. Jeffrey Kluger, 'Staying Sharp: The Surprising Power of the Aging Brain', *Time*, 13 January 2006.

3. Melissa A. Schilling, 'A "Small-World" Network Model of Cognitive Insight', March 2004, p. 26, https://www.researchgate.net/profile/Melissa-Schilling/publication/256062673_A_'Small-World'_Network_Model_of_Cognitive_Insight/links/0046351914b9d24e74000000/A-Small-World-Network-

Model-of-Cognitive-Insight.pdf?_sg%5B0%5D=started_experiment_
milestone&origin=journalDetail

4. Ian Deary, 'The Stability of Intelligence from Childhood to Old Age',
    Current Directions in Psychological Science 23:4 (2014), pp. 239–45. DOI:
    10.1177/0963721414536905

5. Ian Deary, *Intelligence: A Very Short Introduction* (Oxford University Press,
    2020), p. 35.

6. Stuart Ritchie et al., 'Predictors of Ageing-Related Decline across Multiple
    Cognitive Functions', *Intelligence* 59 (November–December 2016), pp. 115–26,
    https://www.sciencedirect.com/science/article/pii/S0160289616302707
    [accessed 12 September 2023].

7. Corley et al., 'Predictors of Longitudinal Cognitive Ageing from Age 70 to 82
    Including APOE e4 Status, Early-Life and Lifestyle Factors: The Lothian Birth
    Cohort 1936', *Molecular Psychiatry* 28 (2023), pp. 1256–71.

8. J. Corley, S. R. Cox and I. J. Deary, 'Healthy Cognitive Ageing in the Lothian
    Birth Cohort Studies: Marginal Gains Not Magic Bullet', *Psychological
    Medicine* 48 (2018), pp. 187–207, doi: 10.1017/S0033291717001489

9. Corley et al., 'Predictors of Longitudinal Cognitive Ageing'.

10. Drew M. Altschul and Ian J. Deary, 'Playing Analog Games is Associated with
    Reduced Declines in Cognitive Function: A 68-Year Longitudinal Cohort
    Study', *The Journals of Gerontology: Series B* 75:3 (March 2020), pp. 474–82,
    https://doi.org/10.1093/geronb/gbz149

11. M. Lövdén, L. Fratiglioni, M. M. Glymour, U. Lindenberger, and E. M.
    Tucker-Drob. 'Education and Cognitive Functioning across the Life Span',
    Psychological Science in the Public Interest 21:1 (August 2020), pp. 6–41. DOI:
    10.1177/1529100620920576. PMID: 32772803; PMCID: PMC7425377.

12. T. J. Krivanek, 'Promoting Successful Cognitive Aging: A Ten-Year Update',
    Journal of Alzheimer's Disease 81 (2021), pp. 871–920, DOI 10.3233/JAD-
    201462

13. Melis Anatürk et al., 'Prediction of Brain Age and Cognitive Age: Quantifying
    Brain and Cognitive Maintenance in Aging', *Human Brain Mapping* 42
    (2021), pp. 1626–40, https://doi.org/10.1002/hbm.25316 [accessed 13
    September 2023].

14. Steven D. Levitt, 'Heads or Tails: The Impact of a Coin Toss on Major Life
    Decisions and Subsequent Happiness', *The Review of Economic Studies* 88:1
    (2016), pp. 378–405.

15. Joshua K. Hartshorne and Laura T. Germine, 'When Does Cognitive Functioning Peak? The Asynchronous Rise and Fall of Different Cognitive Abilities across the Life Span', *Psychological Science* 26:4 (2015), pp. 433–43, https://doi.org/10.1177/0956797614567339 [accessed 13 September 2023].

16. Hartshorne and Germine, 'When Does Cognitive Functioning Peak?'.

17. Mischa von Krause, Stefan T. Radev, and Andreas Voss, 'Mental Speed is High until Age 60 as Revealed by Analysis of over a Million Participants', *Nature Human Behaviour* 6 (May 2022), pp. 700–8.

18. Nicholas A. Christakis and James H. Fowler, *Connected: The Surprising Power of Our Social Networks and How They Shape Our Lives* (Little, Brown, 2009), pp. 240–2.

19. Susan T. Charles and Laura L. Carstensen, 'Social and Emotional Aging', *Annual Review of Psychology* 61 (2009), pp. 383–409.

20. Eric Schniter et al., 'Information Transmission and the Oral Tradition: Evidence of a Late-Life Service Niche for Tsimane Amerindians', *Evolution and Human Behavior* 39:1 (2018), pp. 94–105.

21. Igor Grossmann et al., 'Reasoning about Social Conflicts Improves into Old Age', *Proceedings of the National Academy of Sciences* 107:16 (2010), pp. 7246–50.

22. Wendy Johnson, 'Greatness as a Manifestation of Experience-Producing Drives', in *The Complexity of Greatness: Beyond Talent or Practice*, ed. Scott Barry Kaufman (Cambridge University Press, 2013), pp. 3–16 (p. 7); and Heiner Rindermann, Stephen J. Ceci and Wendy M. Williams, 'Whither Cognitive Talent?: Understanding High Ability and Its Development, Relevance, and Furtherance', in ibid., pp. 43–65 (pp. 51, 58).

23. James C. Kaufman et al., 'Young and Old, Novice and Expert: How We Evaluate Creative Art Can Reflect Practice and Talent', in *The Complexity of Greatness*, pp. 167–72.

24. https://keithsawyer.wordpress.com/2016/11/22/are-you-too-old-to-be-brilliant/ [accessed 13 September 2023].

25. Anders Ericsson and Robert Pool, *Peak: How All of Us Can Achieve Extraordinary Things* (Vintage, 2017), p. 110.

26. The Genius Checklist.

27. Zachary Woolfe, 'Review: A Pianist Explores Mozart the Late Bloomer', *New York Times*, 23 February 2022, https://www.nytimes.com/2022/02/23/arts/music/vikingur-olafsson-carnegie-hall.html?searchResultPosition=57 [accessed 13 September 2023].

28. Brooke N. Macnamara, David Z. Hambrick, and Frederick L. Oswald, 'Deliberate Practice and Performance in Music, Games, Sports, Education, and Professions: A Meta-Analysis', *Psychological Science*, 1 July 2014, doi:10.1177/0956797614535810 [accessed 13 September 2023].

29. M. Fisher and F. C. Keil, 'The Curse of Expertise: When More Knowledge Leads to Miscalibrated Explanatory Insight', *Cognitive Science* 40 (2016), pp. 1251–69, https://doi.org/10.1111/cogs.12280

30. Dean Keith Simonton, 'If Innate Talent Doesn't Exist, Where Do the Data Disappear?', in *The Complexity of Greatness*, p. 19.

31. Ted Underwood, Kevin Kiley, Wenyi Shang and Stephen Vaisey, 'Cohort Succession Explains Most Change in Literary Culture', *Sociological Science* 9 (May 2022), pp. 184–205.

32. https://twitter.com/Ted_Underwood/status/1522195394851188742

33. https://www.chess.com/article/view/chess-grandmaster-hours

34. Roberta Sinatra, Dashun Wang, Pierre Deville, Chaoming Song, and Albert-László Barabási, 'Quantifying the Evolution of Individual Scientific Impact', *Science* 354:6312 (2016).

35. Benedict Carey, 'When It Comes to Success, Age Really Is Just a Number', *New York Times*, 3 November 2016 https://www.nytimes.com/2016/11/04/science/stem-careers-success-achievement.html [accessed 13 September 2023].

36. Sinatra et al., 'Quantifying the Evolution of Individual Scientific Impact'.

37. This point is based on a comment the writer Gwern left on my Substack, *The Common Reader*. https://commonreader.substack.com/p/the-case-for-opsimaths-maybe-late/comments

38. Dean Keith Simonton, 'Creative Productivity: A Predictive and Explanatory Model of Career Trajectories and Landmarks', *Psychological Review* 104:1 (1997), pp. 66–89.

39. Benjamin F. Jones and Bruce A. Weinberg, 'Age Dynamics in Scientific Creativity', *Proceedings of the National Academy of Sciences* 108:47 (7 November 2011), pp. 18910–1, https://doi.org/10.1073/pnas.1102895108

40. Ibid.

41. Matt Clancy, 'Are Ideas Getting Harder to Find Because of the Burden of Knowledge?', https://www.newthingsunderthesun.com/pub/zsc23qxz/release/12 [accessed 13 September 2023].

42. Bruce A. Weinberg and David W. Galenson, 'Creative Careers: The Life Cycles of Nobel Laureates in Economics', Working Paper 11799 (2005), http://www.nber.org/papers/w11799 [accessed 13 September 2023].

43. Benjamin Jones, E. J. Reedy, and Bruce A. Weinberg, 'Age and Scientific Genius', Working Paper 19866 (2014), http://www.nber.org/papers/w19866 [accessed 13 September 2023; also available at https://www.kellogg.northwestern.edu/faculty/jones-ben/htm/Age%20and%20Scientific%20Genius.pdf [accessed 13 September 2023].

44. Ibid., p. 34.

45. G. H. Hardy, *A Mathematician's Apology* (Cambridge University Press, 1940), pp. 11–12, 88, 32–4.

46. For a list of examples, see 'Major Mathematical Advances Past Age Fifty', *MathOverflow.net*, 23 May 2010, https://mathoverflow.net/questions/25630/major-mathematical-advances-past-age-fifty

47. Michael Barany, 'The Fields Medal Should Return to its Roots', *Nature*, 12 January 2018, https://www.nature.com/articles/d41586-018-00513-8 [accessed 26 August 2022].

48. Nancy Stern, 'Age and Achievement in Mathematics: A Case-Study in the Sociology of Science', *Social Studies of Science* 8:1 (February 1978), pp. 127–40 (p. 134), https://www.jstor.org/stable/284859 [accessed 26 August 2022].

49. Stephen Cole, 'Age and Scientific Performance', *American Journal of Sociology* 84:4 (January 1979), pp. 958–77 (p. 958).

50. Ibid., p. 963.

51. Ibid., p. 968.

52. Anthony G. O'Farrell, 'Book Review: *Loving + Hating Mathematics: Challenging the Myths of Mathematical Life* by Reuben Hersh and Vera John-Steiner', *Irish Mathematics Society Bulletin* 67 (2011), pp. 97–8.

53. Alec Wilkinson, 'The Pursuit of Beauty: Yitang Zhang Solves a Pure-Math Mystery', *New Yorker*, 2 February 2015, https://www.newyorker.com/magazine/2015/02/02/pursuit-beauty [accessed 1 July 2022].

54. Thomas Lin, 'After Prime Proof, an Unlikely Star Rises', *Quanta*, 2 April 2015, https://www.quantamagazine.org/yitang-zhang-and-the-mystery-of-numbers-20150402 [accessed 1 July 2022].

55. Michael Segal, 'The Twin Prime Hero', Nautilus, 19 September 2013, https://nautil.us/the-twin-prime-hero-1081/ [accessed 1 July 2022]; *Counting from Infinity: Yitang Zhang and the Twin Prime Conjecture*, documentary, dir. George Paul Csicsery (2015).

56. Genevieve Dean, 'Review: Science and Politics in China: Reflections on One Hundred Thousand Questions', *Science Studies* 4:1 (January 1974), pp. 93–6 (p. 94).

57. *Counting from Infinity.*

58. T. T. Moh, 'Zhang, Yitang's Life at Purdue (Jan 1985–1991)', August 2013 (revised 2018), pp. 2, 4, https://www.math.purdue.edu/~ttm/ZhangYt.pdf [accessed 1 July 2022].

59. Ibid., p. 5.

60. Lin, 'After Prime Proof, an Unlikely Star Rises'.

61. Moh, 'Zhang, Yitang's Life at Purdue', p. 7.

62. Ibid.

63. Ibid.

64. Lin, 'After Prime Proof, an Unlikely Star Rises'.

65. Segal, 'The Twin Prime Hero'.

66. Ibid.

67. Erica Klarreich, 'Unheralded Mathematician Bridges the Prime Gap', *Quanta*, 19 May 2013, https://www.quantamagazine.org/yitang-zhang-proves-landmark-theorem-in-distribution-of-prime-numbers-20130519/ [accessed 1 July 2022].

68. Wilkinson, 'The Pursuit of Beauty'.

69. Ronald Miller, *A View from the Wings* (Weidenfeld & Nicolson, 1993), p. 233.

70. https://slimemoldtimemold.com/2022/02/10/the-scientific-virtues/ [accessed 13 September 2023].

71. Elizabeth L. Bjork and Robert Bjork, 'Making Things Hard on Yourself, But in a Good Way: Creating Desirable Difficulties to Enhance Learning', *Psychology and the Real World* (2009).

72. Ibid.

73. Ibid.

74. Robert Bjork and Elizabeth L. Bjork, 'Desirable Difficulties in Theory and Practice', *Journal of Applied Research in Memory and Cognition* 9:4 (2020), pp. 475–9 (p. 477).

75. Bjork and Bjork, 'Making Things Hard on Yourself, But in a Good Way'.

PART FIVE: MIDLIFE TRANSITIONS

11. Frank Lloyd Wright: The re-examined life and the infinite spiral

1. Frank Lloyd Wright, 'Why I Love Wisconsin', *Wisconsin Magazine*, 1932.

2. Anthony Alofsin, 'Wright, Frank Lloyd (1867–1959), Architect', *American National Biography Online* (Oxford University Press, February 2000), https://www-anb-org.lonlib.idm.oclc.org/view/10.1093/anb/9780198606697.001.0001/anb-9780198606697-e-1700946 [accessed 9 November 2022].

3. Harold Zellman and Roger Friedland, *The Fellowship: The Untold Story of Frank Lloyd Wright and the Taliesin Fellowship* (HarperCollins, 2009).

4. Tom Wolfe, *From Bauhaus to Our House* (Pocket Books, 1981), p. 34.

5. Frank Lloyd Wright, 'Why I Love Wisconsin'.

6. Robert McCarter, *Frank Lloyd Wright* (Phaidon, 1997), p. 277.

7. Mina Marefat, 'Wright in Baghdad', in *Frank Lloyd Wright: From Within Outward*, exh. cat. (Guggenheim, 2009), p. 75.

8. Nicholas Hayes, *Frank Lloyd Wright's Forgotten House: How an Omission Transformed an Architect's Legacy* (University of Wisconsin, 2021), pp. 33–7.

9. McCarter, *Frank Lloyd Wright*, pp. 277–8.

10. *Frank Lloyd Wright: From Within Outward*, p. 174.

11. Frank Lloyd Wright, 'Modern Architecture, Being the Khan Lectures', *The Essential Frank Lloyd Wright*, ed. Bruce Brooks Pfeiffer (Princeton University Press, 2008), p. 180.

12. Cammy Brothers, *Michelangelo, Drawing, and the Invention of Architecture* (Yale University Press, 2007), pp. 1–9.

13. Ibid., pp. 45–6, 50–4.

14. Ibid., p. 9.

15. Ibid., p. 12.

16. Ibid., pp. 10–20.

17. Ibid., pp. 69, 76, 86.

18. Ibid., p. 205.

19. Walt Whitman, 'Song of the Open Road', *Leaves of Grass* (J. M. Dent & Sons, 1947), pp. 125, 127.

20. Frank Lloyd Wright, 'The Architect', *Frank Lloyd Wright Collected Writings Vol 4 (1939–1949)*, ed. Bruce Brooks Pfeiffer (Rizzoli, 1994), p. 290.

21. Anthony Alofsin, *Frank Lloyd Wright The Lost Years: 1910–1922, A Study of Influence* (Chicago, 1993).

22. Ibid., p. 83.

23. Neil Levine, *The Architecture of Frank Lloyd Wright* (Princeton University Press, 1996), p. 27.

24. Donald Hoffmann, *Understanding Frank Lloyd Wright's Architecture* (Dover, 1995), p. 27.

25. Wright quoted in Levine, *The Architecture of Frank Lloyd Wright*, p. 41.

26. Hoffmann, *Understanding Frank Lloyd Wright's Architecture*, pp. 88–93.

27. Frank Lloyd Wright, 'Modern Architecture, Being the Khan Lectures', *The Essential Frank Lloyd Wright*, ed. Bruce Brooks Pfeiffer (Princeton, 2008), p. 180.

28. John Gurda, *New World Odyssey: Annunciation Greek Orthodox Church and Frank Lloyd Wright* (Milwaukee Hellenic Community, 1986), p. 51.

29. Levine, *The Architecture of Frank Lloyd Wright*, p. xvii.

30. Ibid., pp. 55, 93.

31. Ibid., p. 95.

32. Ibid., p. 104.

33. Anthony Alofsin, 'Frank Lloyd Wright and the Aesthetics of Japan', *SiteLINES: A Journal of Place* 4:1 (2008), p. 17, www.jstor.org/stable/24889324 [accessed 14 November 2022].

34. Wright to Martin, 20 August 1922, quoted in Kathryn Smith, 'Frank Lloyd Wright and the Imperial Hotel: A Postscript', *The Art Bulletin* 67:2 (1985), pp. 296–310 (pp. 306, 308), https://doi.org/10.2307/3050913

35. Janzella Zara, 'How Michelangelo Spent His Final Years Designing St. Peter's Basilica in Rome', AD, 25 January 2019, https://www.architecturaldigest.com/story/how-michelangelo-spent-final-years-designing-st-peters-basilica-rome

36. Smith, 'Frank Lloyd Wright and the Imperial Hotel', p. 310.

37. Joseph M. Siry, 'The Architecture of Earthquake Resistance: Julius Kahn's Truscon Company and Frank Lloyd Wright's Imperial Hotel', *Journal of the Society of Architectural Historians* 67:1 (2008), pp. 78–105 (pp. 83–4), https://doi.org/10.1525/jsah.2008.67.1.78

38. Ibid., p. 88.

39. Siry, 'The Architecture of Earthquake Resistance', p. 96.

40. Ibid., p. 99.

41. Whitman, 'Song of the Open Road', p. 131.

42. *Frank Lloyd Wright and Louis Mumford: Thirty Years of Correspondence*, ed. Bruce Brooks Pfeiffer and Robert Wojtowicz (Princeton University Press, 2001), Frank Lloyd Wright [FLW] to Louis Mumford [LM], 6 August 1929, p. 77. All subsequent references to their correspondence are to this edition.

43. Frank Lloyd Wright, 'Form and Function', *Frank Lloyd Wright Collected Writings Vol. 3 (1931–1939)*, ed. Bruce Brooks Pfeiffer (Rizzoli, 1993), p. 188.

44. Whitman, 'Song of the Open Road', p. 134.

45. LM to FLW, 1 July 1930, p. 88.

46. FLW to LM, 7 July 1930, p. 91.

47. Wright to Martin, November 1905, quoted in *Frank Lloyd Wright: From Within Outward*, p. 47.

48. FLW to LM, 7 April 1931, p. 105.

49. Details of the Taliesin apprenticeship can be found in Harold Zellman and Roger Friedland, *The Fellowship: The Untold Story of Frank Lloyd Wright and the Taliesin Fellowship* (HarperCollins, 2009).

50. Frank Lloyd Wright, 'An Organic Architecture', *Frank Lloyd Wright Collected Writings Vol 3 (1931–1939)*, ed. Bruce Brooks Pfeiffer (Rizzoli, 1993), p. 302.

51. Kathryn Smith, *Wright on Exhibit* (Princeton University Press, 2017), p. 109.

52. Ibid., p. 43.

53. Frank Lloyd Wright, 'The Japanese Print', *Frank Lloyd Wright Collected Writings, Volume I: 1894–1930*, ed. Bruce Brooks Pfeiffer (Rizzoli, 1992), pp. 117–18.

54. McCarter, *Frank Lloyd Wright*, p. 193.

12. Reasons to have a midlife crisis

1. Jonathan Rauch, *The Happiness Curve* (St Martin's Press, 2018), p. 21.

2. David G. Blanchflower and Andrew Oswald, 'Is Well-Being U-Shaped over the Life Cycle?', February 2007, NBER Working Paper 12935, http://www.nber.org/papers/w12935

3. Kieran Setiya, *Midlife: A Philosophical Guide* (Princeton University Press, 2017), p. 34.

4. Andrew Jamieson, *Midlife: Humanity's Secret Weapon* (Notting Hill Editions, 2022), p. 27.

5. J. H. Wallis, *The Challenge of Middle Age* (Routledge & Kegan Paul, 1962), pp. 1, 5, 8, 11, 81.

6. Audrey Sutherland, *Paddling My Own Canoe* (University of Hawaii, 1978; Patagonia, 2018), p. 125.

7. Lawrence Levy, *To Pixar and Beyond* (Oneworld, 2016), p. 101.

8. Warren G. Bennis and Patricia Ward Biederman, *Organizing Genius: The Secrets of Creative Collaboration* (Basic Books, 1997), pp. 81–2.

9. Ibid., p. 85.

10. Jobs's verbatim quotations all come from *Make Something Wonderful: Steve Jobs in His Own Words*, published online by the Steve Jobs Archive, https://book.stevejobsarchive.com/

11. Ben Horowitz, *What You Do Is Who You Are* (William Collins, 2019), p. 62.

12. Rebecca Bengal, '*Vogue* Stories: Sarah Jessica Parker, Isabella Rossellini, and Others Recall Their Big Breaks in the Magazine', *Vogue*, 4 September 2012, https://www.vogue.com/article/vogue-stories-sarah-jessica-parker-isabella-rossellini-and-others-recall-their-big-breaks-in-the-magazine

13. Ibid.

14. Alison Beard, 'Life's Work: An Interview with Vera Wang', *HBR*, July–August 2019, https://hbr.org/2019/07/lifes-work-an-interview-with-vera-wang [accessed 13 September 2023].

15. Anne M. Todd, *Vera Wang* (Chelsea House, 2007).

16. Beard, 'Life's Work'.

17. Henry Oliver, 'Robin Hanson Interview', *The Common Reader*, https://www.commonreader.co.uk/p/robin-hanson-interview

18. Lynda Gratton and Andrew Scott, *The 100 Year Life: Living and Working in an Age of Longevity* (Bloomsbury, 2016).

19. Ryan Avent, *The Wealth of Humans* (Allen Lane, 2016), p. 119.

20. Timothy N. Bond and Kevin Lang, 'The Sad Truth about Happiness Scales', *Journal of Political Economy* 127:4 (2019).

21. Osea Giuntella, Sally McManus, Redzo Mujcic, Andrew J. Oswald, Nattavudh Powdthavee and Ahmed Tohamy, 'The Midlife Crisis', Working Paper 30442, http://www.nber.org/papers/w30442 [accessed 13 September 2023].

22. Hannes Schwandt, 'Unmet Aspirations as an Explanation for the Age U-shape in Wellbeing', *Beiträge zur Jahrestagung des Vereins für Socialpolitik 2014*: Evidenzbasierte Wirtschaftspolitik – Session: Redistribution and Subjective Wellbeing, No. A20-V4, ZBW – Deutsche Zentralbibliothek für Wirtschaftswissenschaften, LeibnizInformationszentrum Wirtschaft, Kiel und Hamburg, http://hdl.handle.net/10419/100360 [accessed 13 September 2023].

23. A. J. Reagan et al., 'The Emotional Arcs of Stories are Dominated by Six Basic Shapes', *EPJ Data Science* 5:31 (2016), doi: 10.1140/epjds/s13688-016-0093-1

24. Rauch, *The Happiness Curve*, p. 83.

25. Vivian Nunez, 'Ava DuVernay on How Stepping into Your Power Leaves Room for Changing Your Mind', *Forbes*, 10 December 2021, https://www.forbes.com/sites/viviannunez/2021/12/10/ava-duvernay-on-how-stepping-into-your-power-leaves-room-for-changing-your-mind/?sh=41b4e26193df [accessed 13 September 2023].

26. https://learntocodewith.me/posts/career-change-at-40/ [accessed 13 September 2023].

27. Nicola Bryan, 'Bear Photography Takes Great-grandmother Round the World', *BBC News*, 17 July 2022, https://www.bbc.co.uk/news/uk-wales-62152869 [accessed 13 September 2023].

28. Elaine Moore, 'Silicon Valley: No Country for Young Men', *Financial Times*, 28 August 2022, https://www.ft.com/content/d0349360-723a-475c-9f1f-e9924d72629d [accessed 13 September 2023].

29. Yitzi Weiner, 'The Inspiring Backstory of Eric S. Yuan, Founder and CEO of Zoom', 2 October 2017, https://medium.com/thrive-global/the-inspiring-backstory-of-eric-s-yuan-founder-and-ceo-of-zoom-98b7fab8cacc; Alex Konrad, 'Zoom, Zoom, Zoom! The Exclusive Inside Story of the New Billionaire Behind Tech's Hottest IPO', *Forbes*, 19 April 2019, https://www.forbes.com/sites/alexkonrad/2019/04/19/zoom-zoom-zoom-

the-exclusive-inside-story-of-the-new-billionaire-behind-techs-hottest-ipo/?sh=1271c9234af1 [accessed 13 September 2023].

30. Maureen Dowd, 'At Wimbledon With: Ion Tiriac; Tennis's Grandest Bad Boy', *New York Times*, 24 June 1993, https://www.nytimes.com/1993/06/24/garden/at-wimbledon-with-ion-tiriac-tennis-s-grandest-bad-boy.html?src=pm [accessed 13 September 2023].

31. Henry Oliver, 'Robin Hanson Interview', *The Common Reader*, https://www.commonreader.co.uk/p/robin-hanson-interview

32. https://nowteach.org.uk/

33. Lucy Kellaway, *Re-educated: Why It's Never Too Late to Change Your Life* (Ebury, 2021), p. 116.

34. James C. Kaufman et al., 'Young and Old, Novice and Expert: How We Evaluate Creative Art Can Reflect Practice and Talent', in *The Complexity of Greatness: Beyond Talent or Practice*, ed. Scot Barry Kaufman (Oxford University Press, 2013), pp. 160–7.

35. Kellaway, *Re-educated*, p. 97.

36. Josh Waitzkin, *The Art of Learning* (Free Press, 2007), p. 107.

37. Ibid., p. 113.

38. Olivia Marcus, 'The Coastal Grandmother Aesthetic Makes Me Want to Change My Entire Lifestyle', *Stylecaster*, 13 June 2022, https://stylecaster.com/what-is-a-coastal-grandmother/ [accessed 13 September 2023].

39. Farrah Storr, 'Do You Skew Senior?', *Things Worth Knowing with Farrah Storr*, 21 August 2022, https://farrah.substack.com/p/do-you-skew-senior [accessed 13 September 2023].

40. https://oldster.substack.com/p/whats-it-like-joining-the-peace-corps?s=r [accessed 13 September 2023].

41. https://www.theguardian.com/world/2022/jun/04/japanese-man-kenichi-horie-83-becomes-oldest-person-sail-solo-non-stop-across-pacific [accessed 13 September].

42. Gratton and Scott, p. 179.

Conclusion: be your own interruption

1. Richard Hooker, https://web.archive.org/web/20080605045033/http://www.wsu.edu/~dee/GLOSSARY/ARETE.HTM

2. Aristotle, *Nicomachean Ethics* (Cambridge University Press, 2000), p. 29.

3. https://slimemoldtimemold.com/2022/02/10/the-scientific-virtues/

4. Malcolm X and Alex Hayley, *The Autobiography of Malcolm X* (Penguin, 2001), p. 119.

5. Manning Marable, *Malcolm X: A Life of Reinvention* (Penguin, 2011), p. 38.

6. Ibid., p. 61.

7. Ibid., p. 65.

8. Malcolm X and Alex Hayley, The *Autobiography of Malcolm X*, p. 246.

9. Ibid., p. 247.

10. Ibid., p. 261.

11. Marable, *Malcolm X*, p. X.

12. Ibid., p. 270.

13. Clayborne Carson, 'Malcolm X (19 May 1925–21 February 1965), African-American Religious and Political Leader', *American National Biography*, 1 February 2000, https://doi-org.lonlib.idm.oclc.org/10.1093/anb/9780198606697.article.0801846 [accessed 20 September 2023].

14. Michael T. Martin, 'Conversations with Ava DuVernay – "A Call to Action": Organizing Principles of an Activist Cinematic Practice', *Black Camera* 6:1 (Fall 2014), pp. 57–91, https://www.jstor.org/stable/10.2979/blackcamera.6.1.57

15. Ralph Waldo Emerson, 'Self-reliance', in *Nature and Selected Essays*, ed. and intro. Larzer Ziff (Penguin, 2003).

16. Walter Pater, *Studies in the History of the Renaissance* (Oxford World Classics, 2011).

17. Lorren Walker, *Aging with Strength* (Hawaii, independently published 2012), p. 37.

INDEX